American
Red Cross

Swimming and Water Safety

American Red Cross

This manual is part of the American Red Cross Swimming and Water Safety program. Visit redcross.org to learn more about this program.

The emergency care procedures outlined in this book reflect the standard of knowledge and accepted emergency practices in the United States at the time this book was published. It is the reader's responsibility to stay informed of changes in emergency care procedures.

Published by Krames StayWell Strategic Partnerships Division

Printed in the United States of America

ISBN: 978-1-58480-600-4

ACKNOWLEDGMENTS

This manual is dedicated to the thousands of employees and volunteers of the American Red Cross who contribute their time and talent to supporting and teaching swimming and lifesaving skills worldwide and to the thousands of course participants and other readers who have decided to be prepared to take action when an emergency strikes.

Many individuals shared in the development and revision process in various supportive, technical and creative ways. The Swimming and Water Safety program was developed through the dedication of both employees and volunteers. Their commitment to excellence made this manual possible.

The following members of the American Red Cross Scientific Advisory Council provided guidance and review:

Peter Wernicki, MD
Aquatics Chair, American Red Cross Scientific Advisory Council
Sports Medicine Orthopedic Surgeon, Vero Beach, Florida
Assistant Clinical Professor, Dept. of Orthopedic Surgery, Florida St. University College of Medicine
Chair, International Lifesaving Federation Medical Committee
Medical Advisor, U.S. Lifesaving Association

Linda Quan, MD, FAAP
Vice Chair, American Red Cross Scientific Advisory Council
University of Washington School of Medicine
Seattle Children's Hospital
Seattle, Washington

Peter Chambers, PhD, DO
Member, American Red Cross Scientific Advisory Council
Flight Surgeon, Medical Corps
Patrick Air Force Base, Florida

Roy Fielding
Member, American Red Cross Scientific Advisory Council
The University of North Carolina at Charlotte, Department of Kinesiology
Coordinator, Exercise Science/Director of Aquatics
Charlotte, North Carolina

Louise Kublick
Member, American Red Cross Scientific Advisory Council
Holland Bloorview Kids Rehabilitation Hospital
Operations Manager, Aquatics
Toronto, Ontario, Canada

Stephen J. Langendorfer, PhD
Member, American Red Cross Scientific Advisory Council
Professor, Kinesiology
Bowling Green State University
Bowling Green, Ohio

Terri Lees
Member, American Red Cross Scientific Advisory Council
Aquatic Supervisor
North Kansas City Community Center
North Kansas City, Missouri

William Dominic Ramos, PhD
Member, American Red Cross Scientific Advisory Council
Indiana University
School of Public Health–Bloomington
Director – IU Aquatics Institute
Assistant Professor
Bloomington, Indiana

Special thanks to the following individuals for their expertise as Subject Matter Experts:

Matt Barbini
USA Swimming National Team, High Performance Consultant
Colorado Springs, Colorado

Jason Baumann
USA Diving, Director of Education
Indianapolis, Indiana

Scott Colby
USA Swimming, Sport Performance Consultant
Colorado Springs, Colorado

Tara Eggleston, M.S.
Assistant Division Chief/Countywide Aquatics Coordinator
Maryland-National Capital Park and Planning Commission

Myriam Glez
High Performance Director, USA Synchronized Swimming
Indianapolis, Indiana

Karen Josephson
Illustrator and Synchro Swimming Expert, esynchro.com
Concord, California
U.S. Olympian, 1988 Olympic Silver Medal, 1992 Olympic Gold Medal,
Duet Synchronized Swimming

Russell Mark
USA Swimming National Team, High Performance Consultant
Colorado Springs, Colorado

Photography Credits

Chapter 2 Opener: Image © Michael DeYoung Photography

Chapter 4 Opener: Image © iStockphoto.com/steele2123

Chapter 8 Opener: Image © Mike Powell/Getty Images

Chapter 10 Opener: Image © iStockphoto.com/Juanmonino

Appendix A Opener: © Pete Saloutos/Getty Images

CONTENTS

PART 1:

BEING SAFE IN AND AROUND THE WATER _____ 1

PART 2:

SWIMMING SKILLS _____ 76

INTRODUCTION

In 2014, the American Red Cross celebrates its 100th anniversary of helping people to be safe in, on and around the water. *Swimming and Water Safety* is a resource for American Red Cross Water Safety Instructors during their training as well as a reference after training is complete. In addition, *Swimming and Water Safety* is a valuable resource for anyone who has an interest in participating in aquatic activities. *Swimming and Water Safety* provides information about water safety and drowning prevention; emergency response; hydrodynamic principles; aquatic skills and stroke mechanics; entries, starts and turns; and specialized aquatic interests and activities, such as diving, fitness swimming and competitive swimming.

With this Centennial edition, *Swimming and Water Safety* has been thoroughly updated to reflect the latest science. Chapters have been organized into three thematic units.

Part 1, Being Safe In and Around the Water, describes strategies people can use to prevent and respond to aquatic emergencies. New content includes a definition of water competency and the Circle of Drowning Prevention and Chain of Drowning Survival graphics, which depict steps people can take to lower the risk of death or disability as a result of drowning.

Part 2, Swimming and Diving Skills, describes hydrodynamic principles; basic aquatic skills; stroke mechanics and skills for performing headfirst entries, competitive racing starts, turns and dives. Highly visual, step-by-step explanations accompany the text descriptions. This material has been revised in cooperation with USA Swimming, USA Diving and USA Synchro to reflect the latest science.

Part 3, Aquatics for Health and Fitness, provides information about how people of varying ages and abilities can incorporate aquatic activities into their lives. Information is provided about aquatic programming options and safety considerations for people with disabilities or health conditions. In addition, information is provided about how to incorporate aquatic activities into a fitness program, and about training for competitive events.

PART 1

Being Safe In and Around The Water

CHAPTER 1

Water Safety and Learning to Swim

Swimming and other activities in and around the water enrich our lives in many ways. Time spent at the pool, lake, beach or waterpark offers the opportunity for relaxation and fun, as does time spent enjoying hobbies such as boating, fishing or snorkeling. Water-based sports, such as swimming, diving, water polo and synchronized swimming, allow people to enjoy the camaraderie of a team and the sense of accomplishment that comes from achieving both personal and team goals. Water-based fitness activities, such as fitness swimming or participating in an aquatic fitness class, help many people to improve or maintain their health. But the ability to fully enjoy any of these activities relies on knowing how to swim and how to be safe around the water.

Water Safety Education and Learning to Swim

While aquatic environments and activities are a great source of enjoyment, they are associated with some risks, most notably that of **drowning** (the process of experiencing respiratory impairment from submersion or immersion in liquid). Drowning can be fatal or nonfatal. Death by drowning is a leading public health problem in the United States and throughout the world, but the majority of deaths by drowning can be prevented **(Box 1-1)**. There are two keys to lowering the risk for drowning: water safety education and knowing how to swim.

Box 1-1
International Life Saving Federation (ILS) Position Statement: Swimming and Water Safety Education

1. Death by drowning is a leading public health problem in all countries. Prevention requires public and government support.

2. The vast majority of deaths by drowning can be prevented.

3. Everyone, ideally commencing at a young age and regardless of ability and background, should have access to training in water safety, personal survival and water rescue.

4. Knowledge and understanding of water environments and their associated hazards should be taught to everyone at the earliest possible age.

5. This awareness training should be accompanied by the provision of swimming teaching, in the safest manner possible and to at least a basic level of skill that provides the capacity for survival after unexpected and sudden immersion in water.

6. Acquisition of more advanced water safety knowledge and swimming skills, to include water rescue and competitive swimming, should be encouraged as these enhance aquatic safety.

7. Water hazards should be reduced wherever possible, particularly where swimming and water safety education take place.

8. Trained lifeguards should provide prevention, rescue and treatment where recreational swimming and water safety education take place.

9. Wherever possible, organizations with drowning-prevention expertise, based in high-income countries, should provide assistance to lower-income countries.

10. Accessible and affordable training in water safety and swimming skills should, ideally, be made available for everyone, particularly children, in all countries, to a level consistent with the ILS International Water Safety and Swimming Education Guidelines.

Excerpted from International Life Saving Federation: Lifesaving Position Statement LPS 06. Swimming and Water Safety Education. (www.ilsf.org).

Water Safety Education

Water safety education seeks to give people the knowledge they need to recognize potential risks posed by aquatic environments and activities and teaches them strategies they can use to lower those risks **(Fig. 1-1)**. Water safety education also teaches people personal survival and water rescue skills, which can improve the chances for a positive outcome should an aquatic emergency occur. Research provides evidence of a strong link between water safety education and a reduction in drowning deaths.

Fig. 1-1 Water safety education gives people the knowledge and skills they need to enjoy activities in, on and around the water safely.
Photo: Paul W. Wang/Amboy Guardian

Learning How to Swim

Knowing how to swim is a basic life skill that everyone should possess **(Box 1-2)**. Learning how to swim if you do not already know how can help you to feel more confident when you are in and around water, and it will open up a whole new world of opportunities for enjoying water-based recreational activities. But more importantly, knowing how to swim can save your life or someone else's life.

Choosing a Swim Instruction Program

No one is too old to learn how to swim. And, if you are a parent, enrolling your child in swim lessons helps your child develop this important life skill. Although formal swimming lessons will not "drown-proof" your child, they can significantly reduce the likelihood of your child drowning.

Whether looking for a swim instruction program for yourself or your child, it is wise to do some research to find a program that will best fit your needs. For example, think about whether you would prefer private, semi-private or group lessons. Research the options that are available in your area. Neighbors and health care providers (such as your child's pediatrician) are often knowledgeable about local options for learning how to swim and may be able to offer recommendations. **Box 1-3** summarizes the elements of a good swim instruction program.

Arrange to speak with the swim program coordinators at the facilities you are considering. In addition, ask if you may tour the facility, observe a class in progress or both. Gather information about the following:

- **Program qualities.** The program should have clearly defined objectives, schedules and pricing, and it should seek to accommodate people of all ages and varying abilities. A good swimming instruction program is structured around progressive levels and incorporates basic safety and survival skills, swimming skills and water safety concepts into every lesson.

- **Instructor credentials.** Ask how instructors are trained and what certifications they hold. Instructors should be trained by a nationally recognized training agency, such as Water Safety instructors trained by the American Red Cross.

- **Class assignments.** Find out the criteria used to determine class placement. The program coordinator should be able to tell you what the goals are for each level in a swim instruction program, and what the requirements are to successfully complete that level and advance to the next one. Participants should be grouped with participants of similar ages and abilities.

Box 1-2
Water Competency

Water competency is possessing the basic, minimum skills needed for water safety and survival. Providing participants with the skills they need to achieve water competency should be an objective of every swim instruction program. More than just knowing "how to swim," water competency includes the ability to:

- Enter the water and completely submerge.
- Recover to the surface and remain there for at least 1 minute (floating or treading).
- Turn 360° and orient to the exit.
- Level off and propel oneself on the front or the back through the water for at least 25 yards.
- Exit the water.

The ability to demonstrate the skills that constitute water competency in one aquatic environment may not translate to another. For example, a person who is water competent in a pool may not be water competent in a lake, river or ocean because of different environmental conditions, such as cooler water temperatures or currents. Therefore, the definition of water competency should specify the environmental context.

A definition of water competency allows swim instruction programs to establish specific goals that lead to water competency, and provides participants with the knowledge that after completing a certain level of the swim instruction program, they should possess the minimal skills needed for water competency in that environment.

- **Class size.** The instructor-to-participant ratio should be small enough to allow the instructor to provide each participant with individualized instruction and attention outside of activities that are done as a group. How much time does each participant have to wait for a turn with the instructor? When the instructor is assisting one participant, are the other participants safely practicing the skills they have just learned? "Downtime" should be minimal, even in group classes.

- **Class structure.** Classes should include a variety of teaching methods and activities to keep participants engaged and enhance learning. Time devoted to instruction and practice should be appropriate, with more time given to practice. Time should also be spent reviewing and practicing previously learned skills, as well as learning new ones.

- **Instructor qualities.** Instructors should be professional, encouraging, positive and involved **(Fig. 1-2)**. Instructors should be in the water when they are teaching, unless it is appropriate for them to be on the deck (for example, when demonstrating a skill on dry land before having participants try it in the water). Before and after class, the instructor should be accessible to answer questions. If you are the parent of a child enrolled in the swim class, the instructor should provide you with regular updates about your child's progress.

Fig. 1-2 One sign of a quality swim instruction program is an engaged instructor and participants who are having fun.

- **Attention to safety.** Are certified lifeguards on surveillance duty during the swim lesson? Is the instructor-to-participant ratio small enough to allow the instructor to keep an eye on all of the participants at once? (Even with a lifeguard on duty, the instructor must also be able to adequately supervise and keep track of every participant in the class.) Is the facility clean and well maintained?

Box 1-3
Elements of a Good Swim Instruction Program

- The program has clearly defined objectives, expectations, schedules and pricing and seeks to accommodate people of all ages and varying abilities.
- The program strives to make accommodations and modifications as needed to allow people with disabilities or health conditions to participate in the program.
- Instructors are well trained by a nationally recognized training agency, such as Water Safety instructors trained by the American Red Cross.
- Instructors and other staff members are accessible, knowledgeable, professional and engaged. Instructors are in the water when teaching unless it is appropriate to be on the deck. When the participants are children, the instructor communicates regularly with the parents and provides progress reports and other relevant information.
- Attention is given to safety. The facility is clean and well maintained, and certified lifeguards are on surveillance duty during all swim lessons.
- The instructor-to-participant ratio allows for individualized attention and supervision of all participants.
- Participants are active and engaged throughout each lesson.
- Participants make progress over time.

Supporting a Child Who is Enrolled in a Swim Instruction Program

If you are a parent, there are many things you can do to prepare your child for his or her first swim lesson, and to support learning at home. If you have a young child, parent-and-child classes for infants, toddlers and young preschoolers are great for orienting your child to the water and laying the foundation for learning swimming skills **(Fig. 1-3)**. In addition, you will learn holding and support techniques to use with your child in the water **(Table 1-1)**, and about how to help keep your child safe in and around water.

Fig. 1-3 A parent-and-child aquatics class helps young children get used to being in the water and teaches parents how to keep their child safe in and around water.

As your child progresses through swim lessons, you can help support learning, even though you will no longer be in the pool with your child. Keep in mind that children learn swimming skills at different rates. Praise your child's efforts at the pool and celebrate every accomplishment. Take an interest in what your child is learning—ask her to show you a skill she has learned or to teach you what she has learned about being safe in the water. Help your child to practice and improve by spending time with her in the pool outside of swim lessons. Consider using pool toys, such as kickboards or foam noodles, to stage your own drills and help your child to practice skills she has learned in class **(Box 1-4)**. Your enthusiasm and guidance will go a long way in helping your child benefit the most from swimming lessons.

Table 1-1 Holding and Support Positions

Method	Best For ...	Positioning
Face-to-Face		
Hug Position 	• Water adjustment • Practicing kicking on the front	• Have the child face you, rest his head on your shoulder and place his arms around your neck or on your shoulders. • You support the child's extended legs.
Chin Support Position 	• Practicing bubble blowing and kicking on the front	• Hold the child under the upper chest and shoulders with your fingers and palms. • The child's chin rests on the heels of your palms.
Hip Support on Front Position 	• Water adjustment • Practicing the front glide, front float, bubble blowing, kicking on the front, kicking with the face down unsupported	• Support the child in a face-down, horizontal position by placing your hands under the child's hips and abdomen. • The child's arms are nearly fully extended and rest on top of your arms.
Shoulder Support Position on Front 	• Water adjustment • Practicing kicking on the front, the front glide, bubble blowing, underwater exploration and rolling over	• With your arms nearly extended, hold the child under the armpits.
Back-to-Chest		
Cuddle Position 	• Practicing the back float, back glide readiness, kicking on the back and rolling over	• Have the child rest her head on your shoulder, with her cheek or the side of her head touching or right next to your cheek. • Place one hand on the child's back and the other on her chest. • Hold the child in a horizontal position with her legs extended away from you.

Continued on next page

Table 1-1 Holding and Support Positions *(continued)*

Method	Best For …	Positioning
Hip Support on Back Position 	• Practicing the back float, back glide readiness, kicking on the back	• Have the child rest the back of his head on your shoulder, with his cheek or the side of his head touching or right next to your cheek. • Place your hands on the child's back to bring the body horizontal.
Back Support Position 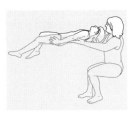	• Practicing the back float, back glide readiness, kicking on the back when maximum freedom of movement is desired	• Support the base of the child's head near the neck with one hand and place the other hand in the middle of the child's back to lift and stabilize the body in a horizontal position. • Tilt the child's head back, extend your arms and move backward slowly to help the child float.
Arm Stroke Position 	• Exploring arm movements in the water	• Sit against the side of the pool or on the steps, or kneel on one knee in shallow water. • Have the child sit on your knee, facing away from you. • Circle the child's chest with one arm to keep him upright. With your other hand, hold the child's wrist from underneath and place your hand on top of the child's hand. Move the child's arm in a paddling motion. • Alternatively, balance a more secure child on your knee and guide both arms in an alternating or simultaneous paddling motion.
Side-to-Side		
Hip Straddle Position 	• Water adjustment • Practicing bubble blowing, water entry and exit	• Have the child face you and straddle your hip. • Support the child by placing your arm around the child's back and holding on to the child's upper thigh. Hold the child's hand with your other hand.
Shoulder Support on the Side Position 	• Water adjustment • Practicing bubble blowing, kicking on the front, front glide, front float, stroking, passing, combining skills	• Hold the child at one side by placing your hands on either side of his chest, under the armpits. Keep the child's head up. • If more support is needed, encircle the child's chest with one arm, placing your palm on the child's chest. Place your other arm underneath the child for additional support.

Box 1-4
Water Orientation and Learn-to-Swim Equipment

- **Swim bar floats (barbells) and noodles** are great for practicing swimming skills and are especially popular for young children.

- **Floating pool toys**, such as rubber ducks or toy boats, can be used to help children adjust to the water and help make spending time in the water more enjoyable.

- **Dive rings and other "sinking" pool toys** can help beginners practice submerging or underwater swimming.

- **Kickboards** help support the upper body and make it easier to breathe while practicing kicking.

The American Red Cross and Water Safety

It is the mission of the American Red Cross to prevent, prepare for and respond to emergencies. Today, the American Red Cross Swimming and Water Safety program helps fulfill that mission by teaching people to be safe in, on and around the water through water safety courses, water orientation classes for infants and toddlers and comprehensive Learn-to-Swim courses for people of different ages and abilities.

The American Red Cross has a long history of helping people to be safe in, on and around the water. In the early 1900s, Wilbert E. Longfellow, the Commodore in Chief of New York City's newly formed U.S. Volunteer Life Saving Corps, identified the need for a nationwide program of swimming and lifesaving instruction and presented a plan for the "waterproofing of America" to the American Red Cross in 1912. Soon after, the Red Cross Life Saving Corps (forerunner of the present-day Red Cross Water Safety courses) was created. Longfellow was appointed to organize the new lifesaving program and was awarded the very first Red Cross Lifesaving Certificate and the lifesaving emblem that has since been earned and proudly worn by millions of people **(Fig. 1-4)**.

Fig. 1-4 Commodore Wilbert E. Longfellow (third from left), with members of the Red Cross Life Saving Corps, made it his life's work to achieve the goal of "Every American a swimmer, every swimmer a lifesaver!"

For the next 33 years, until his death in 1947, Longfellow worked tirelessly in support of the nationwide Red Cross Water Safety program. As a result of his efforts, the nation's drowning rate was cut almost in half—from 8.8 people per 100,000 in 1914 to 4.8 in 1947—and there was a tremendous upsurge in the popularity of swimming, boating and other water activities, to the point where nearly 80 million Americans were participating in some form of aquatic recreation.

As the American Red Cross celebrates its centennial of helping people to be safe in, on and around the water, the Red Cross Swimming and Water Safety program, whose early history is largely the story of the Commodore's contribution through the Red Cross, can point to a proud record. The Red Cross has trained thousands of people to become water safety instructors, and millions of people have taken American Red Cross swimming and water safety classes.

American Red Cross Water Safety Courses and Presentations

The American Red Cross offers a variety of water safety education courses and presentations for adults and children. Topics range from specific interests (such as home pool safety, rip current safety, boating safety and basic water rescue) to general water safety education (such as Longfellow's WHALE Tales, for children between the ages of 5 and 12). Water safety concepts and skills are also incorporated into the American Red Cross Learn-to-Swim program.

American Red Cross Learn-to-Swim Program

The American Red Cross Parent and Child Aquatics, Preschool Aquatics, Learn-to-Swim and Adult Swim courses comprise the American Red Cross Learn-to-Swim program. These courses are designed to meet the needs of participants of all ages and varying abilities. The courses in the American Red Cross Learn-to-Swim program are structured in a logical progression for aquatic skill development. As participants progress through the courses in the program, they build on existing skills and develop new ones, becoming safer and better swimmers. After completing Level 3 of the American Red Cross Learn-to-Swim course, participants should possess the minimal skills needed for water competency in a pool environment. Continuing through the full American Red Cross Learn-to-Swim program helps participants become better, stronger and more competent swimmers in different aquatic environments and under different environmental conditions.

Parent and Child Aquatics

The American Red Cross Parent and Child Aquatics courses help young children between the ages of 6 months and approximately 3 years become comfortable in and around the water so that when the time comes, they are ready to learn how to swim **(Fig. 1-5)**. In addition, parents learn about water safety and how to safely handle their child in and around the water.

American Red Cross Parent and Child Aquatics courses provide the foundation for future aquatic skills. They are not designed to teach children to become good swimmers or even to survive in the water on their own. This is in accordance with the American Academy of Pediatrics statement that recommends that formal swimming lessons not begin until after a child's 4th birthday.

Fig. 1-5 American Red Cross Parent and Child Aquatics courses are for children between the ages of approximately 6 months and 3 years.

Preschool Aquatics

The American Red Cross Preschool Aquatics courses are designed for children about 4 and 5 years old **(Fig. 1-6)**. The Preschool Aquatics course consists of three levels that teach fundamental water safety and aquatic skills. Mastering the skills taught in Preschool Aquatics allows participants to move seamlessly into Learn-to-Swim courses. Participants transitioning from Preschool Aquatics into Learn-to-Swim may enter Learn-to-Swim Level 2 or Level 3, depending on their skill level at the time.

Learn-to-Swim

The American Red Cross Learn-to-Swim course consists of six levels, focused on teaching school-age children and young teenagers how to swim skillfully and safely **(Fig. 1-7)**. In addition, each level of the Learn-to-Swim course includes training in basic water safety and helping others in an emergency. Each level builds on information and skills from the previous level, promoting success and a positive learning experience.

Adult Swim

American Red Cross Adult Swim courses are designed to meet a variety of needs that older teen and adult learners may have **(Fig. 1-8)**. The following courses are available:

- **Adult Swim—Learning the Basics.** This class teaches basic aquatic skills, swimming strokes and water safety concepts to older teens and adults who are novices.
- **Adult Swim—Improving Skills and Swimming Strokes.** This class seeks to help older teens and adults improve on existing skills to become more comfortable in the water, to prepare for specific aquatic activities, or both.
- **Adult Swim—Swimming for Fitness.** This class helps proficient swimmers refine swimming strokes with the goal of participating in a fitness swimming program or competitive event.

Fig. 1-6 American Red Cross Preschool Aquatics courses teach fundamental aquatic skills to 4- and 5-year-olds.

Fig. 1-7 American Red Cross Learn-to-Swim courses teach school-age children and young teenagers how to swim.

Fig. 1-8 American Red Cross Adult Swim courses help older teenagers and adults develop new skills or improve on existing ones.

CHAPTER 2

Preventing Accidents and Injuries In, On and Around the Water

Aquatic environments and activities enrich our lives in countless ways. Enjoying a day at the beach, hosting a pool party for friends, or canoeing or kayaking on a local river are great ways to spend leisure time. But aquatic activities and environments can present special hazards. The key to having a good time *and* staying safe in and around the water is being aware of the potential hazards, and taking steps to prevent injuries or accidents as a result of them.

Lowering the Risk for Drowning

In the United States, drowning ranks fifth among the causes of death from unintentional injury. And, even when a drowning incident does not result in death, it can result in significant long-term disability. Drowning happens quickly and suddenly. Lowering the risk for drowning requires following general principles of water safety **(Box 2-1)** and establishing layers of protection **(Fig. 2-1)**. Having layers of protection in place provides "backup" if one protective strategy fails, reducing overall risk. The American Red Cross has established five layers of protection for lowering the risk for drowning:

- Learn swimming and water safety survival skills.
- Swim in lifeguarded areas.
- Have children, inexperienced swimmers and boaters wear U.S. Coast Guard-approved life jackets.
- Provide close and constant supervision to children who are in or near the water.
- Fence pools and spas with adequate barriers to prevent unsupervised access.

Age is a major risk factor for drowning incidents. In the United States, drowning ranks second, behind motor vehicle crashes, as a cause of death from unintentional injury in children ages 1–14. Children between the ages of 1 and 4 years have the highest rate for drowning. Most of these incidents occur in home swimming pools, but any source of water, including a bathtub or partially filled bucket, is a potential drowning hazard. An infant can drown in as little as 1 inch of water. **Box 2-2** contains tips for lowering the risk for drowning for children.

Box 2-1
General Guidelines for Staying Safe Around the Water

© iStockphoto.com/GlobalStock

- Learn to swim.
- Do not use alcohol or drugs while engaging in aquatic activities.
- Obtain the knowledge and skills you need to prevent, recognize and respond to aquatic emergencies (for example, by taking a boating safety course before operating any watercraft).
- Never swim alone. Swim only in designated areas and areas supervised by a lifeguard.
- Set up specific swimming rules for each member of your family or group based on swimming abilities. Closely supervise children in, on or around the water, even when a lifeguard is present.
- Read and obey all rules and posted signs. Pay special attention to water-depth markings and "no diving" signs.
- Enter the water feet-first, unless you are in an area that is clearly marked for diving and has no obstructions.
- Watch out for the "dangerous too's": too tired, too cold, too far from safety, too much sun and too much strenuous activity.
- Have a means of summoning help (such as a mobile phone) close by. Aquatic emergencies often happen quickly and unexpectedly.
- Get trained in first aid, cardiopulmonary resuscitation (CPR) and automated external defibrillator (AED) use. To enroll in a Red Cross first aid, CPR and AED class, visit www.redcross.org.

Circle of Drowning Prevention

Layers of protection are essential to help prevent drowning.
Plan ahead for aquatic activities:

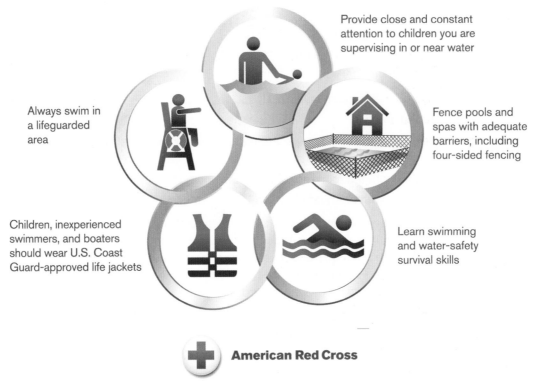

Provide close and constant attention to children you are supervising in or near water

Fence pools and spas with adequate barriers, including four-sided fencing

Learn swimming and water-safety survival skills

Children, inexperienced swimmers, and boaters should wear U.S. Coast Guard-approved life jackets

Always swim in a lifeguarded area

American Red Cross

Fig. 2-1 The American Red Cross Circle of Drowning Prevention highlights the layers of protection that help to lower the risk for drowning.

Box 2-2
Tips for Reducing the Risk for Drowning in Children

- Enroll children in Red Cross Parent and Child Aquatics, Preschool Aquatics and Learn-to-Swim courses. Providing early aquatic experiences to a child is a gift that will have lifelong rewards.

- Young children are curious and their interests and abilities change from day to day. Do not leave a young child unattended near any source of water, even for a moment.

© Tatyana Aleksieva Photography/Getty Images

- Closely supervise children in, on or around the water, even when a lifeguard is present, no matter how well the child can swim or how shallow the water. Stay within an arm's reach of any weak or inexperienced swimmer who is in the water.

- Know each child's swimming ability and set specific rules for each child based on her swimming ability.

Box 2-2 (continued)

- Do not rely on the use of water wings, swim rings, inflatable toys and other items designed for water recreation to replace a U.S. Coast Guard-approved life jacket or adult supervision. These devices can suddenly shift position, lose air or slip out from underneath the child, putting the child at risk for drowning. They may also falsely increase a child's sense of confidence, causing him to venture into water that is too deep.

- Teach children not to engage in competitive underwater games, such as seeing who can hold his or her breath the longest underwater or seeing who can swim the farthest before coming up for air. Hyperventilation (that is, taking a series of rapid, deep breaths before submerging in an effort to hold the breath longer underwater) affects the body's drive to breathe. The child could pass out and then instinctively take a breath underwater, leading to drowning.

- Teach children to stay away from pool drains and other openings that create suction. The suction can hold the child underwater, leading to drowning.

- Prevent access to standing water in the home. Empty bathtubs, sinks, kiddie pools, buckets and other containers immediately after use. Keep toilet lids down and bathroom and laundry room doors closed and secured with safety locks.

- Never leave a child in a bathtub alone; always stay within arm's reach. Do not rely on bathtub floating aids to protect your child from drowning.

- If you own an inground swimming pool, aboveground swimming pool (including inflatable "easy-set"-type pools) or hot tub:
  ○ Surround the entire pool or hot tub area with a fence that is at least 4 feet high, has a self-closing and self-latching gate, and is designed so that a child cannot climb over, under or through it.
  ○ Be sure that all gates, windows and doors leading to the pool or hot tub area are locked.
  ○ Make sure that pools and hot tubs are covered when not in use, and that the cover is secured.
  ○ Keep pool toys out of the water and out of sight. (A child may see a pool toy floating in the water and try to go after it.)
  ○ To prevent the child from climbing over a fence and getting into the pool or hot tub area, keep chairs, tables and other items the child could climb on away from the pool or hot tub enclosure.
  ○ If a child is missing, always look in the pool area first. Seconds count in preventing death or disability.

- If there are bodies of water, fountains or other water features on or near your property or in the community, teach children that these areas are off-limits unless they are accompanied by an adult.

- When visiting another home, check the site for potential water hazards and always supervise your children.

- Never let a child play near storm drains. (Storm drains are especially dangerous after it has rained.)

School-age children often have the opportunity to attend day trips to aquatic facilities that are organized and hosted by a school or community group. In addition, many parents enroll their school-age children in summer camps, where water activities may be a major attraction. In these situations, parents may not be present to directly supervise their children, so it is important for parents to evaluate the host organization's attention to, and provisions for, aquatic safety **(Box 2-3)**.

While pools are a source of danger for younger children, a large number of drowning accidents involving older children, teens and young adults take place in natural bodies of water. The percentage of drowning incidents in natural bodies of water increases with age, with more than half of all the victims in these incidents being 15 years of age and older. Nearly every community has some type of natural body of water, such as a canal, pond, creek, stream, river, lake, drainage basin, reservoir, wetlands area or shoreline that can be accessed easily. In many communities, these areas are frequently features of public parks. Easy access to natural water environments, combined with the growing independence of older children and adolescents, can make these environments especially dangerous to children who are old enough to explore on

Box 2-3
Promoting Safety During Children's Group Aquatic Outings and at Summer Camps

Group outings

Planning and preparation are essential when organized groups attend a day trip to an aquatic environment. Parents can ask the following questions of the group's organizers to evaluate the measures that have been put in place to help keep their children safe during the outing:

- May I have a copy of the written safety plan? (Group organizers should prepare a written safety plan that identifies the safety measures that will be taken and the provisions for appropriate supervision that will be made for maintaining safety during the planned aquatic outing.)

- Will the group be allowed to swim only in designated areas supervised by a certified lifeguard?

- What is the adult chaperone-to-child ratio? (Lifeguards should not be counted as part of this ratio.)

- What activities are planned, and will they be supervised by appropriately trained personnel?

- What system will be used to evaluate each child's swimming ability? Is a system in place for easily identifying each child's swimming ability, such as color-coded tags or caps?

- Are criteria in place (such as height and weight requirements) for attractions such as water slides? How will children be prevented from participating in activities or going on attractions that are beyond their skill level or are otherwise unsafe for them?

- Is there a system (such as roll calls or buddy checks) in place to ensure that staff can quickly account for all children in the group at all times?

- What training and certifications must facility staff (such as lifeguards) have? Do adult chaperones who will be attending the trip know how to swim, and are they trained in water safety and CPR?

Summer camps

Similar information should be sought before enrolling a child in a summer camp. First, make sure the camp meets the government's standards for aquatic safety. Government safety standards for swimming at camps may be covered in state bathing codes or they may be found in separate regulations specific for day and residential camp programs. Because codes vary from state to state, also check to see if the camp follows the aquatic safety standards established by national organizations such as the American Camp Association (ACA), the Boy Scouts of America or the YMCA of the USA. Finally, use the following questions to evaluate the camp's attention to, and provisions for, aquatic safety:

- What is the condition of the pool, waterfront or any other aquatic features? Is the staff properly trained and qualified to supervise and teach aquatic activities?

- What are the aquatic activity areas like? Are they well-designed and maintained, free of obvious hazards and closely supervised by adequate numbers of alert, trained staff? What is the condition of any equipment being used?

© iStockphoto.com/kali9

- Does the camp use a system for easily identifying a camper's swimming ability, such as color-coded tags or caps?
- Are campers classified by their swimming ability? Are instructional and recreational activities consistent with the campers' abilities?
- Is there a system (such as roll calls, buddy checks or buddy tags) in place to ensure that staff can quickly account for all campers at all times?
- Does the camp have a system for promptly accessing emergency personnel and facilities?
- Does the camp require additional information about any temporary or chronic medical condition that might require special precautions in, on or around the water?

Fig. 2-2 Natural bodies of water in the community can be enticing to older children and teens who are old enough to explore on their own. Accidents can happen when children and teens do not know, or fail to appreciate, how dangerous these areas can be.

their own **(Fig. 2-2)**. For this reason, it is important to teach older children and teens about the dangers natural bodies of water in the community present, and to make and enforce rules related to visiting these areas. Also, be aware that aquatic emergencies do not always happen when people are swimming. A hike along a mountain stream or a canoe-camping trip poses just as much risk for an aquatic emergency to develop.

Using Life Jackets

Life jackets, also known as personal flotation devices (PFDs), are not just for boaters. Young children, weak or inexperienced swimmers and nonswimmers should also wear life jackets whenever they are in, on or around the water.

Life jackets are available in many styles and for many different activities. The U.S. Coast Guard has categorized PFDs into five types according to their buoyancy and purpose **(Table 2-1)**.

Table 2-1 Personal Flotation Devices

Type	Description	Advantages	Disadvantages
I: Life jacket 	• Intended for boating on open, rough or remote waters where rescue may be slowed or delayed • May help to turn an unconscious person from a face-down position to a vertical, face-up position or to a face-up slightly tipped back position	• Offers the most reliable flotation • Comes in highly visible colors and may have reflective markings to aid search and rescue	• Bulky in and out of the water
II: Buoyant vest 	• Intended for recreational boating on calm or inland waters where rapid rescue is likely • Suitable for supervised use in pools and waterparks • May help to turn an unconscious person from a face-down position to a vertical, face-up position or to a face-up slightly tipped back position	• More comfortable to wear • Available for infants through adults; good choice for children	• Not recommended for long hours on rough water • Less buoyant than a type I life jacket
III: Flotation vest 	• Intended for fishing or sailing on calm or inland waters where rapid rescue is likely • Suitable for supervised use in pools and waterparks • May help to keep a conscious person in a vertical, face-up position or in a face-up slightly tipped back position; wearer may have to tilt the head back to avoid going face-down	• Most comfortable to wear continuously • Available in many styles • Appropriate for boating and specified water activities	• Must be water-tested by inexperienced swimmers before boating • Wearer may need to tilt head back to avoid turning face-down in the water
IV: Throwable device	• Intended to be thrown to a person in the water; not to be worn • Not intended to take the place of a wearable life jacket	• Able to be thrown from boat or land • Backup to wearable life jackets • Possible use as seat cushions (some styles)	• Not suitable for children, inexperienced swimmers or unconscious victims
V: Special-use device 	• Intended for specific activities such as whitewater rafting • May be worn instead of another life jacket only if used according to the approval condition(s) on its label • Worn continuously	• Designed for specific activities • Continuous wear provides continuous protection	• Limited use

Types I, II, III and V are referred to as life jackets because they are worn on the body, whereas type IV is a throwable device. When choosing a life jacket, select one that has been approved by the U.S. Coast Guard. PFDs that have been approved by the U.S. Coast Guard will have an approval label stamped directly on the device **(Fig. 2-3)**. In addition, consider swimming ability, the planned activity and the water conditions. Type II and type III life jackets are most often used in pool, waterpark and waterfront settings.

Before using a life jacket, make sure that it fits properly. Life jackets are sized according to weight. A properly fitted life jacket feels comfortably snug. Also check to make sure that it is in good condition. Check any buckles or straps to make sure that they function properly and look closely for any rips, tears or holes. Discard any life jacket with torn fabric or straps that have pulled loose. Test the life jacket in shallow water and see how it feels. Practice swimming with it. Then relax and let your head tilt back. Notice if the device can keep your chin above water, allowing you to breathe easily. The life jacket should not ride up on your body in the water.

Water wings and items designed for water recreation (such as inner tubes and inflatable rafts) are not designed or tested for safety and cannot be used as a substitute for a U.S. Coast Guard-approved life jacket and adult supervision **(Fig. 2-4)**. In fact, these pool toys may actually increase a nonswimmer's or an inexperienced swimmer's risk for getting into a dangerous situation in the water, by giving the swimmer a false sense of security. For example, the swimmer may move into water that is too deep, fall off the toy and into the water, or the toy may overturn, setting up the potential for a drowning situation.

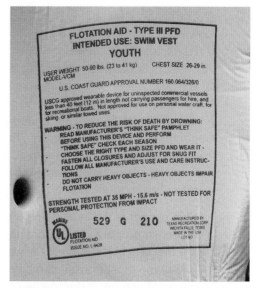

Fig. 2-3 Only use U.S. Coast Guard-approved personal flotation devices (PFDs, or life jackets).

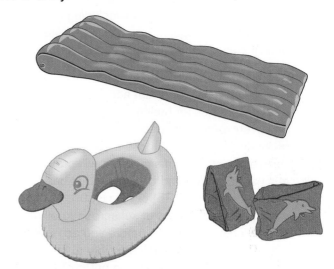

Fig. 2-4 These items are just toys. Do not count on them to provide flotation or to keep a nonswimmer or inexperienced swimmer safe in the water.

Staying Safe from Environmental Hazards

Many aquatic activities provide a great opportunity to get outside and enjoy fresh air and sunshine. Make sure your experience stays enjoyable by being aware of environmental hazards and taking steps to protect yourself from them.

Sun Overexposure

Overexposure to the sun has been linked to multiple health problems, including painful sunburns, skin cancer and eye damage (such as cataracts), and can cause premature aging and wrinkling of the skin. Everyone, regardless of age or skin color, is advised to take steps to limit overexposure to the sun, such as wearing protective clothing, seeking shade when the sun's rays are strongest and consistently using a broad-spectrum sunscreen.

Energy from the sun is called solar radiation. Solar radiation reaches the Earth in a range of wavelengths or rays. Some of these rays are blocked by the atmosphere, but ultraviolet A (UVA) and ultraviolet B (UVB) rays are able to penetrate the atmosphere and reach the Earth's surface. In the past, the ozone layer of the atmosphere offered more protection from dangerous UV rays, but this layer is becoming depleted, permitting greater amounts of UV radiation to reach the Earth's surface. Worldwide efforts are being made to stop the production of chemicals that have contributed to thinning of the ozone layer. The current belief is that with full compliance with these efforts, the ozone layer can return to normal levels by 2050. However, people living and growing up during this timeframe will live most of their lives with increased levels of UV radiation. It is overexposure to UVA and UVB rays that can lead to skin cancer and other health problems.

Skin cancer is the most common type of cancer in the United States, and it is reaching epidemic proportions. According to the American Academy of Dermatology, current estimates are that one in five Americans will develop skin cancer. Despite these statistics, skin cancer is one of the most preventable types of cancer. Of the different types of skin cancer, melanoma is the most serious and also one of the fastest growing types of cancer in the United States. The major risk factor for melanoma is exposure to UV light, and dermatologists think that sunburns experienced in childhood may lead to melanomas later in life. Non-melanoma skin cancers, including basal cell carcinomas and squamous cell carcinomas, are less deadly than melanomas but can be disfiguring and cause more serious health problems if left untreated.

One of the most important actions you can take to reduce your risk for health problems as a result of sun overexposure is to use sunscreen regularly and properly **(Fig. 2-5)**. Choose a sunscreen labeled "broad-spectrum" (this means it will provide protection against both UVA and UVB rays) that has a sun protection factor (SPF) of at least 30. Apply the recommended amount of sunscreen to all exposed skin at least 15 minutes before you go outside, even if it is cloudy out (it is still possible to burn on a cloudy day). Be sure to remember commonly missed areas, such as the lips, ears and the tops of the feet. Reapply sunscreen every 2 hours and after swimming or sweating. Use sunscreen every day, even if you are not going to be outside for long. The sun's rays can also damage your skin through the windows of a car or building. **Box 2-4** summarizes the actions you can take to protect yourself and your family from sun overexposure.

Fig. 2-5 Proper and consistent use of a broad-spectrum sunscreen with a sun protection factor (SPF) of at least 30 can help protect you from the harmful effects of sun overexposure.

Box 2-4
Safe Fun in the Sun

- Use sunscreen regularly and properly. Generously apply a broad-spectrum sunscreen with a sun protection factor (SPF) of at least 30 in ample amounts to all exposed skin 15 minutes before going outdoors, even on cloudy days and even if you do not intend to be outdoors for long. Reapply every 2 hours and after swimming or sweating.

Box 2-4 *(continued)*

- Be aware that sunscreen is not recommended for babies younger than 6 months. If a baby younger than 6 months is outside, it is best to protect the baby from the sun by making sure she is dressed in adequate clothing and by keeping her in the shade (for example, underneath an umbrella or the canopy of a stroller). If you do choose to apply sunscreen to a baby younger than 6 months, apply only a small amount to the baby's face and the back of her hands.

- Wear protective clothing, such as a wide-brimmed hat and sunglasses, when possible. Choose sunglasses that offer 99–100% protection against UV rays. If the temperature is not too warm, long-sleeved shirts and pants can offer some protection from the sun too.

- Pay attention to the UV Index to help you plan your outdoor activities in ways that prevent overexposure to the sun. The National Weather Service calculates the UV Index daily for most zip codes across the United States, predicting the level of solar radiation expected and the risk of possible overexposure, using a scale from 0 to 11+. A UV Index of 0 to 2 indicates a low risk whereas a UV Index of 8 or higher indicates a very high risk.

- Pay attention to the time of day. The sun's rays are strongest between 10 a.m. and 4 p.m. During these hours, avoid exposure to the sun or seek shade, if possible. Follow the Shadow Rule: *Watch Your Shadow. No Shadow, Seek Shade!*

- Know that water, sand and snow reflect the sun's rays, increasing exposure and the risk for sunburn.

- Avoid suntanning and tanning beds. If you want to look like you have been in the sun, use a self-tanning product. Be aware that self-tanning products do not offer protection from the sun so you will also need to use sunscreen.

- Eat foods high in Vitamin D rather than using the sun to get this vitamin.

- Early detection of skin cancer can save your life. Visit a dermatologist for an annual skin exam, and examine all of your skin yourself once a month. Have any new or changing moles evaluated by a dermatologist.

Heat-related Illnesses

Heat-related illnesses can occur on hot, humid days when the body is not able to effectively cool itself through sweating. As a result, the body temperature rises and serious illness can result.

Although it might seem hard to believe that you can overheat while in the water, it can and does happen. Heat-related illnesses occur when fluid is lost during heavy sweating and is not replaced. Just because you are in the water does not mean that you are not sweating, particularly if you are playing or exercising! Working hard or exercising in the heat also increases a person's risk for developing a heat-related illness. And sometimes, just being out in the heat and humidity for a long period of time can be a problem.

Fig. 2-6 Staying hydrated is an important way to ward off heat-related illnesses. *Image © Maridav, 2014. Used under license from Shutterstock.com*

The best prevention strategy for heat-related illnesses is to stay properly hydrated **(Fig. 2-6)**. Staying hydrated helps to make sure the fluids lost from sweating are replaced, which keeps fluid levels in the body balanced and gives body tissues what they need to function well. Water is the best choice of fluid for staying hydrated, but commercial sports drinks, fruit juices or milk are also acceptable. Drink a few ounces every 15–20 minutes or however much you need to not feel thirsty. The feeling of thirst means that the body is already dehydrated. Avoid gulping down fluids quickly. Small amounts taken in slowly work best.

There are three types of heat-related illnesses, of increasing severity:

- **Heat cramps** are painful muscle spasms, usually in the legs and stomach. Heat cramps can quickly turn into heat exhaustion or heat stroke.
- **Heat exhaustion** occurs when the body's cooling system is not able to keep up. The person's skin may be cool and moist, and either very pale or gray, or red. The person may be sweating heavily and may complain of a headache, nausea or dizziness. The person may feel very weak or exhausted.
- **Heat stroke** is the most severe form of heat-related illness. It occurs when the body's cooling system is completely overwhelmed and stops functioning properly. Heat stroke is life threatening! The person's skin will be red and hot, and it may be moist or dry. The person may seem confused, have changes in consciousness or lose consciousness. Breathing may be rapid and shallow, and the pulse may be rapid and weak. The person may vomit.

When a heat-related illness is recognized in its early stages, it usually can be reversed. Move the person to a cooler environment with circulating air. Loosen or remove as much clothing as possible; apply cool, wet cloths and fan the person. If the person is conscious and able to swallow, give small amounts of a cool fluid such as a commercial sports drink, fruit juice, milk or water. If the person's condition does not improve or you suspect heat stroke, call 9-1-1 or the local emergency number immediately. If the person becomes unconscious, be prepared to give CPR.

Hypothermia

In hypothermia, the body is not able to keep itself warm and the body temperature falls far below normal. Hypothermia can lead to death if it is not treated. In an aquatic setting, hypothermia can result from exposure to cold water or air temperatures, or both. The air or water temperature does not have to be below freezing for hypothermia to occur. This is especially true if a person is wet and there is wind. For example, a child who is wet from swimming could develop hypothermia, even in the summertime!

Children and older adults are particularly susceptible to hypothermia. Environmental conditions and prolonged exposure to water or wet clothing (which speeds up the rate at which body heat is lost) can also increase susceptibility to developing hypothermia—even during the summer or in indoor facilities. Immersion in cold water (for example, as a result of breaking through ice, falling off a pier or being thrown into the water from a boat) also puts a person at risk for hypothermia. **Box 2-5** summarizes actions you can take to lower the risk for developing hypothermia when engaging in aquatic activities.

Box 2-5
Lowering the Risk for Hypothermia

- Avoid being outdoors during the coldest part of the day.
- Be aware that many people who fall into cold water never intended to go into the water in the first place. Whenever you are near cold water (for example, playing, working, hunting or fishing), remember that cold water can be dangerous, and take the appropriate precautions.
  - In cooler weather, wear an outer layer that is water-resistant and breathable, a warm hat, and lightweight layers of clothes or insulated clothes.
  - Avoid cotton, which traps moisture. Instead, wear wool or synthetic blends, which help to move moisture away from the skin.

- ○ Know that clothing can help you float and stay warm if you fall into the water (see Chapter 3).
- ○ If you are in a remote area, carry matches in a waterproof container. It may be necessary to build a fire to warm up after a fall into cold water.
- Always wear a U.S. Coast Guard-approved life jacket while boating in cold water.
- Wear a wet suit for skin diving, surfing and kayaking, or other activities that take place in the open water or involve repeated submersion.
- Only participate in aquatic activities when and where it is possible to get help quickly in an emergency.
- Drink warm fluids that do not contain alcohol or caffeine to help the body maintain a normal temperature. Although alcohol may temporarily make you feel warmer, it actually increases loss of body heat and susceptibility to hypothermia.

When a person falls into cold water (for example, as a result of falling through ice), the temperature in the person's arms and legs drops very quickly, due to heat loss through the blood circulating near the skin. The person may have trouble breathing and then may slowly become unable to use the arms and legs. As the person's core temperature continues to drop, function of the heart, brain and other vital organs is affected. The person may become unable to think clearly and lose consciousness. Death from heart failure is possible, but drowning may occur first. In emergencies that involve immersion in cold water, make sure 9-1-1 or the local emergency number has been called and be prepared to give CPR.

Inclement Weather

Weather conditions can change suddenly. Always check the weather forecast before heading out, and know what to do in case inclement weather suddenly arises. You can learn about different kinds of weather events, and how to be prepared for them, by visiting the American Red Cross website (www.redcross.org).

Thunderstorms

Electricity and water do not mix! Leave the water at the first sound of thunder or sight of lightning (**Fig. 2-7**). Remember the 30/30 rule: take cover when the time between a flash of lightning and a roll of thunder is 30 seconds or less, and remain under cover until 30 minutes after the last flash of lightning was seen or the last roll of thunder was heard. If you are outside and cannot reach

Fig. 2-7 If you are in or around water and you hear thunder or see lightning, remember the 30/30 rule: take cover when the time between a flash of lightning and a roll of thunder is 30 seconds or less, and remain under cover until 30 minutes after the last flash of lightning was seen or the last roll of thunder was heard. © iStockphoto.com/Molnár ákos

safety inside of a building, look for a low area. Avoid high ground, tall trees that stand alone, and structures such as sheds, dugouts, bleachers and picnic pavilions. These areas are not safe in a thunderstorm. If no safe shelter is available, squat with your feet together and your arms wrapped around your legs. You want to stay low, but you do not want to lie flat. The less of your body that is in contact with the ground, the better.

Floods

Floods are among the most common water hazards that occur in the United States. Anywhere it rains, it can flood. Being aware of local flood hazards is important for everyone, but especially for people who live near water, in low-lying areas, behind a levee or downstream from a dam. Flooding occurs when waterways such as rivers or streams overflow their banks. It can also occur when rainfall or snow melt exceeds the capacity of underground pipes or drains designed to carry floodwater away from urban areas. Some floods build gradually over a period of days, but flash floods can develop within minutes or hours without any obvious signs of rain. They often produce powerful and destructive walls of water and debris.

Fig. 2-8 Floodwaters are extremely dangerous. Never try to drive or walk through them. *Image © Hank Shiffman, 2014. Used under license from Shutterstock.com*

When a flood watch or warning is in effect, head to higher ground and stay away from the water **(Fig. 2-8)**. If emergency officials advise evacuation, do so immediately. Remember the motto, "*Turn around, don't drown!*" According to the National Weather Service, most of the fatalities during flood events result from people attempting to drive or walk on flooded roadways. It only takes 18 inches of water to lift a vehicle. Once a vehicle becomes buoyant, the water will easily push it sideways and could cause it to tip over. If you are trapped in a car on a flooded road, abandon the car immediately and move to higher ground. Use extreme caution when walking through floodwaters. Six inches of swiftly moving floodwater is enough to knock you off your feet.

Avoid natural bodies of water for 24 hours after heavy rains and flooding, because runoff can contaminate the water with toxic substances. Pay particular attention to children. They are curious and lack judgment about flood-related hazards, such as swiftly moving water and contaminated water.

Recreational Water Illnesses

A **recreational water illness (RWI)** is an illness that is spread by swallowing, breathing or contacting contaminated water. A person can contract an RWI from a natural body of water or from the chlorinated water found in pools and waterpark attractions. In fact, pool water is a very common source of RWIs, especially common ones such as diarrhea, earaches and rashes. In rare cases, RWIs can cause pneumonia, neurological damage and even death.

In a swimming pool or waterpark setting, water contaminated by feces is a primary source of RWIs. Vomit and blood are less likely to cause RWIs. Look for clues to water quality before you get in the water—the pool water should be clean and clear with little or no odor. You should be able to clearly see the main drain on the bottom of the pool, and there should not be a strong chemical odor in the air. Visually inspect surfaces. Pool tiles and attractions such as waterslides should not be sticky or slimy. Lastly, ask the facility staff about the facility's protocols for maintaining water quality, conducting health inspections and training staff members about water quality.

You may also be able to obtain information about water quality in some natural settings, such as at the ocean or lake. Many guarded beaches are tested regularly for pollution and disease-causing organisms. In some areas, water quality flags give information about water conditions. For example, blue flags indicate good swimming conditions and red flags indicate a potential water quality problem.

Diarrhea

Diarrhea is the most commonly reported RWI. When a person with diarrhea swims, the water becomes contaminated. A person who swallows the contaminated water could also then become ill. To lower the risk of infection for others, a person who has diarrhea should not enter

Box 2-6
Six "PLEAs" for Healthy Swimming: Limiting the Spread of RWIs

1. **PLEASE** do not swim when you have diarrhea. This is especially important for children in diapers.

2. **PLEASE** avoid getting pool water in your mouth, or swallowing it.

3. **PLEASE** practice good hygiene.
   - Shower with soap before swimming.
   - Wash your hands after using the toilet or changing diapers.

4. **PLEASE** take your children on bathroom breaks and check diapers often.

5. **PLEASE** change diapers in a bathroom or a diaper-changing area, not at poolside.

6. **PLEASE** wash your children thoroughly (especially the buttocks area) with soap and water before swimming.

Adapted from Centers for Disease Control and Prevention: Six Steps for Healthy Swimming. (http://www.cdc.gov/healthyswimming/)

the water. The Centers for Disease Control and Prevention (CDC) has developed six "PLEAs" to promote safe and healthy swimming in pools and at waterparks **(Box 2-6)**.

When a young child who still wears diapers will be in the water, many facilities require that the child wear swim diapers **(Fig. 2-9)**. Swim diapers are specifically designed to be worn in the water. They are water-resistant and fit snugly around the child's waist and legs. However, if a child has a bowel movement in the diaper, there is still risk for stool escaping and contaminating the water. For this reason, it is important to take frequent breaks to check and change the diaper.

Fig. 2-9 Many facilities require children who wear diapers to wear swim diapers when they are in the pool.

A contamination incident involving feces or vomit that contains solid matter or food particles requires staff to implement decontamination procedures. These procedures include evacuating the pool, removing any solid matter, increasing the chlorine level and maintaining the elevated chlorine level for a set period of time before reducing the chlorine level to its normal level and reopening the pool. For an incident that involves vomit or formed stool, the pool must remain closed for 25 minutes. For an incident that involves diarrhea, the pool must remain closed for 13 hours.

Swimmer's Ear

Swimmer's ear, an RWI that most often affects children, occurs when water remains in the external ear canal for a prolonged period of time. The water usually is contaminated by organisms found in pools and other water environments. The trapped water allows these organisms to grow in the ear canal, causing irritation and infection. Signals of swimmer's ear typically begin within a few days of swimming and may go away on their own without treatment. However, a painful, swollen or full feeling in the ear or even slight hearing loss are reasons to see a health care provider. These signals could indicate a more serious inner ear infection. **Box 2-7** contains tips for preventing swimmer's ear.

Box 2-7
Tips for Preventing Swimmer's Ear

- Wear a swim cap or wetsuit hood, especially for activities that involve frequent submersions (such as surfing).
- Use silicone earplugs. Avoid wax earplugs because these can damage the ear canal and make infection more likely. Do not use any earplugs when surface diving.
- Keep the lining of your ear canals healthy. Do not insert objects (such as cotton swabs or a finger) into the ear canal, because doing so can remove protective earwax and scratch the lining of the ear canal, making infection more likely.
- Remove water from the ears after swimming.
  - Tilt your head to one side (so that one ear is facing down) and jump energetically several times to allow water to escape from your ear. Gently pulling the earlobe in different directions while the ear is facing down may also help the water escape.
  - Use a hair dryer on the low setting: gently pull down the ear lobe and blow warm air into the ear from several inches away.
- Use over-the-counter eardrops that contain one or more agents to evaporate any water, kill the organisms and moisturize the ear canal before and after swimming. Ask your health care provider for recommendations.
- Dry ears thoroughly after swimming by using a towel to gently wipe the outer ear. Do not insert anything (such as a cotton swab) into the ear canal in an attempt to dry it.
- Children who have ear tubes should only participate in aquatic activities that have been approved by their health care providers.

Staying Safe in Specific Aquatic Environments

Throughout the course of a lifetime, a person may have the opportunity to engage in and enjoy aquatic activities in a variety of settings. Every aquatic setting poses specific safety challenges. Being aware of these safety challenges can help you stay safe no matter what aquatic setting you are in.

Swimming Pools and Hot Tubs

Swimming pools and hot tubs may be open to the public or privately owned by homeowners. Public pools and hot tubs include those found in recreation and fitness centers, hotels and motels, and multi-unit housing complexes. Some public pools and hot tubs are supervised by lifeguards and others are not. **Box 2-8** summarizes important tips for staying safe for anyone visiting a public pool or hot tub.

Box 2-8
Safety Tips for Patrons of Public Pools and Hot Tubs

- Read and obey all rules and posted signs. Pay special attention to water-depth markings and "no diving" signs.
- Obey the lifeguard's instructions at all times.
- Supervise members of your own party while they are in the water, especially children, even when a lifeguard is on duty. Take breaks from water activities to give both the swimmers and those supervising them an opportunity to rest.

- Note the location of safety equipment (such as a reaching pole and ring buoy). Remind children not to play with the safety equipment.

- Do not swim in a pool that is overly crowded or with swimmers who are not following the rules.

- Check to see that the pool or hot tub and facility are well-maintained. Reconsider patronizing the facility if there are obvious hazards (such as cracks in the deck, malfunctioning equipment or cloudy water).

Home (residential) swimming pools and hot tubs are an attractive feature for many homeowners **(Fig. 2-10)**. They create a beautiful environment that offers years of fun and activity for families. However, pool or hot tub ownership carries with it the responsibility for ensuring that the pool or hot tub is safe and well maintained.

Fig. 2-10 A pool can be a lovely addition to the landscape and a great place for relaxing and entertaining, but it can also be a safety hazard if the proper precautions are not taken.
Photo: Life Saver Pool Fence Systems, Inc.

Preventing Unsupervised Access to the Pool or Hot Tub Area

Home swimming pools (including inground pools, aboveground pools and "easy-set" inflatable pools) and hot tubs pose a significant threat to young children living in the home, as well to other children in the neighborhood. Most drowning incidents involving children between the ages of 1 and 4 years take place in home swimming pools. Many of these incidents happen very suddenly—about 5 minutes or less after the child goes missing—and while the parents are at home. Homeowners with pools or hot tubs need to take a multi-tiered approach to securing the pool area and minimizing the likelihood that a child will gain unsupervised entry:

- Enclose the pool area on all four sides using an appropriate barrier system **(Box 2-9),** and then make sure the barrier remains secure. Always make sure gates are latched and keep items away from the barrier (such as lawn furniture) that a child could use to climb up and over into the pool area.

- Install pool alarms. These alarms use sensors to detect motion in the water. Underwater pool alarms generally perform better and can be used in conjunction with pool covers. Use remote alarm receivers so that the alarm can be heard inside the house or in other places away from the pool area.

Safety Barrier Guidelines for Home Pools (Pub. No. 362), a resource containing guidelines for choosing and installing fences, gates, covers and audible alarms to prevent unsupervised access to residential swimming pools and hot tubs, is available at no charge from the Consumer Product Safety Commission (CPSC) website (www.cpsc.gov). It is a good idea to check the CPSC site periodically for updated recommendations. Also, be aware that local building codes, regulations and statutes for pools and hot tubs differ from state to state. Many states have pool fence laws. Check with local authorities to find out specific building codes and owner responsibilities.

Preventing Drain Entrapment

Drain entrapment can occur when a pool or hot tub drain is uncovered, or the drain cover is broken or not secured properly. Suction pulls hair, clothing, jewelry, or a body part into or against

Box 2-9
Guidelines for Securing the Pool Area

- Pool fence gates should be self-closing and self-latching and open outward, away from the pool. The latch should be out of a small child's reach.

- Pool barriers should be at least 4 feet high and enclose the entire pool area. They should not have any features that could be used as a hand- or foothold. Solid barriers should not have any features other than normal construction joinery.

- For most fence designs, spacing between vertical members should not exceed 1¾ inches. The opening on chain link fences should not exceed 1¼ inches.

- Horizontal fence support structures that are less than 45 inches apart should be on the pool side of the fence. On fences with horizontal support structures that are greater than 45 inches apart, the horizontal support structures can be on either side of the fence.

- The space under a pool barrier should not exceed 4 inches.

- Any openings in the barrier should not allow a 4-inch sphere to pass through.

- Aboveground pools (including inflatable "easy-set"-type pools) should have a barrier mounted on top of the pool structure that encloses the entire pool. Steps or ladders to the pool should be removable or enclosed by a locked barrier, so that the pool surface is inaccessible.

- Hot tubs should have a lockable structural barrier that completely encloses the top of the hot tub and will not collapse under the weight of a child.

- It is preferable that the house should not form any side of the barrier.
  - In situations where a house does form one side of the barrier, the doors leading from the house to the pool should be locked and protected with alarms that produce a sound when a door is unexpectedly opened.
  - Alarms should continuously sound for 30 seconds and begin within 7 seconds of opening the door.

Adapted from Consumer Product Safety Commission: Safety Barrier Guidelines for Home Pools. (www.cpsc.gov)

the pool drain, leading to entrapment. The suction may be so strong that the person cannot pull away. Drowning can occur if the person's head is underwater and he or she is not able to break free of the drain. Disembowelment can also occur. Beginning in 2008, all public pools and hot tubs were required by law to have anti-entrapment drain covers installed. However, privately owned pools and hot tubs are not subject to the same law, so in many cases, home pool or hot tub drains may not be up to standard.

To protect against drain entrapment, remind people using the pool or hot tub to stay away from the drains and other openings that create suction. Install anti-entrapment drain covers and safety release systems, which offer protection from dangerous drain suction. Consider installing an automatic shutoff system for added protection. Clearly identify the location of the electrical cutoff switch for the pump, know where the pump switch is and know how to turn it off. Check with the Consumer Product Safety Commission (CPSC), Association of Pool and Spa Professionals, the National Swimming Pool Foundation or local authorities to find out more about safe pool and hot tub drainage systems.

Box 2-10
Minimizing Risk for Diving Injuries in Home Pool Settings

Most head, neck and spinal injuries in home pools result from diving into shallow water.

- Prohibit diving in aboveground pools, including inflatable "easy-set"-type pools. These pools are never safe for diving.
- Consult the Association of Pool and Spa Professionals (APSP), state law and local building codes for pool dimension guidelines to help you establish pool rules related to diving in an inground pool. For example:
  - Prohibit all dives into shallow water.
  - Only allow shallow-angle dives from the edge of the pool into deep water.
- Clearly mark the location of the breakpoint between shallow and deep water with a buoyed line and a contrasting stripe on the bottom 12 inches before the breakpoint. Mark the deck with signs that indicate the depth.
- Place "No Diving" signs on the deck near shallow water and on the fence or wall around the swimming pool or on a stand at the entry to the swimming pool area. Signs should be visible to anyone entering the pool or approaching shallow water.
- Prohibit elevated entry from any object not specifically designed for diving, such as chairs, fences or balconies.
- Install a diving board only if there is a safe diving envelope (the area of water in front of, below and to the sides of a diving board that is deep enough to prevent a diver from striking the bottom, regardless of the depth of the water or the design of the pool). The average home pool is not long enough or deep enough for safe springboard diving. It is the diving board manufacturer's responsibility to determine the necessary water envelope for safe diving.

Making, Posting and Enforcing Pool and Hot Tub Rules

Develop a list of pool and hot tub rules, post them prominently and enforce them without exception. Examples of rules you may establish include:

- Children permitted in the pool area only with adult supervision.
- Weak, inexperienced or nonswimmers must wear a life jacket.
- Always swim with a buddy.
- Please do not bring glass bottles or containers into the pool area.
- No running, pushing or rough horseplay.
- No diving (**Box 2-10**).
- Please do not sit or play near the drain.
- Please do not play breath-holding games.

Post depth markers and "No Diving" signs, as appropriate (**Fig. 2-11**). Use a buoyed line to show where the depth changes from shallow to deep, and make sure that weak or inexperienced swimmers stay in the shallow water. Keep extra U.S. Coast Guard-approved life jackets in a variety of sizes on hand for guests who may need them.

Preparing for Emergencies

As a pool or hot tub owner, you need to be prepared to respond should an emergency arise. There are three simple things you can do to prepare for an emergency.

Fig. 2-11 Post "No Diving" signs on the fence surrounding the pool area or at the entry to the pool area.

First, learn American Red Cross first aid and CPR.

Second, stock your pool area with a telephone, emergency contact information and basic water rescue equipment, including:

- Reaching equipment (such as a reaching pole or shepherd's crook) that can be used to pull a person to safety.
- Throwing equipment (such as a ring buoy, heaving jug or throw bag) that can be thrown to a person who is in trouble so that he or she can be pulled to safety.

One way to keep basic water rescue equipment organized and accessible is to make a safety post **(Box 2-11)**.

Box 2-11
How to Make a Safety Post

A safety post can be used to keep basic water rescue equipment organized and easily accessible poolside. To make a safety post, you will need:

- 4 inch × 4 inch post, 6 feet long
- Screw-in hanging hook large enough to hold the throwing equipment
- Throwing equipment, such as a ring buoy or a heaving jug[*]
- Reaching equipment, such as a 10- to 12-foot reaching pole
- Clips to secure the reaching equipment OR two 6-ounce cans with both ends removed and nails
- Plastic zipper bag
- First aid kit
- Emergency contact information, including phone numbers for summoning help and information that will help responders find your location (i.e., the street address and the names of the nearest cross streets)
- Safety poster or first aid booklet (optional)

1. On one side of the post, screw in the hanging hook about 1 foot from the top of the post.

2. On the other side of the post, secure the clips or nail the two open-ended cans, one about 1 foot above the other, no lower than 2 ½ feet from the bottom of the post.

3. Set the post 2 feet in the ground.

4. To make a heaving jug, put ½ inch of water or sand in the 1-gallon plastic jug and screw the top on tightly. (If the jug has a snap-on top, secure it with very strong glue.) Tie the rope to the handle of the jug.

5. Hang the ring buoy or heaving jug and line on the hanging hook.

6. Secure the reaching pole with the clips or put the reaching pole through the cans.

7. Put emergency contact information, the first aid kit and the first aid booklet or poster (if you are including one) in the plastic zipper bag and attach it to the top of the post.

*To make a heaving jug, you will also need a 1-gallon plastic jug with a top and 40–50 feet of lightweight rope.

Box 2-12
Emergency Action Plans

Having an emergency action plan in place and being familiar with the procedures it contains can save precious minutes when every minute counts.

To create an emergency action plan:

1. Identify the types of emergencies that could occur. Think about potential accidents, injuries, illnesses, weather events and other situations (such as power failures) that are likely to occur in your specific setting.

2. Develop and write down the procedure that is to be followed in the event of each emergency. Include:
   - The signal that will be used to indicate that the emergency action plan should be activated (such as a whistle blast, hand signals or both).
   - The steps for responding to the emergency, and who is responsible for each step.
   - The procedure for calling 9-1-1 or the local emergency number and directing emergency medical services (EMS) personnel to the scene.
   - What follow-up actions should be taken, if any.

3. Identify equipment that is needed to respond to the potential emergencies you have identified and stock it close by, in the pool area.

Third, make an emergency action plan **(Box 2-12)**. An **emergency action plan** consists of written procedures for dealing with specific potential accidents or emergency situations. Emergencies that should be addressed include injuries, illness, weather events, and situations such as power failures or drain entrapment. The emergency action plan details information that is needed to get control of the situation, such as:

- What signal will be used to indicate that there is an emergency.
- What equipment is available and where it is located (including the location of cutoff switches for pumps and hot tubs).
- Procedures for summoning emergency medical services (EMS) personnel (including the necessary phone numbers) and directing EMS personnel to the location.
- Procedures for providing aid and getting the situation under control, including what should be done and who should do it.

Review the emergency action plan with family members, guests and neighbors so that they are prepared to help implement the plan should the need arise.

Maintaining the Pool Area

Maintaining the pool area properly is a key safety measure.

- Keep the pool or hot tub water clean and clear. Chemically treat and test the water regularly. Follow the manufacturer's directions and safety instructions for chemical use. Clearly label chemicals and store them in childproof containers in a secured area.
- Keep the pool area properly illuminated.
- Completely secure covers in place immediately after using the pool or hot tub, and completely remove them before using the pool or hot tub.

Hosting Safe Pool Parties

One of the joys of owning a pool or hot tub is inviting others to enjoy it with you. Good planning can help to ensure that everyone has a good, and safe, time at your party. Be familiar with your homeowner's insurance policy. Additional coverage for the event may be required. Make sure that your guests (and their parents or guardians, if the guests are children) know that the party is a pool party. Finally, make arrangements to ensure appropriate supervision during the party.

Consider hiring one or more certified lifeguards to be on duty for the duration of the party. The number of guests and the size of the pool will help you determine how many lifeguards are needed. Contact the local parks and recreation department or local swimming pools to get names of Red Cross-certified lifeguards who are willing to lifeguard at private parties. As the host, you are responsible for checking to verify that the certifications of the lifeguards you have hired are current and providing all appropriate rescue equipment.

Even when lifeguards are on duty, and especially if lifeguards are *not* on duty, children should be actively supervised by parents or other responsible adults. Before the gathering, identify responsible adults to serve as water watchers. The water watcher's job is to supervise the pool when it is in use

Fig. 2-12 A "water watcher" card like this one can be used to identify people who have agreed to serve in this important role, and to remind them of their duties. *Courtesy of poolsafely.gov.*

(Fig. 2-12). Each water watcher must understand and accept responsibility for monitoring the activity in and around the pool and should be trained in first aid, CPR/AED and water safety. Also, remember to review your emergency action plan with your water watchers. Water watchers must agree to avoid distractions while they are on duty (for example using cell phones, socializing or engaging in other activities), and they should refrain from drinking alcohol before and while supervising water activities.

If the swimming portion of the party will go on for more than 1 hour, plan for rest breaks during which everyone is out of the water. Rest breaks are important for the lifeguards and water watchers, and they give the guests who are enjoying the water an opportunity to rest and warm up.

Also remember the importance of establishing and enforcing safety rules. Alcoholic beverages should be strictly prohibited for anyone who is, or will be, supervising or participating in water activities.

Using Hot Tubs Responsibly

In addition to all of the safety considerations detailed previously, hot tubs necessitate some special safety considerations. Although the hot water is relaxing and soothing and can improve circulation, it can also lead to problems if not enjoyed responsibly. Research has shown that high water temperatures can lead to drowsiness or even loss of consciousness, which can lead to drowning. In addition, the hot water can raise body temperature and blood pressure, placing the person at risk for heat-related emergencies. To safely enjoy a hot tub:

- Never use a hot tub when drinking alcohol or using other drugs.
- Never use a hot tub when you are alone.
- Do not increase the water temperature beyond 104°F (40°C).
- Limit your time in the hot tub to no more than 15 minutes.
- Do not use a hot tub if you are pregnant, take medications or have a chronic medical condition (such as high or low blood pressure, heart disease, epilepsy or diabetes) unless you have cleared this activity with your health care provider.
- Do not allow children younger than 5 years to use a hot tub. Children have difficulty adjusting to the extreme water temperature and are at risk for overheating.

The high water temperature in a hot tub provides a good environment for bacterial and parasite growth. If you own a hot tub, be sure to chemically treat and test the water regularly. Shower before entering the hot tub, because substances on the skin (such as dirt, lotion and perspiration) "use up" the chemicals used to treat the water, lowering their levels and increasing the risk for microbial growth in the hot tub. Also, abide by maximum capacity guidelines, because overcrowding of the hot tub reduces the effectiveness of the chemicals used to treat the water.

Waterparks

Waterparks (aquatic amusement parks) are a favorite source of recreation for many families (**Fig. 2-13**). Waterparks feature a wide range of attractions, including high-speed water slides, wave pools, lazy rivers, and water playgrounds or spray pads. Each of these features presents unique risks. While most waterparks go to great lengths to maintain safety, accidents can still happen, ranging from slips and falls on hard surfaces to head, neck or spinal injuries following a collision with another patron or the bottom of the pool.

Fig. 2-13 Waterparks offer varied water-based rides and attractions and are a favorite destination for many people.

For a safe and enjoyable experience at the waterpark:

- Visit the waterpark's website in advance to get information about the attractions and safety rules.
- Dress appropriately. In some cases, this may mean wearing water shoes.
- Follow all posted rules, especially those related to height and weight restrictions and life jacket use. Speak with waterpark staff if you are unsure about any rules or procedures.
- Listen and follow all instructions given by the lifeguards at each attraction.
- Recognize that each attraction may have specific rules that must be followed, in addition to the standard rules. For example, on some attractions (such as certain water slides), life jackets are not permitted, while on other attractions (such as fast-moving winding rivers), life jackets are required.
- Get into the correct position before starting down a water slide: face-up and feet-first. Follow any additional instructions that you may be given to lower your risk for injury. For example, on speed slides, you may be instructed to cross your ankles and fold your arms over your chest to help prevent injuries.
- Do not let children hold onto, or be held by, others when using water slides.

Natural Bodies of Water

Natural aquatic environments offer great beauty and variety, so it is no wonder that people seek these environments out and have found so many different ways to enjoy them. However, nature is unpredictable! To safely enjoy recreational activities in and around natural bodies of water, knowledge of the unique hazards these environments present and respect for the unpredictable ways of nature are necessary.

Rivers, Streams and Creeks

Rivers, streams and creeks offer plenty of choices for recreational activities, such as boating, fishing, rafting and tubing (**Fig. 2-14**). But the feature of rivers, streams

Fig. 2-14 Spending the day on a river is a great way to connect with nature. ©CulturaHughWhitaker/Getty Images

and creeks that makes them so great for these activities—moving water—can also make them dangerous. Knowing how to anticipate and respond to the dangers posed by moving water can help you stay safe when you are enjoying time on or near a river, stream or creek.

Currents

Currents in rivers, streams and creeks are often unpredictable and fast moving. Changes below the surface of the water can cause abrupt changes in the direction and intensity of the current. In addition, the current may not be visible on the surface, even though it may be strong below the surface. Currents can be extremely powerful. Their power increases exponentially with the speed of the water. For example, a current flowing at a rate of 2 miles per hour can exert pressure of up to 33 pounds per square inch, while a current flowing at a rate of 8 miles per hour can exert pressure of up to 538 pounds per square inch! Always respect the power of the water. Avoid wading in water where there is a strong current that could knock you off your feet, and wear a U.S. Coast Guard-approved life jacket when you are fishing, hunting, boating, rafting or tubing. If your boat, raft or tube overturns and you find yourself in a current, float on your back downstream, feet-first. Back-paddle with your arms to steer out of the current, and then swim or wade toward shore.

Entrapments

The bottom of many rivers, streams and creeks is covered with rocks and other submerged objects. The powerful force of the moving water can trap your foot or leg against one of these submerged objects, causing you to fall and get pinned against the object under the surface of the water. Entrapments are a risk even in shallow moving water. Never try to stand up in moving water. If your boat, raft or tube overturns and you find yourself in the water, float on your back with your feet up and pointed downstream to avoid possible entanglement of your feet or legs.

Strainers

A strainer (such as a snarl of tree limbs) is an obstacle in a current that acts like a kitchen colander. If you are upstream of a strainer, you could become trapped in it as the force of the current carries you toward it. If you find yourself approaching a strainer, swim toward the object headfirst, grab any part of the strainer at the surface of the water and try to kick and climb up and over the top.

Hydraulics

Hydraulics are the vertical whirlpools that occur as water flows over an object, such as a low-head dam or waterfall, causing a strong downward force **(Fig. 2-15)**. Whitewater rapids are often filled with dangerous hydraulics. Even if the hydraulic appears small, the reverse flow of the water can trap and hold a person underwater. It is difficult and sometimes impossible to escape from a hydraulic. If you are caught in a hydraulic, resist fighting the current. Instead, try to swim to the bottom, get into the downstream current and then reach the surface.

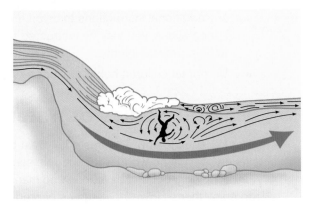

Fig. 2-15 A hydraulic is a powerful rotating force that develops as water flows over an object.

Dams

No dam is ever safe. When you are in, on or around the water, stay away from dams.

A fixed-crest/low-head dam is a barrier built across a river, stream or creek to control the flow of water **(Fig. 2-16)**. Some of the most harmless-looking low-head dams are often the most dangerous. Low-head dams with a thin line of whitewater across the surface can contain powerful hydraulic forces.

The opening of a dam can also create dangerous conditions. When the dam floodgates open, the water level can rise quickly below the dam, creating a wall of water. If the dam is part of a hydroelectric power plant, the current created on opening the dam can pull anyone or anything (including boats) above the dam into danger. The area downstream of dams is also dangerous. Recirculating water currents caused by the movement of water over or through the dam can draw objects back toward the dam.

Lakes and Ponds

Lake and pond water is usually murky, making it difficult to see below the surface. In addition, the bottoms of lakes and ponds often contain hidden hazards (such as rocks, sunken logs or debris, plants and broken glass). Because it is difficult to evaluate the depth of the water or to see underwater hazards, lakes and ponds are generally not safe for diving. The murkiness of the water can also make it difficult to notice a swimmer who is in trouble, especially if the swimmer is submerged.

When enjoying recreational activities in, on or near a lake or pond, enter the water with caution, and always enter feet-first. Wear a U.S. Coast Guard-approved life jacket (if you are boating or if you are a weak or inexperienced swimmer) and protective water shoes. Many lakes have designated swimming areas that may or may not be guarded. If the lakefront has designated swimming areas or lifeguards on duty, swim only in these areas **(Fig. 2-17)**. Be aware that many forms of wildlife also call the lake or pond home and avoid lakes or ponds that are inhabited by animals that can cause injury to humans, such as snapping turtles and alligators **(Box 2-13).**

Fig. 2-16 Stay away from dams. The chances of surviving an aquatic emergency involving a dam are slim.

Fig. 2-17 Some lakes have designated areas for swimming and lifeguard supervision.

Box 2-13
Freshwater Aquatic Wildlife

Many different forms of wildlife live in or near freshwater areas, including rivers, streams, creeks, lakes and ponds.

- Alligators can be found in freshwater in some southern states, such as Florida, Louisiana, Georgia and Texas. They are very dangerous, especially to small children.
- Snapping turtles are large freshwater turtles that often live in and around shallow ponds, lakes and streams. They have powerful jaws and their bites can cause severe injury. Avoid approaching or provoking a snapping turtle.
- Snakes are found in a variety of freshwater habitats, including streams, rivers, lakes and ponds. Snakes rarely pose a threat. Leave them alone and swim away slowly.
- Leeches are usually found in shallow, slow-moving freshwater. You may not see a leech in the water; it is more likely that you will find one on your skin when you come out of the water. Leeches are not harmful. To remove a leech from your skin, gently and slowly pull it off.

Alligator. © iStockphoto.com/Don Fink

Snapping turtle. Image © Ryan M. Bolten, 2014. Used under license from Shutterstock.com

Swimming and other aquatic activities should occur only in areas with good water quality. Conditions in these bodies of water change constantly. Many communities test lakes and ponds regularly for pollution and disease-causing organisms. Obey posted signs and avoid going in the water if the water quality is poor.

Oceans

For many people, a trip to the beach ranks high on their list of favorite things to do. After all, many people plan vacations around visiting a beach or engaging in other activities that take place in or on the ocean, such as boating, fishing, snorkeling, diving or surfing. As with all aquatic environments, however, knowledge of potential dangers is key to staying safe.

Waves

If you plan to swim in the ocean, stick to areas designated for swimming and pay attention to posted signs. These beaches often have lifeguards on duty, but some may not. Even in designated swimming areas, waves at ocean beaches can become quite large. Breaking waves are tremendously powerful, capable of moving large objects and knocking a person over (**Fig. 2-18**). The weight of a wave and the power of the crashing water can hold a person underwater—1 cubic foot of water weighs 62 pounds! Breaking waves near rocky shores are especially dangerous and can cause severe injuries or even death. Avoid swimming along rocky shorelines. When you are walking or playing along any shoreline, pay attention to the waves, and never turn your back on the ocean.

Fig. 2-18 Waves can be powerful, even on beaches designated for swimming and supervised by a lifeguard. Always pay attention to posted signs, and never swim at unguarded ocean beaches or in areas not designated for swimming.

Currents

The action of breaking waves against the beach or coastline creates currents.

Longshore currents

Longshore currents run parallel to the shore. A longshore current can quickly carry you away from your original point of entry. If you find yourself caught in a longshore current, try to swim toward shore while moving along with the current.

Rip currents

Rip currents move water away from the shore or beach and out to sea beyond the breaking waves (**Fig. 2-19**). A visual cue to a rip current is a narrow strip of choppy, turbulent water that moves differently from the water on either side of it. Rip currents typically break apart just past the line of breaking

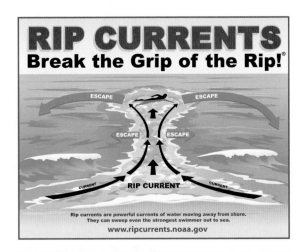

Fig. 2-19 Rip currents are powerful currents of water moving away from the shore. If you are caught in a rip current, swim parallel to the shore until you are free, or let the current take you out and then swim back after the current breaks apart.

waves and are usually no more than 80 feet wide. Under gentle surf conditions, rip currents may be more frequent, but less intense. With periods of high-wave activity, however, rip currents tend to form less often but are much stronger.

Rip currents are dangerous because they are very fast, often faster than a person can swim, and they carry a person away from shore. Even though most rip currents break apart near the shore, they can still take a person into deep water or a frightening distance from the shore. In rare cases, rip currents can sometimes push a person hundreds of feet beyond the surf zone. Rip currents account for more than 80 percent of rescues performed by surf beach lifeguards, and it is estimated that each year more than 100 people die due to rip currents on our nation's beaches.

Rip currents can be a challenge to even the strongest and most experienced swimmers. If caught in a rip current, do not panic! Swim parallel to the shore until free of the current. Once free, turn and swim toward shore. Alternatively, you can just let the rip current take you out to sea, and then swim back after the current breaks apart. If you are too exhausted to swim to shore, signal a lifeguard by calling and waving for help.

Tidal currents

Tidal currents are generated by tides. The change in the water level that occurs as the tide comes in and goes out creates a horizontal current called the tidal current. Tidal currents are somewhat inconsequential in wide areas, such as along an ocean shoreline, but in narrow areas, such as inlets, estuaries and bays, tidal currents can be very strong and fast, and should be avoided.

Because tidal currents are associated with the tides, they are predictable. Tides (and thus, tidal currents) are caused by the gravitational forces of the sun, the moon and the Earth's rotation. The movement of the moon has the strongest influence on tidal currents, which are strongest during a new or full moon (spring tides) and weakest when the moon is in its first or third phases (neap tides).

Aquatic plants

Weeds, grass and kelp often grow thickly in open water, posing a potential source of entanglement for a swimmer. Always stay clear of any patch of plants near the surface. If you find yourself caught up in any aquatic plant life, avoid quick movements, which may worsen the situation. Try to stay horizontal at the surface, swimming slowly and gently out of the plants, preferably along with a current.

Marine life

Before going into any ocean, be knowledgeable about the local marine life. Know which forms of marine life may be dangerous, how to avoid them and how to care for any injuries. On supervised beaches, look for signs alerting you to the presence of hazardous marine life. Shuffle your feet as you enter the ocean to create a disturbance and stir up any marine life that may be resting on the bottom so that you do not accidentally step on it.

Many forms of marine life (such as jellyfish, sea urchins, stinging coral and stingrays) cause stinging wounds. Stings from marine life can have effects that range from merely painful to very serious (such as allergic reactions that can cause breathing and heart problems, paralysis or even death). If the sting occurs in water, move the person to dry land as soon as possible and provide basic first aid to neutralize the toxin and reduce pain **(Box 2-14)**. Call 9-1-1 or the local emergency number if the person has been stung by a lethal jellyfish, does not know what caused the sting, has a history of allergic reactions to stings from aquatic life, has been stung on the face or neck or starts to have difficulty breathing.

Many people also worry about being attacked by a shark while in the ocean. The chance of a shark attack is relatively small, but because the consequences are severe, it is smart to take steps to minimize your risk **(Box 2-15)**.

Box 2-14
Care for a Jellyfish Sting

- Move the person to dry land as soon as possible.
- Offset the toxin by flushing the area as soon as possible. Do not rub the wound or apply fresh water, ammonia or rubbing alcohol because these substances may increase pain.

Bluebottle jellyfish.

  - For most types of jellyfish typically found along the east and west coasts of the United States, flush the injured area with vinegar for at least 30 seconds to offset the toxin. You can also apply a baking soda slurry if vinegar is not available.
  - For bluebottle jellyfish (Portuguese man-of-war), which are found in tropical waters, flush with ocean water instead of vinegar.
- Carefully remove any stingers or tentacles with gloved hands or a towel.
- After deactivating or removing the stingers or tentacles, immerse the affected area in water as hot as can be tolerated for at least 20 minutes or until the pain is relieved. If hot water is not available, use dry hot packs or, as a second choice, dry cold packs to help decrease the pain. Do not apply a pressure immobilization bandage.

Note: Call 9-1-1 or the local emergency number if the person has been stung by a lethal jellyfish, does not know what caused the sting, has a history of allergic reactions to stings from aquatic life, has been stung on the face or neck or starts to have difficulty breathing.

Box 2-15
Staying Away from Sharks

- Stay in a group. Sharks are more likely to attack a solitary person than a group.
- Avoid being in the water at night, dawn or dusk, when sharks are most active and not easily seen.
- Do not enter the water if bleeding from an open wound or if menstruating—sharks are attracted to blood and their ability to detect blood is very keen.
- Do not wear shiny jewelry, because the reflected light resembles fish scales.
- Do not enter the water in areas where there are signs of baitfish, especially those used by sport or commercial fishermen. Feeding areas or areas where sewage, runoff or rivers flow into the sea are also dangerous. Diving sea birds are good indicators of these areas.
- Use extra caution when waters are murky and avoid brightly colored clothing—sharks see contrast particularly well.
- Avoid excess splashing and do not allow pets in the water because their erratic movements may attract shark attention.
- Exercise caution when occupying the area between sandbars or near steep drop-offs—these are favorite hangouts for sharks.
- Do not enter the water if sharks are known to be present and evacuate the water swiftly but calmly if sharks are sighted.
- It goes without saying, but do not harass or provoke a shark if you do encounter one!

Staying Safe While Engaging in Water Activities

Specific activities that are enjoyed in, on or around the water have specific safety considerations.

Swimming

To stay safe while swimming, never swim alone and always swim in a supervised area. In addition, be aware of situations and behaviors that could threaten your safety while swimming.

Exhaustion

One of the dangerous "too's"—too tired—is particularly likely to affect swimmers. Becoming too tired while swimming can put a person at risk for drowning. Exhaustion (also referred to as fatigue) simply means that the person no longer has the energy to keep swimming or floating.

Exhaustion can occur as a reaction to cold water, after being in the sun for too long, as a result of being dehydrated, as a result of swimming too long or too hard, or from any combination of these factors. It is more likely to occur in swimmers who:

- Swim early in the season when the water is cold.
- Swim too much before they are really in shape.
- Do not know which strokes to use to conserve energy (for example, the elementary backstroke takes relatively little energy compared to a front crawl).
- Are young, inexperienced or both.

To prevent exhaustion, take breaks and rest often while swimming or doing other water activities. Be aware of your abilities and environment, and listen to your body.

Hyperventilation and Extended Breath-holding

Some swimmers believe that **hyperventilation** (rapid, deep breathing) before prolonged swimming under water increases the amount of oxygen in the body, allowing the swimmer to hold the breath longer. In fact, hyperventilation is a dangerous practice that may result in drowning. Rather than increasing oxygen levels in the blood, hyperventilation lowers carbon dioxide levels. This is risky because the drive to breathe is controlled by the amount of carbon dioxide in the blood. When a person hyperventilates and then swims underwater, the blood oxygen level can drop to a point that is so low that the swimmer passes out before the brain signals that it is time to breathe. When the person finally does take a breath instinctively, water rushes in and the drowning process begins.

Hyperventilation prior to submerging is an extremely dangerous practice that no swimmer should ever engage in. Also be aware that children who play competitive underwater games (such as trying to see who can hold his or her breath under the water the longest or who can swim the farthest distance underwater before coming up for air) are also at risk for hyperventilation **(Fig. 2-20)**. Teach children that competitive or repetitive underwater games can be extremely dangerous and stop this behavior if you see it occurring.

Fig. 2-20 Hyperventilation (taking a series of rapid deep breaths before submerging in an effort to hold the breath longer while underwater) is an extremely dangerous practice that can lead to drowning.

Diving

Injuries occurring from diving can be very severe or even fatal. For example, head, neck or spinal injuries can result in paraplegia (paralysis from the waist down), quadriplegia (paralysis from the neck down) or drowning.

Most diving injuries take place in water 5 feet deep or less. Many involve the use of alcohol or other drugs. Diving into open water that is shallow, diving into the shallow end of a pool, diving into aboveground pools and unsupervised diving from starting blocks cause most diving accidents.

Fig. 2-21 Aboveground pools are *never* safe for diving.
© Inmagine/imagebrokerrm

Areas that are *never* safe for diving include aboveground pools (including inflatable "easy-set"-type pools) and unfamiliar bodies of water, especially if the water is murky and you cannot evaluate the depth of the water or see hazards under the water **(Fig. 2-21)**. The deep ends of some inground pools are appropriate for diving, but you need to evaluate each pool carefully and obey any posted signs related to whether diving is permitted, and if so, in what areas of the pool. Typical locations of "No Diving" signs are on the deck near the edge of the pool and on walls or fences near shallow water. Many kinds of warnings signs are used, such as the following:

- "No Diving" painted on the deck in contrasting colors
- Tiled lettering embedded into the deck in contrasting colors
- Universal "No Diving" tiles embedded into the deck
- "No Diving" signs mounted on walls, fences or stands

Two common home pool designs are the hopper-bottom pool and spoon-shaped pool **(Fig. 2-22)**. A hopper-bottom pool has a bottom that angles sharply up on all four sides from the deepest point. Thus, the diving envelope (the area that is safe to dive into) is much smaller than it appears **(see Fig. 2-22A)**. Diving into a hopper-bottom pool can be like diving into a funnel. A spoon-shaped pool also may present risks to safe diving because the distance from the end of the diving board or the side of the pool to the slope of the bottom is greatly reduced **(see Fig. 2-22B)**. The bottom contour of the spoon-shaped pool may give a false sense of depth and bottom area throughout the deep end.

Guidelines for lowering the risk for diving injuries are given in **Box 2-16**.

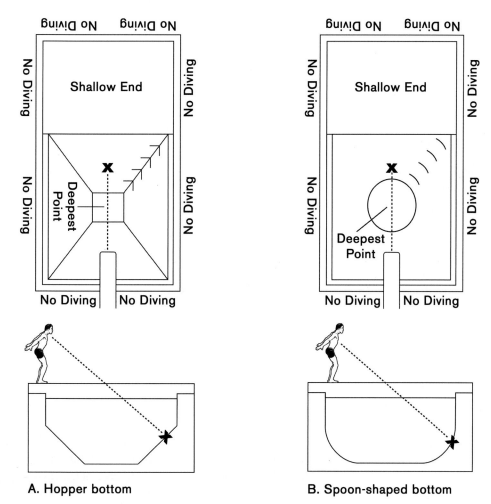

A. Hopper bottom

B. Spoon-shaped bottom

Fig. 2-22 Home pools often feature hopper bottoms or spoon-shaped bottoms, making them unsafe for diving. **(A)** Hopper-bottom pool. **(B)** Spoon-shaped pool.

Box 2-16
Guidelines for Lowering the Risk for Diving-Related Injuries

- Never drink and dive.
- Do not dive alone.
- Do not dive into unfamiliar bodies of water.
- Know the depth of the water (it should be at least 9 feet deep) and the shape of the pool bottom before you dive.
- Dive straight ahead, never off to the side.
- Make sure the area you are diving into is clear of swimmers or other obstacles before you dive.
- Do not dive from a running start.
- Do not dive from any structure that is not specifically designed for diving.
- Do not try to dive headfirst through something (such as an inner tube) or over something.

Derived from the National Pool and Spa Institute: American National Standard for Residential Inground Swimming Pools ANSI/NSPI-5 2003. Alexandria, Virginia: National Pool and Spa Institute, 2003.

Boating

Recreational boating is a term used to describe the operation of open motorboats, cabin motorboats, sailboats, canoes, kayaks, personal watercraft (such as Jet Skis and wave runners; **(Box 2-17)** and other types of watercraft. Boating can be a safe and enjoyable pastime, but it is important to know the dangers. In 2012, the Coast Guard counted 4515 recreational boating accidents, which resulted in 651 deaths and 3000 injuries. Of the deaths, approximately 71 percent were caused by drowning.

Alcohol is a leading contributor to recreational boating accidents, especially those resulting in fatalities. Other contributing factors include operator inattention, operator inexperience, improper lookout, machinery failure and excessive speed.

Preparation and education can go a long way toward preventing recreational boating accidents, and surviving an accident if one should occur. First, check with your state for local laws and regulations related to boating. Second, obtain the proper training before operating a watercraft and stay up-to-date. Training is not just recommended for people

---

Box 2-17
Personal Watercraft Safety

When operating a personal watercraft, wear a U.S. Coast Guard-approved life jacket and develop a float plan before leaving the shore. In addition:

- Know the local laws and regulations. Some states have special laws governing the use of personal watercraft that address operation, life jacket use, registration and licensing requirements, minimum age requirements, education, environmental restrictions and required safety equipment.

- Operate personal watercraft with courtesy and common sense. Pay attention to surroundings and follow the traffic pattern of the waterway. Obey no-wake and speed zones.

Image © Wollertz, 2014. Used under license from Shutterstock.com

- Use extreme caution around swimmers, surfers and other boaters. Run personal watercraft at a slow speed until the craft is away from the shore, swimming areas and docks. Avoid passing close to other boats and jumping wakes. This behavior is dangerous and often illegal.

- Ride with a buddy. Always ride in groups of two or three. You never know when an emergency might occur.

- Always attach the engine cutoff lanyard to yourself and the personal watercraft during operation.

operating large boats—motorboats (both open and cabin type) and personal watercraft are the most common types of vessels involved in reported accidents. Boating safety courses can teach you the fundamentals of safely operating and navigating your vessel, as well as provide information about local water conditions and hazards. Boating safety courses are offered through the American Red Cross (www.redcross.org), U.S. Coast Guard Auxiliary (www.cgaux.org), United States Power Squadrons (www.usps.org) and local state boating authorities. Information about safe boat handling for canoes, kayaks and sailboats can be obtained from the American Canoe Association (www.americancanoe. org) or U.S. Sailing (www.ussailing.org), respectively. The National Association of State Boating Law Administrators (NASBLA; www.nasbla.org), a national nonprofit organization that represents the recreational boating authorities of all 50 states and the U.S. territories, works to establish standards for boating safety education and is a valuable source of information about recreational boating safety courses.

In addition to educating yourself about the safe operation of your watercraft, there are additional steps you can take to promote safety while boating, including wearing a U.S. Coast Guard-approved life jacket, having appropriate rescue and emergency response equipment on hand, creating a float plan, being knowledgeable about local water conditions and hazards and being prepared for changes in the weather.

Wear a Life Jacket

In 2012, 84 percent of the people who died from drowning as a result of a recreational boating accident were not wearing life jackets. This statistic underscores the importance of always wearing a U.S. Coast Guard-approved life jacket when boating. Most boating emergencies happen suddenly, leaving you little to no time to "put on a life jacket if you need it." Put your life jacket on at the dock and do not take it off until you return **(Fig. 2-23)**. Even good swimmers should wear a life jacket when boating because the potential always exists for falling or being thrown into cold or dangerous water, or for sustaining a head injury following a collision. In cold water, having a life jacket on can be the

Fig. 2-23 When boating, put your life jacket on before you leave the dock and do not take it off until you return to shore, even if you are an experienced swimmer. © *Andersen Ross/Getty Images*

single most important factor in surviving the incident. Many states have laws requiring life jacket use for people being towed on water skis, tubes or similar devices, and for people who are operating personal watercraft.

Be Prepared with Rescue and Emergency Response Equipment

Make sure your watercraft is stocked with equipment that can help you in case you run into trouble. In addition to extra life jackets and equipment for throwing and reaching assists, keep equipment for signaling distress on board. Equipment for communicating distress visually (such as flags, flares or lights) and sound-producing devices (such as an air horn or an athletic whistle) is required for some boats per U.S. Coast Guard regulations. Fire extinguishers may also be required on board per U.S. Coast Guard regulations.

It is also important to have a reliable way to communicate with the shore and other boats in case of an emergency. In many boating emergencies, a nearby boat may be able to provide assistance and can respond quickly. A marine very high frequency (VHF) radio is a two-way communication device that allows boaters to contact other boaters, bridge operators and harbor officials. In addition, many of these devices can provide rescue personnel with your exact location. All marine rescue personnel and commercial ships use this type of radio, and in many locations, the U.S. Coast Guard monitors VHF channel 16 at all times, 24 hours a day, 7 days a week. Also consider installing marine cell phone signal boosters to extend the range of your cell phone signal while you are on the water.

Finally, make sure the boat has the proper equipment to assist with reboarding, should that become necessary. Larger boats may have a rope ladder or dock line available. Canoes and kayaks may have short lengths of rope attached to the ends of the canoe or kayak (called "painters") and end loops that look like handles that may be helpful for righting and reentering the craft.

Create a Float Plan

A float plan is a written document that provides the details of a boating trip. It contains information about the vessel, the people on board and the planned itinerary. Before you leave shore, create a float plan and leave it with a responsible person on land who can initiate rescue efforts if you fail to return or check in on time.

Be Knowledgeable about Local Water Conditions and Hazards

It is important to understand local water conditions and hazards. Changing tides can cause significant changes in water depth. Sandbars, currents, aquatic life and bottom conditions are constantly changing and creating new hazards. Certain areas may become crowded with commercial traffic. In some aquatic environments, it may be necessary to pass under a drawbridge or go through a lock. The U.S. Coast Guard, U.S. Army Corps of Engineers, marina staff and local authorities can provide helpful information about local water conditions and hazards.

Be Prepared for Changes in the Weather

In many open-water environments, the weather and water conditions can change rapidly and dramatically. Bad weather is always dangerous, but it can be deadly for boaters far away from the shore. Large waves, high winds and changing currents can make travel difficult and may lead to capsizing.

Remember the adage, "*Know before you go.*" Always check the weather before leaving and then keep an eye on the weather throughout the day. Boats equipped with marine VHF radios can monitor local forecasts. In addition, be alert to environmental cues to incoming weather changes, such as changes in cloud cover or sky color, a sudden drop in temperature, abrupt changes in wind speed or direction or a falling barometer. **Box 2-18** summarizes actions to take if severe weather develops.

Box 2-18
Boating Safety: If Severe Weather Develops

- Slow down and maintain enough boat speed to steadily move forward but still stay in control.
- Check to make sure that everyone on board is adequately dressed and wearing a properly fitting life jacket.
- Turn on the boat's navigation lights.
- Head into waves at a 45° angle; if on a personal watercraft, approach waves at a 90° angle.
- Have passengers sit low in the boat or on the floor near the centerline. Keep your shoulders between the gunwales on small boats. Do not sit on the gunwales, bow, seatbacks or any other area not designed for seating.
- Remain still and do not move about the boat.
  - If you must move, maintain three points of contact.
  - Do not stand up in small boats.
- Anchor the boat, if necessary and safe to do so.

Tubing and Rafting

Tubing and rafting are popular river sports. Depending on the river and the time of year, the experience may range from leisurely drifting downstream on calm waters to an adrenaline-packed thrill ride over whitewater rapids **(Fig. 2-24)**. If you are planning to tube or raft with a tour company, check to make sure that the tour guide is qualified and well-trained. The local chamber of commerce can provide information about accredited tour guides and companies. In addition, following these guidelines can help you have a safe and enjoyable rafting or tubing trip:

Fig. 2-24 Whitewater rafting tours are popular with those seeking a thrill.
Image © VILevi, 2014. Used under license from Shutterstock.com

- Never go tubing or rafting after a heavy rain or if flood or flash flood warnings are posted.
- Wear a U.S. Coast Guard-approved life jacket, a helmet (if required) and water shoes.
- Do not consume alcohol while tubing or rafting.
- Always abide by the specifications regarding the number of people the raft or tube can accommodate. Never overload your raft or tube.
- Create a float plan and leave it with a responsible person on shore if you are setting out on your own.

Fishing and Hunting

In most fishing- and hunting-related accidents involving the water, the person never intended to get in the water. To lower your risk of drowning as result of a water-related accident while hunting or fishing:

- Take a boating safety course if you plan to use a boat to fish or hunt.
- Always wear a U.S. Coast Guard-approved life jacket if you intend to be in a boat or near the water.
- Do not consume alcohol while hunting or fishing.
- Always hunt or fish with a friend.
- When you are in a boat, keep a wide base of support and a low center of gravity and use your hands to maintain your balance.
- Be especially careful of your footing when walking near water.
- Dress properly for the weather.
- Have a reaching or throwing device on hand.

Outdoor Ice Sports and Activities

In parts of the country when natural bodies of water freeze during the winter months, people often enjoy outdoor ice sports and activities, such as skating, ice fishing and snowmobiling **(Fig. 2-25)**.

There is no such thing as 100 percent safe ice. Ice on smaller, shallower and slower-moving bodies of water tends to be more solid than ice on larger, deeper and fast-moving bodies of water. Ice that forms over open water may be unsafe if the following are present:

- Springs or fast-moving water
- Wind and wave action
- Waterfowl and schooling fish
- Decomposing material in the water
- Water bubblers (devices designed to keep the water near boat docks from freezing thick)
- Discharge from an industrial site or power production facility
- Objects protruding through the ice, such as tree stumps

Fig. 2-25 Even in cold parts of the country, people find ways to enjoy outdoor aquatic activities all year long. *Image © Stephen McSweeney, 2014. Used under license from Shutterstock.com*

Do not go out on ice that has recently frozen, thawed and then frozen again. This happens in the spring and early winter as temperatures change often. Wait until the outside temperature has been below freezing long enough that at least 4 inches of solid ice forms over the entire area. Always check the ice thickness before going out using a chisel, cordless drill or ice auger. Ice should be solid and at least 4 inches thick if you are planning to walk on it. However, this thickness is not enough for snowmobiles, all-terrain vehicles or other vehicles, or if more than one person will be on the ice. Be aware that the thickness may not be the same over the entire area, so always use caution, even if the ice is thick enough in the place where you took your measurement.

Dress in several loose-fitting, lightweight layers, instead of one heavy layer. Wear a hat, boots and a water-resistant outer layer. Wear a life jacket under your outer layer, unless you will be driving onto the ice in an enclosed vehicle, such as a truck or car. If the truck or car were to fall through the ice, a life jacket worn under your clothes could hinder your ability to escape from the vehicle quickly.

Whenever you are planning on going out on the ice, always go with a friend and let someone on shore know where you are and when you will return. Look for objects sticking up through the ice and mark them as hazards. Be prepared in case the ice breaks. Have something at hand to throw or extend to a person who needs help, such as a rope with a weighted end, a long tree branch, a wooden pole or a plastic jug with a line attached.

When ice breaks, it usually occurs suddenly and without warning. The sudden surprise of falling through the ice coupled with the shock of the cold water often causes the person to panic. Almost immediately, the exposure to the cold water reduces the ability to move the arms and legs, which can further increase panic as any effort to get out of the water becomes even more difficult. Ice rescue picks (ice claws), which are handles with sharp metal spikes that a person can use to climb back onto the ice after falling through, can be invaluable in this situation and are a wise investment if you plan on going out on the ice.

If you fall through the ice, try to stay calm. Turn toward the direction you came from, since the ice is likely to be strongest there, and quickly get into a floating position on your stomach. Bend your knees to help trap air in your pant legs and boots. Reach forward onto the broken ice, but do not push down on it. (If you have ice rescue picks, dig the points of the picks into the ice.) Use a breaststroke or other kick to push your body farther onto the ice. Once you are on the ice, roll away from the break area. If a companion falls through the ice, encourage the person to remain calm and use a reaching or throwing assist (described in detail in Chapter 3) to help pull the person to safety.

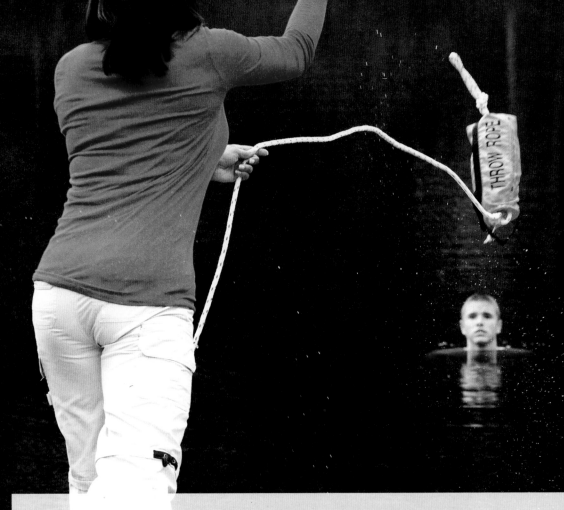

Recognizing and Responding to Aquatic Emergencies

Many Americans live, work and play in or near water. In fact, nearly 40 percent of our nation's population lives in counties directly on a shoreline, and this number is getting bigger each year. That's not even counting our access to lakes, rivers, pools and other aquatic environments.

Now, more than ever, knowing how to recognize and respond to an aquatic emergency is as important as knowing how to prevent one.

Recognizing an Emergency

An emergency can happen to anyone in or around the water, regardless of swimming ability. For example, a strong swimmer can get into trouble in the water because of sudden illness or injury. Or, a nonswimmer playing in shallow water can be knocked down by a wave or pulled into deeper water by a rip current. The key to recognizing an emergency is staying alert and being able to recognize when a person is having trouble in the water.

Staying Alert

Staying alert means using all your senses when observing others in and around the water. For example, you may see a swimmer acting oddly. Or, you may hear a scream or sudden splash. Keep in mind that the signals of an emergency might be what you *do not* see or hear. For instance, it may surprise you to learn that most people who are in trouble in the water cannot or do not call for help. They spend their energy just trying to keep their heads above water to get a breath. Likewise, a person who is experiencing a medical emergency might slip underwater quickly and never resurface.

The more alert you are, the faster you can respond to an emergency and potentially save a life.

Identifying When a Person Needs Help

A person who needs help may be drowning, or he may be swimming but in distress. It is essential to identify what is going on so you can respond appropriately. **Table 3-1** compares and summarizes the typical behaviors and appearances of distressed swimmers, drowning victims who are active and drowning victims who are passive. Early recognition and response greatly increases the chances of survival for a person who is drowning **(Fig. 3-1)**.

Chain of Drowning Survival

A person who is drowning has the greatest chance of survival if these steps are followed:

Recognize the signs of someone in trouble and shout for help

Rescue and remove the person from the water (without putting yourself in danger)

Call emergency medical services (EMS)

Begin rescue breathing and CPR

Use an AED if available and transfer care to advanced life support

American Red Cross

Fig. 3-1 Following the steps outlined in *Chain of Drowning Survival* from the American Red Cross can increase a person's chances of surviving a drowning incident.

Drowning Victim—Active

A drowning victim who is struggling to remain at the surface of the water has distinctive arm and body positions. These are efforts to try to keep the mouth above the water's surface in order to breathe. This universal behavior is called the *instinctive drowning response*.

A drowning victim who is struggling to remain at the surface of the water cannot call out for help because his efforts are focused on getting a breath **(Fig. 3-2)**. In fact, a drowning in progress is often silent. The person works to maintain a vertical position and keep his

Fig. 3-2 A drowning victim who is struggling to stay at the surface of the water and to breathe has no energy left to call out for help.

Table 3-1 Recognizing When a Person Needs Help

	Distressed Swimmer	Drowning Victim—Active	Drowning Victim—Passive
Head position	Above water	Tilted back with face looking up	• Face-up or face-down in the water • Submerged
Appearance	• Trying to support self by holding or clinging to a lane line or safety line • Concerned facial expression	• Struggling to keep or get the head above the surface of the water • Struggling to reach the surface, if underwater • Panicked or wide-eyed facial expression	• Limp or convulsion-like movements • Floating or submerged • Eyes may be closed • If submerged, may look like a shadow
Breathing	Breathing	Struggling to breathe	Not breathing
Arm and leg action	• Floating, sculling or treading water • May wave for help	Arms at sides or in front alternately moving up and pressing down	None
Body position	Horizontal, vertical or diagonal, depending on means of support	Vertical, leaning slightly back	Horizontal or vertical
Locomotion	• Little or no forward progress • Increasingly less able to support self	None	None
Sounds	Able to call for help but may not do so	Cannot call for help	None
Location in water	At the surface	At the surface, underwater or sinking	Floating at the surface, sinking or submerged on the bottom

face above the water by pressing down with his arms at his sides or in front. However, the person's mouth may slip underwater, often repeatedly. Young children may tip forward into a horizontal face-down position and be unable to keep the mouth above the surface of the water at all. The person will not make any forward progress in the water, and may only be able to stay at the surface for 20–60 seconds, if at all. The person may continue to struggle underwater but eventually will lose consciousness and stop moving.

Some drowning victims are not at the surface when the problem occurs. For example, the person may slip into water over his head, incur an injury, or experience a sudden illness and struggle underwater to reach the surface. These drowning victims may look like they are playing or floating underwater. It may be difficult to recognize a drowning victim when the person is underwater.

Drowning Victim—Passive

Some people who are drowning do not struggle. They suddenly slip underwater (for example, as a result of a sudden illness or injury or a dangerous behavior such as hyperventilation and prolonged underwater breath-holding). The use of alcohol or other drugs is also frequently a contributor to this type of drowning incident.

A person who is drowning but not struggling may be floating face-down at the surface of the water, or she may be underwater in a face-down or face-up position, or on her side. The person may be limp or have slight convulsive movements. The person is not moving or breathing. It can be difficult to see a

Fig. 3-3 A drowning victim who is underwater can be difficult to see. The person may look like a shadow, a smudge or an object like a towel.

drowning victim who is underwater, especially if the person is at the bottom of the pool or in a natural body of water where the water is murky. In a pool, the person may look like a shadow or an object like a towel on the bottom **(Fig. 3-3)**.

Distressed Swimmer

A distressed swimmer is someone who is not drowning, but needs help. A swimmer can become distressed for several reasons, including exhaustion, cramping or a sudden illness. A swimmer who is distressed may be afloat and able to breathe and call for help. However, you will notice that she is making little or no forward progress. She may be treading water or clinging to a line for support. A distressed swimmer may be unable to reach safety without assistance. Without help, a swimmer in distress may soon become a drowning victim.

Responding to an Emergency

In an emergency, your role is to recognize the emergency, decide to act, call emergency medical services (EMS) personnel for help and give assistance consistent with your knowledge and training until EMS personnel arrive and take over **(Box 3-1)**. If you work at an aquatic facility, you are a member of the safety team, which works to prepare for, prevent and respond to emergencies. As such, you are responsible for being familiar with the facility's emergency action plan, as well as your role in implementing it should an emergency occur.

Deciding to Act

In an emergency, deciding to act is not always as simple as it sounds. People are often slow to act in an emergency because they are not exactly sure what to do or they think someone else will take action. In an emergency situation, your decision to act could make the difference between life or death for the person who needs help.

Box 3-1
The Emergency Medical Services (EMS) System

The emergency medical services (EMS) system is a network of professionals linked together to provide the best care for people in all emergencies, both in and out of the water.

The system begins when someone sees an emergency and decides to take action by calling 9-1-1 or the local emergency number.

This action allows the EMS dispatcher to take down information about the emergency and provide it to the trained EMS professionals who will respond to the scene.

EMS professionals may include paramedics (trained to give advanced-level medical care at the scene of an emergency); emergency medical technicians (EMTs; trained to give mid-level medical care at the scene of an emergency); emergency medical responders (EMRs; trained to give basic-level care at the scene of an emergency); police officers; firefighters and other professional rescuers (for example, ski patrollers, park rangers).

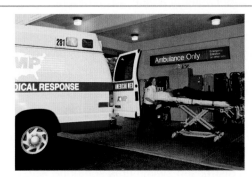

© ChadBaker/JasonReed/RyanMcVay/Getty Images

Once on the scene, these professionals will take over the care of the person, including transportation to a hospital or other facility for the best medical care if needed.

In the excitement of an emergency, it is easy to become frightened or confused about what to do. Remember to stay calm; you can help. In any emergency situation, follow the three action steps, **CHECK—CALL—CARE:**

- **CHECK** the scene and the person.
- **CALL** 9-1-1 or the local emergency number.
- **CARE** for the person. Give care according to the conditions that you find and your level of knowledge and training.

Let's take a look at the first step: check. First, check the scene. Be on the lookout for other victims, and for signals that the scene is unsafe. Look for clues as to what happened. Also check for bystanders who may be able to help you. *Never* rush into a dangerous situation, or you risk becoming a victim yourself. After you check the scene, check the person.

An aquatic emergency can take place on land or in the water. If the person is in the water, you must decide whether he or she needs help getting out of the water. Only help the person get out of the water if you can do it safely (for example, by using a reaching or throwing assist, which you will learn about later in this chapter). Do not enter the water to help the person unless you are specifically trained to perform in-water rescues. Your safety must be your top priority. If you cannot safely help the person out of the water, get help from a trained responder, such as a lifeguard, or call 9-1-1 or the local emergency number and wait for help.

Calling for Help

Once you have checked the scene and the person, take the second emergency action step: call 9-1-1 or the local emergency number to activate the EMS system. Whenever possible, send another person to make the call while you continue to stay with the person. Whether you make the call yourself or send someone else to call, be prepared to give the dispatcher the following information:

- Your name (or the name of the person making the call)
- The telephone number of the phone being used
- The location of the emergency (the exact address, city or town; nearby intersections or landmarks; the name of the facility)
- A description of what happened
- A description of the number of victims
- A description of what help has been given so far

Stay on the phone with the dispatcher until the dispatcher tells you it is all right to hang up. The dispatcher may need additional information from you, or he or she may be able to help by giving you first aid instructions over the phone.

The following conditions and situations are serious and require a call to 9-1-1 or the local emergency number to activate the EMS system:

- Fatal or nonfatal drowning
- Injury or suspected injury to the head, neck or spine
- Trouble breathing
- Persistent chest or abdominal pain or pressure
- Unconsciousness
- Severe bleeding, vomiting blood or passing blood
- Seizures that occur in the water or last more than 5 minutes
- Severe headache or slurred speech
- Poisoning
- Possible broken bones
- Multiple injuries

If you are unsure about whether professional help is needed, act on the side of caution and activate the EMS system.

Giving Assistance

The final emergency action step is to give care according to the conditions that you find and your level of knowledge and training **(Box 3-2)**. Make the person comfortable until EMS personnel arrive and take over.

Box 3-2
Learn Lifesaving Skills!

Many different types of first aid emergencies can occur in aquatic settings, ranging from the relatively minor (such as an abrasion or jellyfish sting) to the life-threatening (such as sudden cardiac arrest or anaphylaxis). People who experience sudden cardiac arrest or other serious first aid emergencies have a better chance of surviving when those around them know how to respond and give care until trained personnel arrive to take over. Unfortunately, many people do not know how to provide basic first aid and emergency cardiovascular care or are uncomfortable providing this care.

Red Cross first aid, CPR and AED (automated external defibrillator) training programs are designed to give you the confidence to respond in an emergency situation with skills that can save a life. By taking a Red Cross course, you learn from the best. Red Cross materials are developed in collaboration with leading educational and medical authorities and incorporate the latest science in first aid and emergency cardiovascular care. Courses are taught by certified instructors and, upon successful completion, participants earn nationally recognized certificates. Spanish-language courses are also available. To enroll in a Red Cross first aid, CPR and AED class visit www.redcross.org.

In an aquatic emergency such as drowning, knowing how to do full CPR (cycles of chest compressions and rescue breaths) is critical.

Basic Water Rescue: Helping Others in an Aquatic Emergency

Learning basic water rescue skills is important for anyone who lives, works or plays near water. There are many different ways to help a person who is in trouble in the water to safety. The method you will use depends on your level of training and the situation. Always take care to choose an assist that helps the person, while keeping you as safe as possible as you respond.

Reaching and Throwing Assists

Reaching and throwing assists allow you to help a conscious person who is in trouble without entering the water yourself. These types of assists are the safest assists for responders who are not professionally trained lifeguards to perform during an aquatic emergency. They are also the best type of assist to use when someone has fallen through ice (**Box 3-3**). To keep yourself safe, always remember "*Reach or throw, don't go!*"

When doing a reaching or throwing assist:

- Start the rescue by talking to the person, if possible. Let the person know help is coming.
- Use gestures to communicate with the person if it is too noisy or if the person is too far away to hear.
- Tell the person what he or she can do to help with the rescue, such as grasping a line, rescue buoy or other floating device.
- Encourage the person to move toward safety by kicking or stroking. Some people are able to reach safety by themselves with calm encouragement from a person on the deck or shore.

Reaching Assists

If the person is close enough, use a reaching assist to help him or her out of the water. To do a reaching assist, use any available object that will extend your reach and give something for the person to grab so you can pull the person in. Items that work well for reaching assists include a pole, an oar or paddle, a tree branch, a shirt, a belt or a towel. Community or hotel pools and recreational areas often have reaching equipment, such as a shepherd's crook (an aluminum or fiberglass pole with a large hook on one end), located close to the water.

You can perform a reaching assist from the pool deck, pier surface or shoreline. If no equipment is available and you are close enough, you may be able to perform a reaching assist by extending your arm to the person. You can also perform a reaching assist from a position within the water by extending an arm or a leg to the person, if you are already in the water and you have something secure to hold onto. **Water Rescue Skill Sheet 3-1** describes how to perform a step-by-step reaching assist.

Throwing Assists

A throwing assist involves throwing an object that the person can grasp so you can pull him or her to safety. A floating object with a line attached is ideal for a throwing assist; however, lines and floats can also be used alone. Rescue devices that are meant for throwing assists include a heaving line, ring buoy, throw bag or heaving jug **(Fig. 3-4)**. In some situations, you may have to improvise with an object that floats but is not specifically meant for throwing assists, such as a rescue tube (a vinyl, foam-filled tube with an attached tow line that is standard equipment for lifeguards), life jacket or cooler. If possible, keep a throwing object with a coiled line in a prominent location that is accessible to the water, so that anyone can quickly access it to throw to someone in trouble. All boats should

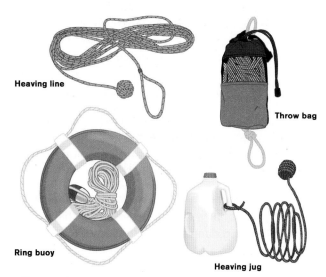

Fig. 3-4 A variety of items can be used for a throwing assist.

have rescue equipment for throwing assists onboard. **Water Rescue Skill Sheet 3-2** describes how to perform a step-by-step throwing assist.

Box 3-3

Using a Reaching or Throwing Assist to Help a Person Who Has Fallen Through Ice

Never go out onto the ice in an attempt to rescue a person who has fallen through the ice. Because a person has just fallen through it, the ice is unsafe. A responder who rushes out onto the ice is likely to become a victim as well. Instead, follow these guidelines:

1. Send someone to call EMS personnel immediately. Trained responders may be needed to get the person out of the ice. Even if you are successful in rescuing the person from the ice without the help of EMS personnel, the person will still need medical care.

2. From a secure place on land, try a reaching or throwing assist. Use anything at hand that the person can grasp for support, such as a tree branch, pole, life jacket or weighted rope. Act quickly. Within 1 minute, the person's hands may be too numb to grasp the object.

3. Pull the person to shore and give first aid for hypothermia. If it is not possible to safely pull the person to shore, reassure the person and make sure he or she is as secure as possible until help arrives.

Wading Assists

If a throwing assist does not work and the water is shallow enough for wading (that is, less than chest deep), you can try a wading assist **(Fig. 3-5)**. A wading assist involves wading into the water and using a reaching assist to help pull the person to safety. Objects that may help extend your reach and give the person something to grab on to include rescue equipment (such as a rescue tube or ring buoy), kickboard, life jacket, tree branch, pole, air mattress or paddle.

Fig. 3-5 A wading assist can be used when the water is less than chest deep and there are no conditions that make wading dangerous. For your own safety, wear a life jacket when performing a wading assist. Take an object to extend to the person to hold on to so that the person does not have to hold on to you.

You can also use a wading assist to rescue an unconscious or submerged person who is in water that is less than chest deep. When the person is unconscious or submerged, instead of using a reaching assist to pull the person to safety, use a flotation device to keep the person at the surface of the water and support him while you tow him to safety.

For your own safety, wear a life jacket if one is available when attempting a wading assist. Only perform a wading assist in water that is less than chest deep. If a current or soft bottom makes wading dangerous, do not enter the water. **Water Rescue Skill Sheet 3-3** describes how to perform a step-by-step wading assist.

Sloped Entry Assists

A walking assist or a beach drag may be used to remove a person from shallow water along a sloping beach, shore or pool entry. A walking assist can also be used to help a person out of the water using the steps of a pool. Use a walking assist when the person is conscious and able to support some or all of his weight. Use a beach drag when the person is unconscious or otherwise unable to bear weight. **Water Rescue Skill Sheet 3-4** describes how to perform these step-by-step assists.

Two-person Removal from the Water Using a Backboard

A backboard is the standard piece of equipment used by lifeguards to remove a person from the water when the person is unable to exit the water on his or her own or when the person has a possible injury to the head, neck or spine. Usually this type of rescue is performed by two lifeguards, but if a second lifeguard is not available, a bystander may be required to assist. **Water Rescue Skill Sheet 3-5** describes how to assist a lifeguard in removing a person from the water using a backboard.

Manual In-line Stabilization

Manual in-line stabilization is a technique used to minimize movement of a person's head, neck and spine when a head, neck or spinal injury is present or suspected **(Box 3-4)**. Injuries to the head, neck or spine can be serious because they may result in lifelong disability

Box 3-4
Recognizing Head, Neck and Spinal Injuries

If you are unsure whether a person has a head, neck or spinal injury, think about what the person was doing and what happened to cause the injury when checking the scene. In aquatic settings, head, neck or spinal injuries are usually caused by high-impact, high-risk activities, such as:

- Entering head-first into shallow water
- Falling from greater than standing height
- Entering the water from a height, such as a diving board, waterslide, embankment, cliff or tower
- Striking a submerged or floating object
- Receiving a blow to the head
- Colliding with another swimmer
- Striking the water with high impact, such as falling while water skiing or surfing

In addition to noting the circumstances of the injury, observe the person for signals of a possible head, neck or spinal injury. These include:

- Changes in level of consciousness
- Severe pain or pressure in the head, neck or spine
- Loss of balance
- Partial or complete loss of movement of any body part
- Back pain, weakness, tingling or loss of sensation in the hands, fingers, feet or toes
- Persistent headache
- Unusual bumps, bruises or a depression on the head, neck or spine
- Impaired breathing or vision
- Nausea or vomiting
- Bruising of the head, especially around the eyes and behind the ears
- The person is holding his head, neck or back
- Behavior resembling intoxication

(e.g., paralysis) or death. If possible, let a lifeguard or a person with more advanced training respond first. However, if such a person is not around, you will need to act. If you suspect a head, neck or spinal injury, follow these general guidelines:

- Have someone call 9-1-1 or the local emergency number immediately.
- If the person is in the water and breathing, use an in-line stabilization technique to minimize movement of the head, neck and spine and keep the person's face out of the water. If the person is on land, place your hands on both sides of the person's head and support it in the position in which you found it. Continue to immobilize the person's head until EMS personnel arrive and take over.
- If the person is in the water and not breathing, immediately remove the person from the water and give care according to the conditions you find and your level of knowledge and training.

Manual in-line stabilization techniques that are used to minimize movement of the person's head, neck or spine when the person is in water include the hip and shoulder support and the head splint. The hip and shoulder support (**Water Rescue Skill Sheet 3-6**) is used for a person who is face-up. The head splint (**Water Rescue Skill Sheet 3-7**) provides better stabilization than the hip and shoulder support and can be used for a person who is face-up or face-down.

Basic Water Rescue: Helping Yourself in an Aquatic Emergency

An aquatic emergency can happen to anyone, even someone who has a great deal of experience being in and around the water. A swimmer can develop a physical condition, such as cramping or fatigue, which hinders his or her ability to keep swimming. A boating accident, mechanical malfunction or rough water can cause the craft to capsize, tossing its occupants into the water. In fact, many people who find themselves involved in an aquatic emergency never intended to go into the water in the first place. A car may go off the road into a body of water, or ice may crack, causing an ice skater to fall through. If you find yourself in trouble in the water, knowing what you can do to help yourself is imperative.

Relieving Muscle Cramps

Muscle cramps can occur when muscles become tired or cold from swimming or other activity. A cramp is an involuntary muscle contraction, usually in the arm, foot or calf. A muscle cramp can occur at any time, in any depth of water. If you develop a muscle cramp in shallow water, try to relax the muscle by stopping or changing the activity. Get out of the water, begin floating or change to a different swimming stroke. Changing the position of the affected limb to stretch the cramped muscle and massaging the area may also help to relieve the cramp. If you develop a muscle cramp in deep water, take a deep breath, roll forward so that you are face-down and float. Extend your leg and flex the ankle or toes while massaging the cramped muscle **(Fig. 3-6)**.

Fig. 3-6 If you experience a muscle cramp in deep water, position yourself face-down, extend the affected leg, flex the ankle or toes and massage the area.

Abdominal cramps are rare, but can happen. If you experience an abdominal cramp, try to relax and maintain your position in the water until the cramp passes.

Using Clothing as a Flotation Aid

If you find yourself in the water fully clothed and without a life jacket, you may be able to use an article of clothing that you are wearing as a makeshift flotation device **(Fig. 3-7)**. Once filled with air, articles of clothing such as a shirt, jacket or pants can aid floating, as well as provide protection against cold water, marine life, sun exposure and fuel spills. If shoes are light enough to allow swimming comfortably, leave them on. But if your shoes are too heavy or if you intend to use your pants as a flotation device, assume a jellyfish float position (see Chapter 5, Fig. 5-6A) and remove them. **Water Rescue Skill Sheet 3-8** describes step-by-step how to use articles of clothing to aid flotation.

Fig. 3-7 Articles of clothing inflated with air can aid floating.

Self Rescue in Warm Water

In warm water, you may decide to try to swim to safety, or to float in place until help arrives. Remember that swimming long distances to safety should only be used as a last resort. If you decide to swim, use the survival swimming stroke, which will allow you to cover a considerable distance while using a minimal amount of energy, whether you are buoyant or not. Use survival floating to rest while you are making your way to safety. If it is not possible to reach safety and you must wait for help, use survival floating alone. **Water Rescue Skill Sheet 3-9** describes the survival float step-by-step, and **Water Rescue Skill Sheet 3-10** describes the survival swimming stroke.

Self Rescue in Cold Water

Cold water presents several challenges. It is not possible to swim as far in cold water as it is in warm water. If you are in open water or a great distance from the shore, floating in place until help arrives is the best way to survive a cold water emergency. If you do decide to attempt to swim, consider your swimming ability, the amount of insulation you have and the water conditions. When the water is 50° F (10° C) or colder, even a good swimmer may have difficulty reaching shore, so only attempt to swim if you can reach the shore in a few strokes. Keep in mind that in emergencies it is often hard to judge distance, so be careful not to underestimate the distance to shore. If you do attempt to swim to safety, use a stroke with an underwater arm recovery (such as the breaststroke or elementary backstroke) to help maintain heat.

In cold water, keep all of your clothes on, including a hat if you are wearing one **(Box 3-5)**. Tight-fitting foam vests and flotation jackets with foam insulation help to retain heat and can double survival time. Even wet clothes help retain body heat, and if you are not wearing a life jacket, you can try inflating your clothing with air for flotation. Avoid splashing in an attempt to warm up. Splashing increases blood circulation in the arms and legs and will drain energy, resulting in heat loss. Similarly, treading water chills the body faster than staying still. In cold water, tread water only if it is necessary. Keep your face and head above the water, and turn your back toward waves to help keep water off of your face. Look around for a log or anything floating for support. In the event of a boating accident, try to right the boat and reenter. If that is not possible, climb up onto the capsized boat to keep more of your body out of the water.

If you are not in immediate danger but you are far from shore, stay still and let your life jacket provide support until help arrives. When you are wearing a life jacket, you can use the heat escape lessening posture (HELP) (if you are alone) or the huddle position (if you are in a group of two or more people) to stay warmer. The HELP and the huddle positions can increase the

---

Box 3-5
Falling Into the Water Fully Clothed

People who fall into the water wearing winter clothes, especially heavy boots or waders, usually panic because they think they will sink immediately. But winter clothes and outdoor gear (such as a snowmobile suit, hip boots or waders) can actually trap air and aid floating, in addition to helping to delay hypothermia. If you fall into the water wearing hip boots, waders or rubber boots, relax and bend your knees—the trapped air in the boots will bring you back to the surface quickly.

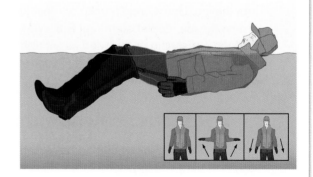

Then lie back, spread your arms and legs and perform a "winging" motion with your arms to move toward safety.

Fig. 3-8 The HELP and the huddle positions can be used to reduce exposure to cold water. (**A**) HELP position. (**B**) Huddle position.

chances of survival when floating in cold water by reducing the amount of body surface area that is directly exposed (**Fig. 3-8**).

- To get into the HELP position, draw your knees up to your chest, keeping your face forward and out of the water. Hold your upper arms at your sides and fold your lower arms against or across your chest (**see Fig. 3-8A**).
- To get into the huddle position, put your arms around the other person so that your chests are together. If you have a group of three or more people, put your arms over one another's shoulders so that the sides of your chests are together (**see Fig. 3-8B**). If there is a child or older adult in the group, put the child or older adult in the middle.

The HELP and huddle positions should not be used in swift river currents or white water. If you are wearing a life jacket and you are caught in a current, remain calm and try to swim to safety if the current is carrying you toward some danger. Float on your back and go downstream feetfirst until your breathing slows (sudden immersion in cold water can cause the breathing rate to increase). Breathe normally for a few seconds before starting to swim to shore.

Self Rescue: Falling Through Ice

If you fall through ice, try to stay calm and resist the urge to climb out onto the ice. It is likely to be weak in the area where the fall took place. Instead, turn toward the direction you came from, since the ice is likely to be strongest there. Quickly get into a floating position on your stomach. Bend your knees to help trap air in your pant legs and boots. Reach forward onto the broken ice, but do not push down on it. If you have ice rescue picks ("ice claws"), dig the points of the picks into the ice. Use a breaststroke or other kick to push your body farther onto the ice. Once you are on the ice, do not stand up! Roll away from the break area until a rescuer on shore is able to perform a reaching or throwing assist to help you the rest of the way, or until you are well clear of the broken area. Because of the risk for hypothermia, call 9-1-1 or the local emergency number if this has not been done already.

Self Rescue: Falling Into Moving Water

If you fall into moving water, do not stand up—the force of the water can entrap your feet or legs and hold you in place. A modest amount of water volume and velocity can exert significant force. Instead, float downstream on your back feetfirst to fend off obstacles and avoid entrapment of your feet and legs. Use your arms to back-paddle to slow down and steer out of the main current. Swim or wade toward the shore when you are out of the main current, or as soon as it is safe to do so. Because of the force of the current, this will result in a slightly downstream path **(Fig. 3-9)**. If you fell into the water because the boat you were in capsized, try to hold onto the boat, staying upstream of it, and swim with the boat to shore **(Fig. 3-10)**. However, if it is unsafe to continue holding onto the boat, let it go.

Self Rescue: Capsized Boat

It is important to stay calm if your boat capsizes. If you are not wearing a life jacket, put one on immediately.

If you can right the boat, do so. Once you right the boat, try to reboard:

- On larger boats, use the ladder or swim platform to reboard. If the weight in the boat is distributed correctly, climb up over the transom (i.e., the wide, flat area at the back of the boat). Be careful not to injure yourself on the boat's propeller or outboard engine.

- For smaller boats (like canoes, kayaks and rowboats), pull yourself over the middle of the boat and lie across it. Once the boat is stabilized, roll your legs into the boat. Canoes, kayaks and rowboats can often be rowed to shore even when filled with water.

If you cannot right the boat or reboard, stay with the boat and wait for rescue. If the water is cold, climb on top of the overturned boat to keep as much of your body out of the water as possible. Staying with your boat will help you conserve energy (because the boat will help you float) and make you more visible to rescue personnel. If you filed a float plan at your launch site and do not return on time, someone should notice when you are missing and look for you.

If the boat sinks or floats away, stay where you are if it is safe to do so. Make sure your life jacket is securely fastened, remain calm and wait for help. If you are not wearing a life jacket, look for another buoyant item, such as a cooler, oar, paddle or decoy, to use as a flotation aid instead, or consider inflating your clothes. If the water is warm, you also may need to use survival floating, survival swimming or both.

Self Rescue: Sinking Vehicle

If you are in a vehicle that plunges into water, staying calm, knowing what to do and acting quickly can save your life. Many people who find themselves going off the road into a body of water try to call 9-1-1 or the local emergency number for help. This is a waste of valuable time. A heavy vehicle will float for 30 seconds to 2 minutes before the water reaches the bottom of the side windows. Use that time to do the following:

1. Leave your seatbelt on until the vehicle hits the water. Then immediately unfasten it. If you are traveling with a child, unfasten the child's seatbelt after you have unfastened your own.

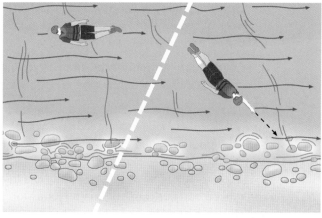

Fig. 3-9 If you are caught in a current, float downstream on your back, feetfirst. Back-paddle with your arms to break free of the main current. Once free of the main current, swim or wade toward the shore. This will result in a slightly downstream path because of the force of the current.

Fig. 3-10 If your boat capsizes in moving water, try to hold onto the boat, staying upstream of it. *Image © Steve Heap, 2014. Used under license from Shutterstock.com*

2. Open or break the window. A window-break tool kept within reach in the car can make quick work of breaking the window, and requires no strength or force to use. (Never open the doors, because this can cause the vehicle to sink very quickly.)

3. Exit through the window as soon as you have opened or broken it. If you are traveling with a child, push the child through the open window and then follow behind.

If you cannot open a window and escape during the initial floating phase, your chances of survival decrease significantly. When a vehicle starts to sink, it can be difficult or impossible to open the door because of the water pressure pushing on it from the outside. You will need to wait for the water level inside the car to rise so that the pressure equalizes. As the vehicle starts to sink, it will tilt engine-end down until it is in a nearly vertical position. Move to the higher end so that you can continue to breathe for as long as possible. Water pressure will be equal when the vehicle is nearly full of water. When the pressure equalizes, open the door. If you are traveling with a child, push the child through the open door and then follow behind.

Water Rescue Skill Sheet 3-1
Reaching Assist

Reaching Assist with Equipment	1. Brace yourself on the pool deck, pier surface or shoreline. 2. Extend the object to the person: ○ When using a rigid object such as a pole or oar, sweep it toward the person from the side until it makes contact with the person's arm or hand. ○ When using a shirt or towel, lie down and flip it into the person's hands. 3. When the person grasps the object, slowly and carefully pull the person to safety. Keep your body low and lean back to avoid being pulled into the water. 
Reaching Assist without Equipment	1. Brace yourself on the pool deck or pier surface. 2. Extend your arm and grasp the person. 3. Pull the person to safety. 
Reaching Assist without Equipment from a Position in the Water	1. Hold onto a secure object (such as a pool ladder, gutter or piling) with one hand. 2. Extend a free hand or one leg to the person. Do not let go of the secure object or swim out to the person. 3. Pull the person to safety. 

Water Rescue Skill Sheet 3-2

Throwing Assist

1. If the line has a wrist loop, place your nonthrowing hand (the hand that will be holding the line) through it. If there is no wrist loop, step on the nonthrowing end of the line. Hold the coil of the line in the open palm of your nonthrowing hand.

2. Grasp the side of the object with your throwing hand. Holding the object vertically, step back with your leg on the throwing side and then swing the object backward and then forward for an underhand toss.

Step 2

3. Aim the throw so that the object lands just beyond the person with the line lying on the person's shoulder. If there is a crosswind or current, throw upwind or up current of the person.

4. Tell the person to grab the object. After the person has a firm grasp on the object or line, drop the remaining coil, if any, and slowly pull the person to safety while offering reassurance.

   o As you pull, keep your body low and lean back to avoid being pulled into the water.

   o Reach out with one hand and grasp the line with your thumb inward. Pull the line in to your side with that hand while reaching out with the other. Continue the alternate pulling and reaching action until the person is at the side or is able to stand in shallow water.

Step 3

Step 4

Water Rescue Skill Sheet 3-3

Wading Assist

Wading assists are used in water that is less than chest deep. Do not attempt a wading assist if there is a current or a soft bottom that will make wading dangerous.

Wading Assist: Conscious Person

1. Put on a life jacket, if one is available. Select an object to use for the reaching assist.
2. Wade into the water and extend the object to the person.
3. Tell the person to grab the buoyant object and to hold on tightly.
4. Pull the person to safety, keeping the object between yourself and the person (this will help to prevent the person from grasping you).

Wading Assist: Unconscious Person

1. Put on a life jacket, if one is available. Select a buoyant object to assist with moving the person to safety.
2. Wade into the water and turn the person face-up.
3. Position the buoyant object under the person's shoulders.
4. Move the person to the edge of the pool or the shoreline, keeping the person's mouth and nose out of the water.
5. Remove the person from the water.
6. Give first aid according to the conditions you find and your level of knowledge and training.

Wading Assist: Submerged Person

1. Put on a life jacket, if one is available. Select a buoyant object to assist with moving the person to safety.
2. Wade into the water.
3. Reach down, grasp the person and pull her to the surface.
4. Turn the person face-up.
   - If the person is unconscious, position the buoyant object under her shoulders.
   - If the person is conscious, tell the person to grab the buoyant object and to hold on tightly.
5. Move the person to the edge of the pool or the shoreline, keeping the person's mouth and nose out of the water.
6. Remove the person from the water.
7. Give first aid according to the conditions you find and your level of knowledge and training.

Sloped Entry Assists

Sloped entry assists are used to remove a person from the water in areas where there is a gently sloping entry and exit point.

Walking Assist

1. Place one of the person's arms around your neck and across your shoulder.

2. Grasp the wrist of the arm that is across your shoulder, and wrap your free arm around the person's back or waist.

3. Maintain a firm grasp, and help the person walk out of the water.

Beach Drag: One Responder

1. Stand behind the person, and grasp him or her under the armpits. Support the person's head with your forearms, if possible.

2. Walk backward slowly, dragging the person out of the water. Use your legs, not your back, to power the movement. If you are not able to move the person completely out of the water, at least make sure the person's head and shoulders are out of the water.

Beach Drag: Two Responders

1. Both responders stand on either side of the person, facing the shoreline.

2. Place one hand under the person's armpit and use the other hand to support the person's head. Have your partner do the same.

3. Lift the person's torso up, using your legs, not your back. Walk forward slowly, dragging the person out of the water.

Water Rescue Skill Sheet 3-5

Two-Person Removal from the Water Using a Backboard

1. Bring a backboard (with the head immobilizer and straps removed, if possible) to the side of the pool.

2. The lifeguard brings the person to the side of the pool and turns the person to face the wall.

3. Cross your hands and grab the person's wrists, pulling the person up slightly to keep the person's head above the water and away from the wall.

Step 3

4. The lifeguard ensures that the person's face is out of the water, and then climbs out of the pool, removes the rescue tube and gets the backboard.

5. The lifeguard guides the backboard, foot-end first, into the water along the wall next to the person.

Step 5

6. Immediately turn the person onto the backboard by uncrossing your hands. Allow the backboard to float up beneath the person.

Step 6

7. Grab one of the person's wrists and one of the handholds on the backboard while the lifeguard does the same on the other side.

Step 7

Continued on next page

Two-Person Removal from the Water Using a Backboard

8. On the lifeguard's signal and working together, pull the backboard and the person onto land, resting the underside of the board against the edge of the pool. Remember to lift with your legs, not your back.

9. Together, step backward and carefully lower the backboard to the ground.

Step 8

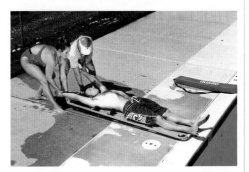

Step 9

Water Rescue Skill Sheet 3-6

Hip and Shoulder Support

With this manual in-line stabilization technique, support the person at the hips and shoulders to keep the face out of the water and minimize movement of the head, neck and spine. Use it for a person who is face-up.

1. Approach the person from the side and lower yourself to about shoulder depth.

2. Slide one arm under the person's shoulders and the other arm under his hips. Hold the person's body horizontally, keeping the person's face out of the water.

3. Do not lift the person. Hold the person still in the water until help arrives.

Head Splint

This manual in-line stabilization technique provides better stabilization than the hip and shoulder support. Use it for a person who is face-up or face-down.

Head Splint: Face-Up Victim

1. Approach the person from behind. Stand behind the person's head and lower yourself to about shoulder depth.

2. Grasp the person's arms midway between the shoulder and elbow. Grasp the person's right arm with your right hand and the person's left arm with your left hand.

3. Gently move the person's arms up alongside the person's head, so that the person's head is supported in between the person's arms.

4. Position yourself to the person's side with the person's head close to the crook of your arm. Squeeze the person's arms against the person's head to help hold the head in line with the body. Do not move the person any more than is necessary.

5. Check for consciousness and breathing:

   ○ If the person is not breathing, immediately remove the person from the water, call 9-1-1 or the local emergency number and provide resuscitative care according to your level of knowledge and training.

   ○ If the person is breathing, hold the person still in the water until help arrives.

Step 2

Step 3

Step 4

**Head Splint:
Face-Down
Victim**

1. Approach the person from the side.

2. Grasp the person's arms midway between the shoulder and elbow. Grasp the person's right arm with your right hand and the person's left arm with your left hand.

3. Gently move the person's arms up alongside the person's head, so that the person's head is supported in between the person's arms. Squeeze the person's arms against the person's head to help hold the head in line with the body.

4. If you are in shallow water, lower yourself to about shoulder depth. Glide the person slowly forward, turning the person until he or she is face-up. To do this, push the person's arm that is closest to you under the water while pulling the person's other arm across the surface toward you.

5. Position yourself to the person's side with the person's head close to the crook of your arm. Squeeze the person's arms against the person's head to help hold the head in line with the body. Do not move the person any more than is necessary.

6. Check for consciousness and breathing.

   ○ If the person is not breathing, immediately remove the person from the water, call 9-1-1 or the local emergency number and provide resuscitative care according to your level of knowledge and training.

   ○ If the person is breathing, hold the person still in the water until help arrives.

Step 2

Step 4

Step 5

Self-Rescue with Clothes

Shirt or Jacket: Blowing Air Method

1. Tuck the shirt or jacket in or tie the shirttail ends together around your waist.

2. Unbutton the collar button if you are using a shirt. Take a deep breath, bend your head forward into the water, pull the shirt or jacket up to your face and blow into it.

3. Keep the front of the shirt or jacket under water and hold the collar closed.

4. Repeat steps 1–3 to reinflate the shirt or jacket as necessary.

Step 2

Shirt or Jacket: Striking Air Method

1. Fasten the buttons or close the zipper up to the neck.

2. Hold the bottom of the shirt or jacket out with one hand, keeping it just under the surface of the water, and lean back slightly.

3. From above the surface of the water, strike the water with your cupped free hand, following through so that the air caught by your hand is pulled to a point below the bottom of the shirt or jacket.

4. Keep the front of the shirt or jacket underwater and hold the collar and the bottom of the shirt or jacket closed.

5. Repeat steps 1–4 to reinflate the shirt or jacket as necessary.

Step 3

Step 4

Self-Rescue with Clothes

Pants: Striking Air Method

1. Take a deep breath, lean forward into the water and reach down and remove your shoes.

2. Loosen your waistband and belt.

3. Take another deep breath, lean forward and reach down. Take off your pants one leg at a time without turning them inside out. Lift your face from the water and take a breath whenever necessary.

4. Once you have removed your pants, either tie both legs together at the bottom or tie a knot in each leg as close as possible to the bottom. Then zip or button the pants to the waist.

5. Hold the back of the waistband underwater with one hand. Keeping the pants on the surface of the water, strike the water with your cupped free hand, following through so that the air caught by your hand is forced into the waistband opening below the surface. You can also inflate the pants by submerging them and then blowing air into the open waistband below the surface of the water.

Step 5

6. Once the pants are inflated, gather the waistband together with your hands or by tightening the belt. Slip your head in between the pant legs where they are tied together or, if they are each tied separately, place one pant leg under each arm for support.

7. Repeat steps 1–6 to reinflate the pants as necessary.

Step 6

Water Rescue Skill Sheet 3-9
Survival Float

The survival float is used in warm water while awaiting rescue or to rest while swimming.

1. Take a breath, then place your face down into the water. Allow your arms and legs to hang freely. Rest in this position for a few seconds.

2. When you are ready to breathe again, slowly lift your arms to about shoulder height and separate your legs, moving one leg forward and one leg back (stride position).

3. Gently press down with your arms while bringing your legs together. This movement lifts your mouth above the surface of the water, allowing you to take a breath.

4. Take a breath, and then return to the resting position.

Step 1

Step 2

Step 3

Survival Swimming

If a person is very buoyant, it can take several minutes to complete the following sequence of movements, which helps to conserve energy. A person who is not very buoyant must perform this sequence of movements slightly faster to prevent sinking before the breath.

1. Start in the survival float position. After taking a breath, bend forward at the waist and bring your hands up alongside your head.

2. Separate your legs, moving one leg forward and the other back (stride position). Extend your arms forward, then bring your legs together again to propel yourself diagonally toward the surface.

3. Sweep your arms out and back to your thighs and glide near and almost parallel to the surface.

4. When you need to breathe, bend your legs and draw them toward your torso while bringing your hands up alongside your head. If you do not float well, pull hard with your arms, downward and outward. Take a breath, and then quickly return to the survival float position.

5. Extend your arms forward and separate your legs into the stride position once again. Tilt your head back and prepare to breathe out, as in survival floating.

6. Repeat steps 1–5.

Step 1

Step 2

Step 3

Step 4

PART 2

Swimming Skills

CHAPTER 4

Understanding Hydrodynamic Principles

If you ask a swimmer what he or she likes about swimming, you might get an answer such as "the feeling of gliding effortlessly through the water" or "the sense of weightlessness that comes from being in the water." Being in the water allows us to experience movement in ways that are not possible on solid ground. For example, on dry land, gravity is a force that pulls us down toward the Earth, whereas in water, buoyancy is a force that lifts us up. Let's review some basic principles of physics as they apply to the aquatic environment.

Buoyancy

Buoyancy is the upward force that water places on an object when the object is in water. Water's buoyancy opposes gravity's downward force, which has the effect of lessening body weight in the water. Buoyancy is one reason aquatic therapy (physical therapy performed in the water) can be so effective for helping to restore or maintain function. The buoyancy of the water helps to support the person's weight during exercise, reducing stress placed on joints. Buoyancy is also the reason that many people who have mobility impairments on land find it much easier to move in the water, because the buoyancy of the water helps to support the person's body weight. Buoyancy allows swimmers to spend most of their energy producing forward movement rather than supporting themselves.

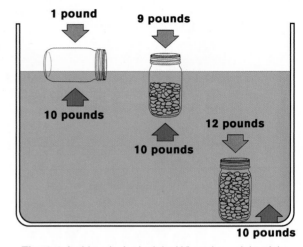

Fig. 4-1 Archimedes' principle: When the weight of the displaced fluid is more than the weight of the object, flotation occurs.

Archimedes' principle explains how buoyancy works **(Fig. 4-1)**. This principle states that the buoyant force on an object is equal to the weight of the fluid displaced by the object. When the weight of the displaced fluid is more that the weight of the object, flotation occurs. Imagine three containers of the same size and shape. Each weighs 1 pound and can displace 10 pounds of fluid. The first container is left empty, sealed and placed in the water. It bobs high in the water with most of the container visible above the surface of the water. The second container is filled with 8 pounds of pebbles, sealed and placed in the water. This container also floats, but much lower in the water than the first container. The third container is filled with 11 pounds of pebbles, sealed and placed in the water. This container sinks because the weight of the container (12 pounds) exceeds that of the displaced fluid (10 pounds). Yet, if you tried to lift the third container while it was underwater, it would feel as if you were lifting only 2 pounds, instead of 12.

Specific Gravity

The amount of buoyancy exerted on an object is primarily determined by the object's specific gravity. **Specific gravity** is the ratio of the weight of the object to the weight of the water it displaces. Think back to the containers. Recall that the first two containers floated at different heights in the water even though buoyancy pushed them both up. Although they both displaced the same amount of water, they had different specific gravities, which caused them to float differently.

Pure water has a specific gravity of 1. The specific gravity of other objects is the ratio of their density to that of water—the object's density divided by the density of water. Objects with a specific gravity that is less than 1 will float. Objects with a specific gravity that is greater than 1 will sink. The first container, which weighs only 1 pound but displaces 10 pounds of water, has a specific gravity of 0.1. This container floats high on the surface of the water because its specific gravity value is much lower than that of water. The second container, which weighs 9 pounds but displaces 10 pounds of water, has a specific gravity of 0.9. This container floats just above the surface of the water because its specific gravity value is only slightly lower than that of the water. The third container, which weighs 12 pounds but displaces 10 pounds of water, has a specific gravity of 1.2. Because its specific gravity value is greater than 1, the third container sinks.

Specific gravity explains why some people can float easily while others cannot **(Fig. 4-2)**, and why it is easier to float in salt water than in fresh water. Specific gravity varies from one person to another because people have varying amounts of body fat, muscle mass and bone density. Adipose tissue (body fat) has a specific gravity that is less than 1.0 and promotes floating. Muscle and bone tissue, on the other hand, have specific gravity values that are slightly greater than 1.0 and promote sinking. People with more body fat float more easily, whereas those with little body fat who are muscular or who have a dense bone structure do not float easily and may even sink. Age and gender can also play a role in how easily a person floats. In general, children are more buoyant than adults (because they do not have as much muscle mass and their bones are less dense) and women are more buoyant than men (because women's bodies tend to have a higher percentage of body fat).

The water also can make a difference in how a person floats. Salt water has more buoyant force because it has a higher specific gravity than fresh water. For this reason, a person who has trouble floating in a pool may find it easier to float in the ocean. Similarly, a person who floats easily in a pool will float even higher in the ocean.

Box 4-1 describes an easy way to check for buoyancy. If you are a person who does not naturally float easily, there are adjustments you can make to improve your ability to float. For example, inhaling deeply and holding your breath lowers your body's specific gravity, enhancing your ability to float—although some people will still have difficulty floating, even with a full breath of air. Kicking slightly, making sculling or finning movements (described in Chapter 5) with your arms and hands, or a combination of kicking and arm movements can also help you to stay near the surface. Finally, wearing a life jacket can increase your buoyancy because the life jacket displaces a large amount of water with only a minimal increase in weight.

Fig. 4-2 Depending on body composition and other factors, a person's natural floating position may be (**A**) horizontal, (**B**) diagonal or (**C**) nearly vertical.

Box 4-1
Try It

Evaluating Your Natural Buoyancy

1. Move into a tuck float position (see Chapter 5, Fig. 5-6B). Hold your knees against your chest until your body stops rising or sinking. Recover to a standing position.

   Did your back rise above the surface? If so, you float easily.

2. Take a large breath of air, hold it and return to the tuck float position. Recover to a standing position.

   Did your back rise above the surface this time? If so, you have some difficulty floating and when floating on your back, you probably float more in a diagonal position than a horizontal one.

3. Take a large breath of air, return to the tuck float position, then slowly let the air out through your mouth and nose. Recover to a standing position.

   Did your body drift down as you exhaled? If so, you do not float easily and are likely to sink while trying to float motionlessly.

4. Move into a back float with your arms at your sides. Recover to a standing position.

   Did your body remain mostly horizontal in the water? If so, you float easily.

Center of Mass and Center of Buoyancy

Specific gravity is not the only factor that affects how you float. Two other factors affect the position of your body when you float: your center of mass (sometimes called your center of gravity) and your center of buoyancy.

Two large forces act on the body when a person is floating. One is the downward force of gravity. The other is the upward force of buoyancy. In reality, both forces occur all over the body. But to help understand how these forces affect floating, we can assume that the **center of mass** is the location of all downward force and the **center of buoyancy** is the location of all upward force. When the center of mass is directly below the center of buoyancy, a person is able to float in a stable position. This happens because the two forces act on the body along the exact same line. If the center of mass is not directly below the center of buoyancy, the body will rotate until it achieves this alignment.

In a standing position with the arms at the sides, for most people, the center of mass is located near the hips and the center of buoyancy is located in the chest **(Fig. 4-3)**. In the water, a person's natural floating position (vertical, diagonal or horizontal) depends on the location of the center of mass relative to the center of buoyancy **(Fig. 4-4)**. Moving the center of mass and the center of buoyancy so that they are closer together increases stability during a horizontal float by minimizing the tendency of the body to rotate **(Box 4-2)**.

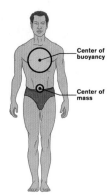

Fig. 4-3 When a person is standing with his arms at the sides, the center of buoyancy is typically located in the chest and the center of mass is typically located near the hips.

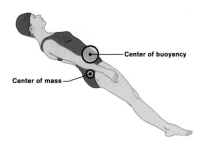

Fig. 4-4 The body rotates until the center of mass is directly below the center of buoyancy, which is why some people float in a diagonal or nearly vertical position.

Box 4-2

Try It

Changing the Relationship Between Center of Mass and Center of Buoyancy

1. Float on your back with your arms at your sides.

2. Move your arms above your head.

3. Flex your wrists so that your hands (or fingers) are out of the water.

4. Bend your knees.

What happened? Did making these changes in body position make it easier for you to float in a horizontal position? These changes in position move body tissue with a specific gravity of less than 1 (e.g., fat, air-filled lungs) toward your feet and body tissue with a specific gravity of greater than 1 (e.g., bones, muscle) toward your head, moving the center of mass and the center of buoyancy closer to one another and increasing stability.

Drag

Drag is the force that opposes movement through the water. Water, which is denser than air, creates resistance as a person tries to move through it. A participant in an aquatic fitness or rehabilitation program may use drag to his or her advantage, exercising against the resistance created by the water to improve muscular strength and endurance. However, swimmers seek to minimize drag because doing so helps them to swim faster and more efficiently. There are three main types of drag: form drag, wave drag and frictional drag.

Form Drag

Form drag is the resistance created by a swimmer's body shape as the swimmer moves through the water. Form drag is the most significant contributor to overall resistance to movement through the water. However, form drag is the one factor that all swimmers can control to improve their efficiency when swimming.

A tight, narrow body shape helps to reduce form drag **(Fig. 4-5)**. A pointed, rather than blunt, front end reduces the amount of frontal surface area that is pushing through the water **(Box 4-3)**. To reduce form drag while swimming

Fig. 4-5 To reduce form drag, narrow your shape from your fingers to your toes.

Box 4-3

Try It

Experiencing Form Drag

Activity 1

Stand in chest-deep water.

1. With your elbows at your sides and your palms facing down, bring your hands together and apart several times.

2. Now repeat this movement with your thumbs up and palms facing each other.

You probably noticed that the second movement was more difficult. This is because when your hands were horizontal (as in the first move), form drag was reduced because the area pressing against the water was narrow. But when your hands were vertical (as in the second move), form drag was increased because the area pressing against the water was wider.

Activity 2

1. Push off on the surface of the water in a streamlined position (arms extended overhead, hands clasped together with your arms against your ears, legs extended together behind you with your toes pointed) and glide as far as possible.

2. Push off underwater in a streamlined position and glide as far as possible.

3. Push off underwater with your hands apart and glide as far as possible.

4. Push off underwater in a streamlined position, then flex your feet, pointing your toes downward.

5. Push off underwater with your arms in a streamlined position, but with your legs apart, and glide as far as possible.

6. Push off underwater with both your arms and legs spread apart and glide as far as possible.

7. Push off underwater in a streamlined position, then separate your legs and move your arms so that they point straight down and glide as far as possible.

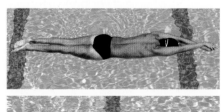

In the first step, you are in position to glide the farthest. With each progressive step, form drag increases, shortening the distance that you are able to glide.

on the surface, keep your entire body as horizontal as possible. Most people's hips and legs naturally float lower in the water. Controlling your center of mass by maintaining a neutral head position (looking down toward the bottom of the pool, with your neck relaxed) helps to keep your hips and legs at the surface. In addition, keeping your head in a neutral position helps to prevent excessive side-to-side or up-and-down body motion, another cause of form drag.

Wave Drag

Wave drag is the resistance caused by turbulence in the water. Other swimmers and activity in the water can cause turbulence, resulting in wave drag. As you swim, your movement through the water also creates waves that add resistance to forward progress. You cannot prevent those waves from occurring, but you can reduce the resistance they cause by using good technique. For example, wave drag is reduced when you take smooth, even strokes and limit the amount of splashing. Wave drag is also reduced, but not completely eliminated, when you move underwater, such as during starts and turns and in underwater swimming.

Frictional Drag

Frictional drag refers to the resistance created by a swimmer's body surface as it moves through the water. Wearing loose clothing while swimming dramatically increases this type of drag, which is why competitive swimmers wear smooth, tight-fitting swimwear or racing suits. Similarly, wearing a swimming cap and even shaving body hair can reduce frictional drag.

Propulsion

Propulsion is the action of pushing or driving forward. Swimmers are propelled through the water through a combination of kicking the legs and pulling water with the arms. The forward movement that results is due to two types of propulsive forces at work: drag forces and lift forces. In the past, many thought that lift forces played the major role in propulsion. However, research has demonstrated that drag forces are actually the dominant form of propulsion in swimming.

Drag Propulsion

Drag (paddle) propulsion is based on one of Isaac Newton's three laws of motion: the law of action and reaction. This law states that for every action there is an equal and opposite reaction. One example of drag propulsion is the backward push of a paddle blade moving a canoe forward. Another is when a diver presses down on the end of the diving board and the board recoils, lifting the diver into the air.

Fig. 4-6 In swimming, the arms act like paddles to push the water backward and move the swimmer forward. Facing your hands and forearms toward your feet during the arm pull results in the greatest propulsion.

To improve the efficiency and effectiveness of your swimming stroke, focus on maximizing drag propulsive forces. In swimming, your limbs act as paddles to push water backward and move your body forward **(Box 4-4)**. To create the greatest drag propulsive force when swimming, your hands and forearms should face toward your feet **(Fig. 4-6)**. For example, when swimming the front crawl, focus on moving your arms straight back through the power phase of the arm stroke, with minimal sideways motion.

Box 4-4
Try It

Experiencing Drag Propulsion

Stand in chest-deep water.

1. With your arms in front of your body and your palms and forearms facing down, press downward with your arms.

2. With your arms in front of your body and your palms angled slightly inward, press downward with your arms.

3. With your arms in front of your body and your palms angled slightly outward, press downward with your arms.

You probably noticed that the first time you pressed your arms down, you felt the most resistance, but you also experienced the most propulsion. This is because when your hands and forearms are flat, you are able to push against the greatest amount of water, creating the greatest drag propulsive force.

Lift Propulsion

While drag propulsion plays the dominant role in forward movement, lift propulsive forces help in overall propulsion. The basic principle behind lift propulsion as it relates to swimming is that as fluid moves around an object, the individual particles within the fluid speed up or slow down to stay parallel with the particles on either side of the object. The faster moving particles tend to lift the object as they try to remain parallel with the slower moving particles on the other side of the object. Lift propulsion is the natural result of several movements used in swimming.

Sculling (described in Chapter 5) is an example of lift propulsion **(Box 4-5)**. In sculling, the swimmer moves the hands, wrists and forearms to manipulate the flow of water and achieve lift.

Box 4-5
Try It

Experiencing Lift Propulsion

1. Stand in shallow water, anywhere from waist- to shoulder-deep.

2. Bend your elbows with your hands in front, palms facing down. Your elbows should be about 5 to 7 inches from your waist.

3. Hold your hands about 6 inches beneath the surface. Keep your hands flat with your fingers loosely held together and your arms relaxed.

4. Rotate your palms between 20 and 50 degrees to press water out and then in. The total distance your hands move is about 12 inches. Although it may look as if your palms are flat and facing the bottom of the pool, they rotate from facing out to in, with almost no time spent facing flat toward the bottom. Keep your upper arms relatively still with a small rotation on each scull. Avoid "locking" your upper arms in place. Maintain a continuous movement, without stopping and starting at the in and out points of each scull.

5. Keep your hands moving with an even tempo and pressure. When you get good "grab," you may see a whirlpool develop over your fingers.

6. Continue to scull and lift your feet off the bottom.

What happens when you lift your feet off the bottom while making sculling movements with your arms?

When sculling, the swimmer keeps the hands pitched at a slight angle and presses them toward the body. During this motion, the water that passes over the top of the hand must cover a greater distance than the water on the other side of the hand. As a result, the water flowing over the top of the hand accelerates to remain parallel with the slower moving water on the other side of the hand. Lift propulsion also takes place when the hands and feet move outward away from the body and then back inward toward the body or as the hands and feet move deep in the water and then back up toward the body. Moving the arms through the water with the hands positioned so that the palms are facing back and slightly tilted toward the feet results in lift propulsion as well.

Law of Inertia

The second of Isaac Newton's laws of motion is the law of inertia. The law of inertia states that an external force is needed to get a body at rest to begin movement, to stop a moving body, and to change the direction of a moving body. Let's look at each of these principles as they relate to swimming.

1. An external force is needed to get a body at rest to begin movement. This simply means that more energy is needed to start a stroke than to maintain a stroke. Therefore, it is more efficient to keep moving forward, rather than starting and stopping repeatedly. Strokes that involve continuous motion, like the front crawl and back crawl, are most efficient but tiring. In strokes that incorporate a glide, like the elementary backstroke and sidestroke, inertia allows the swimmer to rest while still moving forward. However, if the glide is too long and the swimmer slows down too much, more work will be required to start the next stroke. Swimmers must find a balance between continuous arm movements and glides to manage their energy.

2. An external force is needed to stop a moving body. The water is an external force that can stop a moving body. Swimmers need less force to keep moving when they are in a streamlined position than they do in other positions that create more drag.

3. An external force is needed to change the direction of a moving body. Inertia keeps a swimmer moving in the same direction. To change the direction of travel, the swimmer must apply force to change the direction of his or her body. As speed increases, more and more force is needed to change direction. Incorrect body position, improper stroke mechanics or both can act as an external force on a moving body, causing the body to change direction unnecessarily. This is one of the reasons why beginning swimmers often have difficulty swimming in a straight line.

Law of Acceleration

Newton's third law of motion, the law of acceleration, states that the change in speed of an object depends on the amount of force applied to it and the direction of that force (Box 4-6). This law relates to swimming in two ways.

First, the more force a swimmer applies when pushing water back, the faster he or she will swim. Second, concentrating all propulsive force in one direction and maintaining that direction makes swimming more efficient. Incorrect body position, improper stroke mechanics or both can direct propulsion away from the swimmer's intended direction. This pushes the swimmer off course, and additional energy is needed to readjust body motion and get back on track.

Box 4-6

Try It

Experiencing the Law of Acceleration

Activity 1

1. Forcefully push off the pool wall and move into a streamlined position. Do not kick or stroke with your arms. Allow your body to slow to a stop.

2. Forcefully push off the pool wall and move into a streamlined position. Start swimming the front crawl as fast as possible.

Forcefully pushing off the wall causes rapid acceleration from a stationary position to a full glide speed. But without any kicking or arm action, the glide slows to a stop (due to drag resistance). In the second step, when you begin to swim after pushing off the pool wall and reach your maximum speed, the additional acceleration produced by your arm and leg action is counterbalanced by the deceleration caused by drag resistance. The net effect is no acceleration. This is why in the second step, you are able to continue to move through the water without slowing to a stop.

Activity 2

1. Swim the elementary backstroke one length of the pool.

2. Return, using only one arm for each stroke (i.e., alternate arms, keeping the opposite arm at your side).

Did you notice a difference between the first length and the second? Most likely, you were able to move down the length of the pool quickly, efficiently and in a straight line when you were performing the elementary backstroke with proper stroke mechanics. But when swimming the elementary backstroke using alternating arms, you probably moved in a zigzag pattern and had to spend a great deal of energy to adjust your direction of motion, rather than using this energy to accelerate forward.

Law of Levers

A lever allows a person to do more work using less force. Examples of mechanical levers include crowbars and seesaws. Arms, legs and other body parts can also act as levers. A lever consists of a pivot point and one or two rigid parts, called arms. For example, think of a seesaw: the pivot point is in the center, and the arms extend on each side. Force applied to one side results in movement on the other side.

The law of levers states that the product of the force applied and the length of the force arm is equal to the product of the resistance encountered and the length of the resistance arm **(Fig. 4-7)**. The force arm is the part of the lever to which force is applied. Its length is equal to the distance from the pivot point to the point where force is applied. The resistance arm is the part of the lever that moves against weight or some other type of resistance.

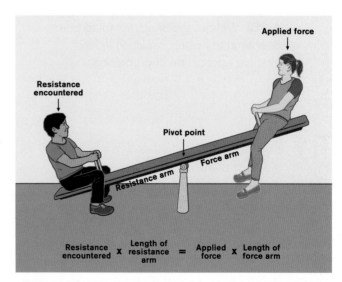

Fig. 4-7 The law of levers relies on four variables: force applied, the length of the force arm, the resistance encountered and the length of the resistance arm. The force applied multiplied by the length of the force arm is equal to the resistance encountered multiplied by the length of the resistance arm.

Its length is equal to the distance from the pivot point to the point where the resistance is encountered.

As it applies to swimming, the law of levers suggests that to be most effective, forces of propulsion should be applied close to the body **(Box 4-7)**. The law of levers is the reason why arm strokes are more efficient and provide better propulsion when the hands and wrists stay close to the body, as opposed to going out to the sides or down deep in the water. The law of levers also explains why bending the arms while treading water provides more upward force than straight arms. Similarly, kicks are more efficient when the legs are kept close to the centerline of the body, rather than going out too wide, and near the surface, rather than going too deep.

Applying the law of levers helps researchers analyze strokes to find the best limb positions and motions for effective swimming. For example, think about the front crawl. In the front crawl, the arm acts as a lever, with the shoulder as the pivot point. The shoulder muscles are the applied force and the length of bone between the shoulder and shoulder muscle attachment is the force arm **(Fig. 4-8A)**. The resistance encountered is the water resistance against the arm, and the resistance arm is the distance from the shoulder to the middle of the forearm. In the front crawl, bending the elbow during the pull shortens the resistance arm, reducing the force needed to propel the swimmer forward **(see Fig. 4-8B)**. Without the bend, the hand goes deeper in the water, resulting in less efficient application of propulsion.

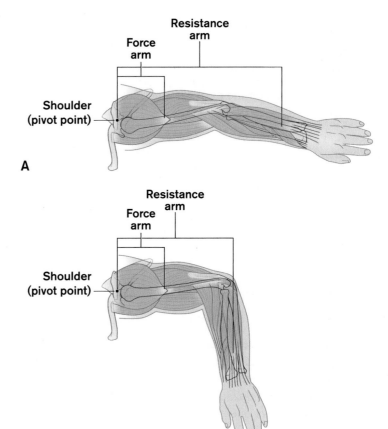

Fig. 4-8 In the front crawl, the arm acts as a lever with the shoulder as the pivot point. (**A**) When the arm is straight, the distance from the shoulder to the middle of the forearm (i.e., the resistance arm) is greater. Therefore, more force needs to be applied to propel the swimmer forward. (**B**) When the arm is bent, the distance from the shoulder to the middle of the forearm is reduced, decreasing the amount of force that needs to be applied to move the swimmer forward.

Box 4-7
Try It

Experiencing the Law of Levers

1. In shallow water near the side of the pool, place your hands on the edge of the pool deck.

2. With your arms straight, try to lift out of the water without pushing off from the bottom of the pool.

3. Now, bend your arms at the elbows and try to lift out of the water.

Did bending your arms at the elbows make it easier for you to lift your body out of the water? By bending your arms, you shortened the length of the resistance arm, reducing the force needed to lift yourself out of the water.

CHAPTER 5

Basic Aquatic Skills

Basic aquatic skills, such as controlling breathing, floating, gliding, and changing direction and position in the water, are second nature to experienced swimmers. But new swimmers need to learn these important skills. Not only are these fundamental skills necessary for staying safe and feeling comfortable and confident in the water, they are the building blocks for learning more advanced swimming strokes. In addition, many of these skills can be essential survival skills in the event of an aquatic emergency.

Entering and Exiting the Water

The most basic of the "basic aquatic skills" is simply getting into and out of the water. New swimmers need to learn how to adjust to the water, as well as safe techniques for getting into and out of the water.

Water Adjustment

Some new swimmers can hardly wait to get into the water. Others will be more hesitant. Learning strategies for adjusting to the water, both physically and mentally, can help fearful swimmers feel more confident and comfortable.

Physical Adjustment

Physical adjustment to the water involves gradually getting used to the water temperature. Most aquatic environments are much cooler than bathwater. Even relatively warm pool water (83–86° F) may feel cool. Getting wet gradually helps your body physically adjust to the cooler water temperature **(Fig. 5-1)**. You can adjust to water temperature by:

Fig. 5-1 To adjust to the water temperature, sit on the edge of the pool (or stand in thigh-deep water) and splash or scoop water onto your upper body.

- Entering on the steps, ramp or slope until you are thigh-deep and then scooping water onto your arms, chest, neck and face.
- Sitting on the edge of the pool and scooping water onto your body.

Mental Adjustment

Many inexperienced swimmers feel afraid around the water and are often apprehensive about entering it. When a person is feeling anxious or stressed, breathing patterns change. An anxious person tends to breathe more rapidly and take shallower breaths. This, in turn, increases feelings of anxiety. Once in the water, the coolness of the water may cause breathing to quicken, and the pressure of the water around your chest may make breathing feel difficult. These effects can also increase anxiety.

It is possible to lessen anxiety by making a conscious effort to breathe slowly, deeply and regularly. This type of breathing, which mimics how a person normally breathes when relaxed, can have a calming effect. Using the following breathing techniques before getting in the water can help reduce anxiety:

- Breathing in and out slowly and deeply while sitting on the edge of the pool
- Taking a deep breath, holding it for a couple of seconds, and then slowly exhaling

Techniques for Entering and Exiting the Water

The best method to use for entering the water depends on the body of water, your surroundings, your size and swimming ability, and your purpose for getting into the water. Beginning swimmers should only enter the water feetfirst. In most pools and some other swim areas, this can be done by using a ladder, steps or a ramp. You can also enter the water from the deck by sitting down on the side of the pool, rolling onto your stomach and sliding into the water **(Fig. 5-2)**.

You can exit the pool the same way you entered it—using a ladder, steps or ramp—or you can pull yourself onto the deck. To exit the pool by pulling yourself onto the deck, face the deck.

Place both hands on the overflow trough or deck and push down to lift your upper body out of the water, place a knee or foot onto the overflow trough or deck, and then climb out. Young swimmers and those with less upper body strength can pull themselves up to their elbows, then onto their stomach, and then put one leg up on the side and continue to climb out of the water until they can stand or sit on the deck safely.

Some swimmers with physical disabilities may use a hoist or lift to enter and exit the water. However, many are able to use ladders, steps or a ramp or modified techniques from the deck to enter and exit the pool. A swimmer with a disability may need varying degrees of support while entering and exiting the water, or no support at all.

Fig. 5-2 Feet-first entries (such as by sitting on the deck, rolling onto your front and sliding into the water) are safest for beginners.

Bobbing and Breath Control

Most aquatic skills require you to briefly hold your breath and submerge your face. The ability to hold your breath for short periods of time is an important safety skill and it contributes to coordinated breath control (which is necessary to swim well). While swimming, holding your breath for a long time is not necessary, but it is important to be able to breathe in and out rhythmically and steadily. **Bobbing** is a skill swimmers can use to practice breath control while in the water **(Fig. 5-3)**.

To practice bobbing:

1. Hold onto the overflow trough or pool wall in chest-deep water.

2. Take a breath.

Fig. 5-3 Bobbing helps to develop breath control, which is essential for swimming.

3. Bend your knees and fully submerge your head, and then straighten your legs to resurface. As you come back up, gently exhale through your mouth and nose.

4. When your mouth rises above the surface of the water, take another breath, and then repeat the sequence of submerging and resurfacing.

When you are comfortable bobbing in chest-deep water while holding onto the overflow trough or pool wall, move to chin-deep water and practice bobbing away from the wall.

Floating

Practicing floating helps novice swimmers explore the effects of buoyancy and develop water confidence (that is, a comfort level with being in the water). Floating is also an important safety skill. In an aquatic emergency, floating allows you to stay near the surface of the water and to rest while you are waiting for help to arrive.

Not everyone floats easily. Physically and mentally adjusting to the water before entering and keeping your body relaxed makes floating easier. Understanding and applying the hydrodynamic principles of floating (see Chapter 4) will help you to make adjustments that will help you stay closer to the surface of the water.

Floating on Your Back

The back (supine) float is especially useful for survival or for resting between strokes **(Fig. 5-4)**. Keeping your lungs full of air creates extra buoyancy and makes floating on your back easier.

To float on your back:

1. Submerge to your neck in chest-deep water.

2. Hold your arms overhead and slightly out to your sides.

3. Lay your head back until your ears are in the water.

4. Without pushing off the bottom, arch your body gently at your hips, pushing your chest and stomach toward the surface and letting your body move to its natural floating position—horizontal, diagonal or nearly vertical (see Chapter 4, Fig. 4-2).

5. Keep your legs relaxed, knees slightly bent and feet beneath the surface. Breathe rhythmically in and out through your mouth every few seconds.

6. When you want to recover to a standing position, take a breath, tuck your chin toward your chest, bring your knees toward your chest and sweep your arms back, down and forward in a circular motion **(Fig. 5-5)**. Exhale and then stand up.

Fig. 5-4 One of the main benefits of the back float is that this position keeps your nose and mouth out of the water. (Photo: Alexandra Clark)

Fig. 5-5 To recover to a standing position from a back float, tuck your chin, bring your knees to your chest and sweep your arms back, down and forward in a circular motion, as if you were pulling up a chair to sit in.

If your natural floating position is diagonal or nearly vertical, you can float in a more horizontal position by keeping your arms in the water and moving them above your head, flexing your wrists so your hands (or fingers) are out of the water and bending your knees (see Chapter 4, Box 4-2). If you have trouble floating and tend to sink, you can use sculling or finning motions (described later in this chapter) to help stay near the surface with little effort.

Floating on Your Front

Examples of front floats include the jellyfish float, the tuck (turtle) float and the front (prone) float **(Fig. 5-6)**. The jellyfish and tuck floats are useful for introducing new swimmers to the effects of buoyancy. The front (prone) float also helps new swimmers become accustomed to the face-down, horizontal position that is the basis for the front crawl and other swimming strokes done on the front. The ability to float on the front is an important survival skill; both the survival float and survival swimming (see Chapter 3) involve floating on the front.

Jellyfish Float

In the jellyfish float, the arms and legs dangle, much like the tentacles of a jellyfish **(see Fig. 5-6A)**.

To do the jellyfish float:

1. Submerge to your neck in chest-deep water.

2. Take a deep breath, bend forward at the waist and put your face in the water.

3. Flex your knees slightly to raise your feet off the bottom.

4. Allow your back to rise to the surface of the water, and let your arms and legs hang naturally.

5. To recover, drop your feet, exhale slowly and stand up.

Tuck (Turtle) Float

In the tuck float, the knees are tucked to the chest and the arms are wrapped around the legs **(see Fig. 5-6B)**.

To do the tuck float:

1. Submerge to your neck in chest-deep water.

2. Take a deep breath, bend forward at the waist and put your face in the water with your chin on your chest.

3. Flex your hips and bring your knees to your chest, wrapping your arms around your legs. At first, you may sink a few inches but your shoulders will slowly rise toward the surface until they are just above or below the surface of the water.

4. To recover, let go of your legs, exhale slowly and stand up.

Front (Prone) Float

In the front float, the arms and legs are extended so that the body is in a horizontal position **(see Fig. 5-6C)**.

To do the front float:

1. Submerge to your neck in chest-deep water with your arms extended in front of you, palms facing down.

Front Floats

Fig. 5-6A Jellyfish float.

Fig. 5-6B Tuck (turtle) float.

Fig. 5-6C Front (prone) float.

2. Take a breath, bend forward at the waist and put your face in the water until your ears are covered. To keep your nose from filling with water, gently blow a small amount of air out through your nose.

3. Keeping your arms extended in front of you, gently push off the bottom and let your feet and legs float to the surface.

4. To recover, exhale slowly, lift your head, press down with your arms, pull your knees under your body toward your chest and place your feet on the bottom to stand up.

Beginning swimmers may find it easier to learn the front float in water that is shallow enough to allow them to touch the bottom with their hands when they are in the prone position. However, people who tend to float in a diagonal or nearly vertical position may find it difficult to keep their toes off the bottom in water this shallow.

To do the front float in shallow water:

1. Lie face down with your hands on the bottom.

2. Take a breath, then put your face in the water until your ears are covered. To keep your nose from filling with water, gently blow a small amount of air out through your nose.

3. Slowly lift your hands off the bottom and then extend your arms in front of you. If your toes are still on the bottom, relax your legs and gently push up off the bottom to get your toes to rise.

4. To recover, exhale slowly, lift your head and press down with your arms, pull your knees under your body toward your chest and place your feet on the bottom to stand up.

Moving Forward, Moving Backward and Staying in Place

Basic skills for moving forward, moving backward or staying in place in the water include gliding, finning, sculling and treading. These skills are essential survival skills and also form the basis for learning more advanced swimming techniques.

Gliding

Gliding involves pushing off the side or bottom and moving through the water in a **streamlined position**. In the streamlined position, your arms are extended in front of you, pressed against your ears with your hands clasped together. Your legs are together and extended behind you, with your toes pointed. You can glide on your front or your back **(Fig. 5-7)**.

To glide:

1. Begin in the front float position (to glide on your front) or the back float position (to glide on your back).

2. Push off the side or bottom with your feet, bringing your arms and legs into a streamlined position.

3. Glide until your momentum slows, and then start swimming.

Fig. 5-7 When you glide, you move through the water in a streamlined position. (**A**) Front glide. (**B**) Back glide.

Finning

Finning, a pushing motion with the arms, is a basic skill for creating movement as well as staying in position while floating on your back.

To practice finning:

1. Move into a back float position with your head back and your arms at your sides, palms down. Your hands are relaxed and under the surface of the water.

2. Bend your elbows and slowly move your hands away from your sides.

3. Flex your wrists and push the water toward your feet using short strokes. Your arm movements can be simultaneous or slightly alternating.

Sculling

Sculling is a motion of the arms that creates a force to sustain the body in water or to move the body in any direction, usually horizontally or vertically. The hands move in a figure-eight path that creates a lift force as a result of the flow of water over the hands.

In sculling, as in swimming, the swimmer tries to establish "grab" or "catch" on the water. "Grab" or "catch" on the water can be described as a feeling of pressure on the hands and forearms that gives the swimmer the ability to press the torso away from the hands, going up, down or across the surface. Some swimmers also describe "grab" or "catch" as a feeling of controlling the water in the palm of the hand, as if holding a small ball in the palm, pushing it out and catching it before it gets away, and then pressing it in toward the torso and again catching it. Once a swimmer gets "grab" or "catch," the hands will automatically move through the figure-eight path.

The sculling motion originates with a rotation in the shoulders combined with a bending and straightening of the elbows **(Fig. 5-8)**. Your upper arms stay relatively still, but should not be locked in place. Your elbows should be about 5 to 7 inches away from your torso.

Keep your hands flat, with your fingers held lightly together. It is acceptable to have small spaces between your fingers. Too much tension in your hands and arms may prevent you from establishing catch on the water and cause you to slice your hands in and out through the water, eliminating the figure-eight path and limiting the force or propulsion generated. Your palms should rotate between 20 and 50 degrees to get the most efficient and effective sculls.

Sculling is an important water survival skill, because it can help keep your mouth above water while you are resting or moving to safety. Sculling is also a fundamental skill used in all the swimming strokes, in water polo, and in synchronized swimming. To learn and practice the sculling motion:

1. Stand in shallow water, anywhere from waist- to shoulder-deep.

2. Bend your elbows with your hands in front, palms facing down. Your elbows should be about 5 to 7 inches from your waist.

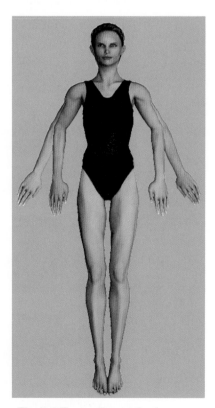

Fig. 5-8 The sculling motion is produced by rotation of the shoulders combined with a bending and straightening of the elbows. The upper arms remain relatively still. *Art courtesy of esynchro.com.*

3. Hold your hands about 6 inches beneath the surface. Keep your hands flat with your fingers loosely held together and your arms relaxed.

4. Rotate your palms between 20 and 50 degrees to press water out and then in. The total distance your hands move is about 12 inches. Although it may look as if your palms are flat and facing the bottom of the pool, they rotate from facing out to in, with almost no time spent facing flat toward the bottom. Keep your upper arms relatively still with a small rotation on each scull. Avoid "locking" your upper arms in place. Maintain a continuous movement, without stopping and starting at the in and out points of each scull.

5. Keep your hands moving with an even tempo and pressure. When you get good "grab," you may see a whirlpool develop over your fingers.

Once you understand how the basic sculling motion feels, try sculling on your back **(Fig. 5-9)**. The standard (back) scull is the most basic scull, done in a back floating position. By changing the position of your hands, you can propel yourself headfirst (headfirst back scull) or footfirst (footfirst back scull). Additional sculling techniques are described in **Box 5-1**.

Standard (Back) Scull

To do a standard scull:

1. Get in a back floating position with your arms by your sides. Gently press your head and upper back down to help bring your feet to the surface.

2. Bend your elbows and rotate your arms so your elbows are pointing down, toward the bottom of the pool. Your elbows should be about 5 to 7 inches from your waist.

3. Hold your hands at about the depth of your buttocks (4 to 10 inches beneath the surface), palms facing the bottom of the pool **(see Fig. 5-9A)**. Keep your hands flat with your fingers loosely held together and your arms relaxed.

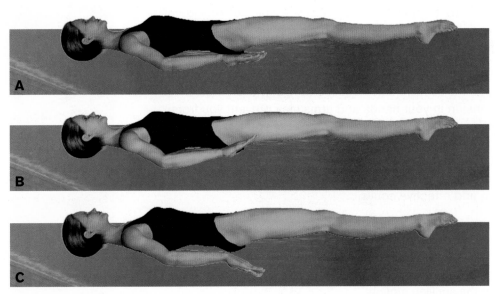

Fig. 5-9 Changing the direction your palms face as you scull determines whether you maintain your position, move forward or move backward. (**A**) In the standard scull, facing the palms toward the bottom of the pool helps you to maintain your position without moving. (**B**) In the headfirst scull, lift your fingers so that your palms face toward your feet. This directs the force of the water toward your feet, moving you headfirst through the water. (**C**) In the feetfirst scull, flex your wrists and point your fingers toward the bottom of the pool. This directs the force of the water toward your head, moving you feetfirst through the water. *Art courtesy of esynchro.com.*

4. Rotate your palms between 20 and 50 degrees to press water out and then in. Keep your upper arms relatively still with a small rotation on each scull. Avoid "locking" your upper arms in place. Maintain a continuous movement, without stopping and starting at the in and out points of each scull.

5. Keep your hands moving with an even tempo and pressure.

Headfirst Back Scull

The headfirst back scull is the standard scull with a small adjustment in the hands to create headfirst propulsion.

To do a headfirst back scull:

1. Get in a back floating position with your arms by your sides. Gently press your head and upper back down to help bring your feet to the surface.

2. Bend your elbows and rotate your arms so your elbows are pointing down, toward the bottom of the pool. Your elbows should be about 5 to 7 inches from your waist.

3. Hold your hands at about the depth of your buttocks (4 to 10 inches beneath the surface). Bend your wrists to lift your fingers toward the surface **(see Fig. 5-9B)**. Any amount of bend will create headfirst movement, but to move quickly, an angle of about 45 degrees is best. Keep your hands flat with your fingers loosely held together and your arms relaxed.

4. Rotate your palms between 20 and 50 degrees to press water out and then in. Keep your upper arms relatively still with a small rotation on each scull. Avoid "locking" your upper arms in place. Maintain a continuous movement, without stopping and starting at the in and out points of each scull.

5. Keep your hands moving with an even tempo and pressure.

Footfirst Back Scull

The footfirst back scull is the standard scull with a small adjustment in the hands to create headfirst propulsion.

To do a footfirst back scull:

1. Get in a back floating position with your arms by your sides. Gently press your head and upper back down to help bring your feet to the surface.

2. Bend your elbows and rotate your arms so your elbows are pointing down, toward the bottom of the pool. Your elbows should be about 5 to 7 inches from your waist.

3. Hold your hands at about the depth of your buttocks (4 to 10 inches beneath the surface). Bend your wrists to point your fingers toward the bottom **(see Fig. 5-9C)**. Any amount of bend will create footfirst movement, but to move quickly, an angle of about 30 to 45 degrees is best. Keep your hands flat with your fingers loosely held together and your arms relaxed.

4. Rotate your palms between 20 and 50 degrees to press water out and then in. Keep your upper arms relatively still with a small rotation on each scull. Avoid "locking" your upper arms in place. Maintain a continuous movement, without stopping and starting at the in and out points of each scull.

5. Keep your hands moving with an even tempo and pressure.

Box 5-1
Additional Sculling Techniques

Front (Canoe) Scull

The front (canoe) scull is used to maintain a stationary position or move forward on your front. To canoe scull, start on your front with your arms extended along your sides and your face in the water. Press down gently with your chest to raise your head above the surface of the water and squeeze your buttocks to help raise your feet toward the surface. Bend your elbows and lower your hands in the water. Your hands should be at

Front (canoe) scull

about chest-to-shoulder position, slightly wider than your shoulders. Your elbows are about 5 to 7 inches away from your torso. Bend your wrists so that your fingertips point straight ahead (if you want to stay still) or at about a 45-degree angle toward the bottom of the pool (if you want to move forward). Keep your hands flat with your fingers loosely held together and your arms relaxed. Rotate your palms between 20 and 50 degrees to press water out and then in. Keep your upper arms relatively still. The size of the scull depends on the size of the swimmer and varies from 10 to 18 inches. Keep your hands moving with an even tempo and pressure. It is better to use a gentle pressure that is just enough to support your body and hold your head up (if desired), than to scull very hard.

Torpedo Scull

The torpedo scull is done on your back with your hands overhead to move in a footfirst direction. To torpedo scull, start on your back with your face, hips, thighs and feet at the surface and your arms extended over your head. Press your hands and arms beneath the surface about 4 to 8 inches. Your elbows should be at the sides of your head, next to your ears but not touching them. You can keep your elbows relatively straight, or slightly bent. Bend your wrists 30 to 45 degrees so that your palms face away from your head. Keep your hands flat with your fingers loosely held together and your arms relaxed. Rotate your palms between 20 and 50 degrees to press water out and then in. Keep your upper arms relatively still, about 6 to 12 inches away from your ears. Keep your hands moving with an even tempo and pressure. A faster tempo and more pressure will generate faster propulsion.

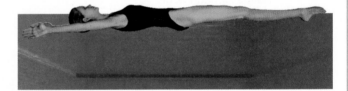

Torpedo scull

Support Scull

The support scull is the scull that synchronized swimmers use to support their legs above the surface. It is most often done in an inverted (upside down) position with one or both legs above the surface. The range of motion of the forearms and hands varies depending on the position of the torso and legs. In the standard support

Support scull

Art courtesy of esynchro.com.

Box 5-1 (continued)

scull in a vertical position (legs together with the body in vertical alignment), the hands move from about straight out to the sides of the torso to anywhere from 45° to 90° forward.

You can learn the support scull standing upright in shallow water before trying it in an inverted position. To learn the support scull standing upright, stand in chest- to shoulder-deep water with your arms at your sides. Rotate your arms so your palms face away from your body and bend your elbows so your forearms are about horizontal and your palms face up. Your upper arms are about 5 to 7 inches away from your waist. Keep your hands flat with your fingers held lightly together. Initiating the rotation from your shoulders, move your hands and forearms forward and back. Your palms stay relatively flat toward the surface with some rotation back on the out sculls and forward on the in sculls. When standing upright, your hands move down toward the bottom on the out scull with your elbows nearly straightening. As your hands scull in, your elbows bend more and you pull your hands up toward the surface. Your hands move in a "figure-eight" path, not directly side to side. As in the other sculls, once you achieve "grab," your hands will automatically move in the "figure-eight" pattern. Scull in and out, or forward and back, in a continuous motion with an even tempo. The surface of the water should appear to "boil up" over your hands.

It is easiest to learn the inverted support scull in a position with the legs at the surface of the water. This can be done in a tabletop position: torso vertical with head pointing toward the bottom and both knees bent so the shins lay flat on the surface of the water. The arm position is the same as when standing, but your palms will now be facing toward the bottom of the pool. Begin with your forearms and hands straight out to the sides of your body. Your hands move up toward the surface on the out scull, with your elbows nearly straightening. Your hands move down toward waist-level on the in scull as your elbows bend.

Treading

Treading is an important personal safety skill, because it allows you to remain upright in deep water with your head above the surface. **Treading** typically combines a scissors, breaststroke or rotary (eggbeater) kick with sculling or finning movements of the hands and arms **(Fig. 5-10)**. However, with practice, it is possible to tread using only the arms or legs. Whichever movements are used, treading should be done using just enough movement to keep your body vertical.

To tread:

1. Stay nearly vertical, with your upper body bent slightly forward at the waist.

2. Make continuous sculling movements with your hands a few inches below the surface in front of your body, with your palms facing downward and your elbows bent. When sculling to maintain your position while treading water, your reach will be much wider than it is when you are sculling to maintain your position while floating on your back.

Fig. 5-10 Treading typically combines arm movements (sculling or finning) and leg movements (a scissors, breaststroke or rotary kick) to keep the body upright and the head above the surface.

3. Kick using either a scissors kick, a breaststroke kick, or a rotary kick **(Fig. 5-11)**:

   - **Scissors kick.** Separate your legs, moving one toward the front and the other toward the back, and then bring them together **(see Fig. 5-11A).**

   - **Breaststroke kick.** Start with your legs extended straight down and together. Bend your knees and draw your legs up so that your thighs are parallel to the bottom of the pool. As you draw your legs up, separate your knees and flex your feet, then push outward in a circular motion. To complete the kick, extend your legs toward the bottom of the pool and bring your feet together again **(see Fig. 5-11B).**

   - **Rotary kick:** Because the rotary kick has no resting phase, it provides continuous support. This strong kick is also used in water polo, synchronized swimming and lifeguarding. To do a rotary kick, bend your knees and draw your legs up so that your thighs are parallel to the bottom of the pool. Your knees should be slightly wider than hip-width apart. Rotate your lower legs at your knees, one leg at a time, making large circular movements with your foot and lower leg. Move one leg clockwise and the other counterclockwise **(see Fig. 5-11C).** As each foot moves sideways and forward, extend it sharply outward. The power of your kick comes from lift forces created by the inward sweeping action of your foot. As one leg kicks, the other leg recovers. Kick just hard enough to keep your head out of the water.

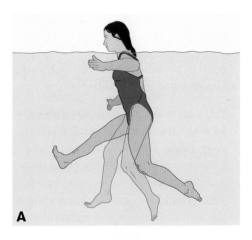

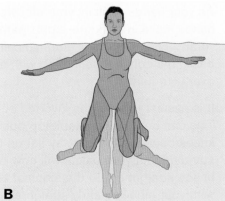

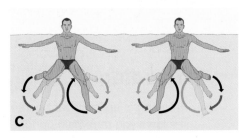

Fig. 5-11 Different kicks can be used when treading. (**A**) Scissors kick. (**B**) Breaststroke kick. (**C**) Rotary kick.

Starting, Changing Direction and Turning Over

All beginning swimmers need to know how to start or resume swimming, how to change direction while swimming and how to turn over.

Starting

You can start swimming by moving from a vertical to a horizontal position, or by pushing off from the pool wall.

Starting from a Vertical Position

Moving from a vertical to a horizontal position on your front

To move from a vertical to a horizontal position on your front:

1. Take a breath.

2. Lean forward and put your face in the water until your ears are covered.

3. Extend your arms in front of you, in the direction you intend to go.

4. Push off the bottom or kick your legs to help move your body into a horizontal position, and then start swimming.

Moving from a vertical to a horizontal position on your back

To move from a vertical to a horizontal position on your back:

1. Move your arms overhead and slightly out to the side.

2. Lay your head back until your ears are covered.

3. Arch your body gently at the hips, pushing your chest and stomach toward the surface.

4. Push off the bottom or kick your legs to help move your body into a horizontal position, and then start swimming.

Starting from the Pool Wall

Starting on the front from the pool wall

To push off from the pool wall on your front:

1. Grasp the overflow trough or the pool wall with one hand.

2. Extend your other arm in front of you, in the direction you intend to go. Rotate your body and lean forward slightly, so that your shoulder and extended arm are under the surface.

3. Place your feet against the pool wall, about hip-width apart with one foot higher than the other **(Fig. 5-12A)**.

4. Take a breath and put your face in the water.

5. Let go of the wall and rotate your body into a face-down position.

6. Extend your arms into a streamlined position **(Fig. 5-12B)** and push off the wall with both feet. Keep your legs together and your toes pointed.

7. Glide until your momentum slows to swimming speed and then start swimming.

Starting on the back from the pool wall

To push off from the pool wall on your back:

— Starting on the Front from the Pool Wall —

Fig. 5-12A Starting position.

Fig. 5-12B As you let go and push off, rotate your body into a face-down, streamlined position and glide before starting to swim.

1. Hold onto the overflow trough or pool wall with both hands about shoulder-width apart.

2. Tuck your body and place your feet against the pool wall just under the surface of the water about hip-width apart. Your knees are inside your arms **(Fig. 5-13A)**.

3. Bend your arms slightly, put your chin on your chest and pull your body closer to the wall.

4. Take a breath, then lean your head back into the water and arch your back slightly.

Fig. 5-13A Starting position.

Fig. 5-13B As you let go and push off, bring your arms into a streamlined position and glide before starting to swim.

5. Let go of the wall, bring your hands close to your body and push off the wall while keeping your back slightly arched.

6. If you are going to start swimming the back crawl, move into a streamlined position with your arms over your head and glide until your momentum slows to swimming speed **(Fig. 5-13B)**. If you are going to start swimming the elementary backstroke, glide with your arms at your sides.

Starting on the side from the pool wall

To push off from the pool wall on your side:

1. Grasp the overflow trough or pool wall with one hand.

2. Extend your other arm in front of you, in the direction you intend to go.

3. Place your feet against the pool wall, about hip-width apart with one foot higher than the other.

4. Push off with both feet, maintaining a side-lying position and placing the hand used to hold the pool wall against your thigh.

5. Glide until your momentum slows to swimming speed and then start the sidestroke.

Changing Direction

The ability to change directions while swimming on the front or the back is an important safety skill because it allows you to orient yourself (for example, to swim toward an exit) and to avoid obstacles in the water.

To change direction when swimming on your front:

1. Reach one arm in the desired direction.

2. Look toward that arm (in the direction you want to go) and pull slightly wider with your opposite arm during the arm stroke.

To change direction when swimming on your back:

1. Tilt your head in the desired direction.

2. Make a stronger stroke with your opposite arm.

Turning Over

The ability to turn from your front onto your back (or vice versa) while swimming allows you to change strokes or to rest in a floating position.

To turn over while swimming on your front:

1. Exhale slowly into the water.

2. Lower one shoulder and turn your head in the opposite direction. (To turn counterclockwise, lower your left shoulder and turn your head to the right. To turn clockwise, lower your right shoulder and turn your head to the left.) The momentum from the stroke helps to complete the turn.

3. Breathe normally and rest by floating on your back, or continue swimming on your back.

To turn over while swimming on your back:

1. Take a breath.

2. Lower one shoulder and turn your head in your same direction.

3. Keeping your arms underwater, reach across your body in the direction of the turn until you are positioned on your front.

Underwater Skills

Swimmers need to know how to move deeper in the water (that is, toward the bottom from the surface of the water), and how to swim underwater. Underwater skills are useful for exploring the underwater world, avoiding surface hazards and retrieving lost objects. If you are a person who floats easily, it may take more time for you to develop underwater skills. To lower your risk for injury when surface diving and swimming underwater:

- Protect your head by keeping at least one hand extended above your head when descending and ascending.

- Keep your eyes open so that you can see potential hazards. If you wear contact lenses, remove them before opening your eyes underwater. Avoid wearing goggles when submerging to a depth of 5 feet or more **(Box 5-2)**.

- Never hyperventilate before swimming underwater, and never engage in competitive or repetitive breath-holding games or activities. Prolonged breath-holding while swimming underwater can cause even an accomplished swimmer to lose consciousness and possibly drown.

Surface Diving

Surface diving is a technique used to go under the water when swimming on the surface. It is the quickest and most effective way to go underwater. This skill can be used to retrieve objects from the bottom and for certain activities, such as snorkeling.

A surface dive can be done feetfirst or headfirst. Either way, the key to an effective surface dive is to raise part of your body above the surface so that your weight out of the water forces your body downward. Exhaling through your nose while descending prevents water from entering your nose. If you experience ear pain or pressure while descending or swimming underwater, pinch your nostrils and gently attempt to blow air out through your nose. If this does not relieve the pain or discomfort, swimming to shallower water or to the surface is necessary to prevent damage to the ears.

Box 5-2
Goggles and Face Masks

Goggles and face masks are pieces of equipment designed to improve visibility while swimming. Each has a specific purpose.

Goggles

Goggles, which only cover the eye socket, improve visibility at the surface of the water. They are not made for underwater swimming and should not be used when you are submerging to a depth of 5 feet or more. Swimming underwater in goggles can cause blood vessels in the eyes to break because there is no way to equalize the pressure inside the goggles with the increasing water pressure outside the body. The air volume inside the goggles tends to compress. This compression tends to "pull" the eyeball out of the eye socket to effectively reduce the trapped air volume, causing blood vessels to break.

Face Masks

Face masks used for snorkeling and diving are intended to improve visibility at and below the surface of the water. These protective devices encase the eyes and the nose. As the outside water pressure increases with depth, the diver can exhale through the nose, forcing additional air into the space behind the lens. This increases the pressure inside the mask until it is equalized with the pressure outside.

Feetfirst Surface Dive

For safety, use a feetfirst surface dive if the water is murky, or if you are not sure how deep the water is.

To do a feetfirst surface dive:

1. Start by treading water in a vertical position.

2. While performing a strong scissors or breaststroke kick, press down forcefully with both hands at the same time, bringing them to the sides of your thighs. This helps you to rise in the water for a better descent.

3. When your body reaches its maximum height out of the water, take a breath **(Fig. 5-14A)**.

Feetfirst Surface Dive

Fig. 5-14A Raise your body above the surface of the water by pressing down forcefully with your arms (bringing them alongside your thighs) while doing a strong scissors or breaststroke kick.

Fig. 5-14B After you are completely underwater, turn your palms outward and sweep your arms upward to propel yourself toward the bottom.

4. Keep your body vertical and in a streamlined position as you start moving downward. Turn your palms outward, then sweep your hands upward for more downward propulsion **(see Fig. 5-14B)**. This sweeping action occurs completely underwater. Additional hand sweeps may be necessary to reach the desired depth.

5. Once your momentum slows, tuck your body, roll into a horizontal position, extend your arms and legs and begin to swim underwater.

Tuck Surface Dive

The tuck surface dive is a head-first surface dive. If you do not know the depth of the water, or if the water is less than 8 feet deep, keep one arm extended over your head when moving toward the bottom.

To do a tuck surface dive:

1. Use a swimming stroke or glide to gain forward momentum.

2. Take a breath, sweep your arms backward to your thighs and then turn your palms downward.

3. Tuck your chin to your chest, bend your body at a right angle at your hips and draw your legs into a tuck position.

4. Roll forward until you are almost upside down.

5. Press your arms and hands forward with your palms facing the bottom **(Fig. 5-15A)** while extending your legs upward **(Fig. 5-15B)**.

6. Use the breaststroke arm pull (a sweeping "circular" motion with both arms) to go deeper after your momentum begins to slow.

Pike Surface Dive

The pike surface dive is similar to a tuck surface dive, except the legs are extended perpendicular to the body in a pike position rather than drawn to the chest in a tuck position. As with the tuck surface dive, keep one arm extended over your head as you move toward the bottom if the water is less than 8 feet deep, or if you are not sure how deep the water is.

To do a pike surface dive:

1. Use a swimming stroke or glide to gain forward momentum.

2. Take a breath, sweep your arms backward to your thighs and turn your palms downward.

Tuck Surface Dive

Fig. 5-15A From the tucked position, extend your arms toward the bottom and...

Fig. 5-15B Extend your legs toward the surface.

Fig. 5-16A From a horizontal position, tuck your chin to your chest and flex at the hips sharply while reaching your arms forward and downward toward the bottom.

Fig. 5-16B Lift your legs upward, keeping them straight and together, until your body is in a streamlined, nearly vertical position.

3. Tuck your chin to your chest and flex at the hips sharply while reaching your arms forward and downward toward the bottom **(Fig. 5-16A)**.

4. Lift your legs upward, keeping them straight and together, so that your body is in a fully extended, streamlined and nearly vertical position **(Fig. 5-16B)**. Allow the weight of your legs and forward momentum to cause descent.

Swimming Underwater

Many different types of strokes and modified strokes are used to swim underwater. A modified breaststroke is commonly used **(Fig. 5-17)**. The breaststroke can be modified for underwater swimming in several ways. Common modifications include:

Fig. 5-17 Many people use a modified breaststroke for swimming underwater.

- Using a breaststroke arm pull with a scissors or dolphin kick.

- Extending the arm pull all the way back to the thighs, or using the arm pull and kick together followed by a glide with your arms at your sides. These methods help make your stroke longer and stronger underwater.

- Shortening the arm pull or not using it at all and keeping your arms stretched out in front of your body. These methods allow you to feel for obstacles if visibility is poor.

To change direction or depth while swimming underwater, turn your head in the direction you want to go and reach your arms in that same direction, then pull them back. Flexing or extending your hips also helps direct your body up or down.

CHAPTER 6
Basic Swimming Strokes

Whether you are a proficient swimmer looking to improve, or a new swimmer just starting out, one of the best ways to develop your swimming technique is by focusing on how to propel your body through the water with little wasted effort. Moving easily and efficiently through the water is the goal, whether you are swimming for recreation, fitness or competition. This chapter takes a look at six basic swimming strokes—the front crawl, back crawl, breaststroke, butterfly, elementary backstroke and sidestroke—and offers tips for refining your technique.

Stroke Mechanics

Stroke mechanics are the basic elements of a swimming stroke: body position and motion, breathing and timing, arm stroke and kick. The focus of stroke mechanics is on making the most of propulsive movements while maintaining efficient body position and good body alignment. Although the way you perform a stroke will vary depending on a number of factors, including your size, strength, flexibility and body composition, understanding the basic elements of each stroke is the key to becoming a better, more efficient, swimmer.

Every swimming stroke has a power phase and a recovery. The **power phase** is the part of the stroke where the arm or leg is moving the body in the right direction. The power phase of the arm stroke has three parts: the catch, the mid-pull and the finish. The **recovery** is the part of the stroke where the arms or legs relax and return to their starting position. Some strokes may also have a "**glide**," a part of the stroke where the body keeps moving without any effort from the swimmer.

Front Crawl (Freestyle)

When most people think of swimming, the first stroke they think of is often the front crawl **(Fig. 6-1)**. Sometimes called **freestyle** (because it is the most commonly used stroke in the freestyle category of competitive swimming), the front crawl is the fastest stroke performed face-down in the water. It is also one of the most popular and usually the first to be learned.

The front crawl is performed with the body horizontal and prone (face-down). **Body roll** (a rotating movement around the midline of the body) helps the swimmer maintain proper

Fig. 6-1 The front crawl (freestyle) stroke is what most people think of when they think of "swimming."

body position, gives a good rhythm to the stroke and makes taking a breath easier. Most of the propulsive movement of the front crawl comes from alternating arm strokes that drive forward on entry and then apply force backward during the underwater arm motion. Additional propulsion is supplied by a flutter kick. The kick also helps to stabilize the body by keeping the legs close to the surface of the water.

Body Position and Motion

A prone, horizontal and streamlined body position and good body roll are the foundation for the front crawl.

Good body position makes this stroke more efficient. To maintain correct body position, pay attention to the position of your head. Where your head goes, the rest of your body follows. When you are in the prone position, look toward the bottom of the pool or slightly forward, keeping your neck in a relaxed and neutral position, as if standing up straight **(Fig. 6-2)**. The water line should be at about the middle of the top of your head, about even with your ears.

Fig. 6-2 To maintain good body position in the front crawl, look toward the bottom of the pool or slightly forward, keeping your neck in a neutral position, as if standing up straight. The water line should be at about the middle of the top of your head.

Unless you are turning your head to breathe, keep your head still. If your head moves from side to side, your body will move from side to side. If your head bobs up and down, your hips will do the same. Any unnecessary movement increases the resistance of the water against your body, requiring you to use extra energy to move forward. Keeping your head facing down and your neck relaxed helps keep your hips and legs at the surface, which allows for good body position, an effective kick and efficient swimming. An ineffective kick can cause poor body position, and conversely, poor body position can make it difficult to have an effective kick.

Body roll is a rotating movement around the **midline** of the body, an imaginary line from head to feet that divides the body equally into left and right parts. This rotating movement is very important to several aspects of the front crawl. First, it allows for a dynamic reach forward as the arm enters the water and helps to maintain the body's forward movement. Second, body roll improves arm propulsion by allowing more force to be generated during the arm stroke. Much as a person pulling a rope with outstretched arms is able to generate more force by rotating the hips, a swimmer can generate more force with each arm if the body rotates during the arm stroke. Finally, this rotation allows for a relaxed arm recovery with a bent elbow.

In good body roll, your whole body, not just your shoulders, rotates around the midline while your head stays still, facing the bottom of the pool. In the front crawl, the shoulders and torso rotate to the side about 30–40° from the surface of the water **(Fig. 6-3)**. The legs also rotate to the side, but to a lesser degree, staying naturally in line with the shoulders and torso. At the point of maximum rotation, the shoulder stays next to the cheek and the body remains facing more toward the bottom than the side. If there is too much rotation, the arm stroke will be less effective, the kick is likely to pause and falter, and it becomes difficult to maintain balance.

Evolution of the Front Crawl

English swimmer John Trudgen developed a hand-over-hand stroke that became known as the trudgen. He copied the stroke from South American Indians and introduced it in England in 1873. In this new technique, each arm recovered out of the water as the body rolled from side to side. The swimmer did a scissors kick with every two arm strokes. The stroke is now acknowledged as the forerunner of the front crawl. The inefficiency of the trudgen kick led Australian Richard Cavill to try new methods of kicking. He used a stroke that he observed natives of the Solomon Islands using, which combined an up-and-down kick with an alternating overarm stroke. He used the new stroke in 1902 at the International Championships to set a new world record (100 yards in 58.4 seconds). The stroke he used became known as the "Australian crawl." At the 1956 Olympic Games in Melbourne, the Australian men's swimming team introduced a front crawl stroke that took advantage of body roll and increased speed through the water.

Fig. 6-3 In good body roll, the shoulders and torso rotate about 30–40° from the surface of the water. The lower body rotates as well, but to a lesser extent.

Breathing and Timing

Most swimmers learn to time their breathing to correlate with each arm cycle (e.g., they take a breath each time the right arm recovers out of the water). However, some swimmers time their breathing so that it occurs every 1½ arm cycles. This results in breathing on alternate sides and helps promote a balanced technique between the right and left arm strokes. Whichever technique you choose, coordinate your breathing so that there is no pause in the stroke to take a breath.

The position and motion of the head are the keys to breathing and timing. Proper head motion for breathing lets the head remain low in the water, which helps maintain good body position. Start by turning your head toward the recovery arm as it exits the water. Look to the side or slightly toward your feet, keeping your head aligned with your neck and the water line at the top of your head. One ear stays in the water—do not lift your head up to breathe. The head turn should not make your body twist or rotate more to one side than the other.

As you rotate your head to breathe, you create a trough that allows you to take a breath (Fig. 6-4). Inhale as your recovery arm is starting to recover and your opposite arm is starting the catch phase of the arm stroke. You do not need to take a deep breath because the next opportunity to take a breath is coming soon. After inhaling, quickly return your face to the water before the recovery arm reenters the water. Exhale slowly underwater through your mouth and nose between breaths so that you are prepared to inhale on the next head rotation. If you do not exhale underwater, you will have to exhale and then inhale when your head is turned for a breath, causing a pause in the stroke. The resultant impact on timing will affect all other parts of the stroke, making the stroke less efficient and increasing the energy needed to continue swimming.

Fig. 6-4 Turning—not lifting—your head creates a trough in the water that allows you to take a breath.

Arm Stroke

The arm stroke consists of the power phase and the recovery:

- During the power phase, you use your entire arm to push water backward and propel your body forward. For good form, it is important to move your arm straight back, without letting it cross the midline of your body. As your arm moves water toward your feet, your body rotates so that the opposite hip moves toward the bottom. As your arm moves through the power phase (from the catch to the finish), your hand accelerates so that it is moving fastest at the end of the power phase.

- During the recovery, your arm recovers out of the water to its starting position. While your arm recovers to the starting position, your arm, hand and finger muscles can relax. Tensing these muscles causes them to tire more quickly, and the recovery will be stiff and mechanical.

Power Phase

The power phase of the arm stroke begins as your hand enters the water at an angle, fingers first, followed by your bent elbow. The point where your hand enters the water is about three-fourths as far as you can reach with your arm fully extended (Fig. 6-5A). Allow your hand to enter the water smoothly, keeping your elbow higher than the rest of the arm. The elbow enters the water last. Think of this part of the stroke as the forearm going through a hole that your hand makes in the water's surface with little to no splash. Your hand should be relaxed with the fingers straight.

Fig. 6-5A Your hand enters the water at a point about three-fourths as far as you can reach with your arm fully extended.

Fig. 6-5B Begin the catch with your arm fully extended, and then...

Fig. 6-5C Bend your elbow so that your palm and forearm face toward your feet.

Fig. 6-5D During the mid-pull, continue pressing your palm and forearm directly backward along the side of your body.

Catch

The **catch** is where the power starts. To initiate the catch, extend your arm forward in front of your shoulder or slightly wider **(Fig. 6-5B)**. Bend your elbow so that your palm and forearm face toward your feet, and press backward with your fingertips pointing down **(Fig. 6-5C)**. Pointing your fingertips down causes your elbow and hand to naturally move slightly outside your shoulder. Your body starts to rotate along the

Fig. 6-5E During the finish, keep your hand facing back for as long as possible.

midline as soon as the catch position is established. When your hand is pitched effectively and your body is allowed to roll, the catch seems to lead your body forward automatically. You will feel tension in your wrist and pressure on your palm and forearm.

Mid-pull

Continue pressing your palm and forearm directly backward **(Fig. 6-5D)**. As your arm travels backward, keep your elbow slightly wider than your hand and shoulder so your elbow remains bent with your palm and forearm facing back. Your elbow remains higher than your hand and wider than your shoulder throughout the pull.

Finish

As you finish the power phase, keep your palm pressing toward your feet and your fingertips pointed toward the bottom for as long as possible **(Fig. 6-5E)**. Your hand moves upward as your elbow bends toward the surface. Avoid extending your arm fully at the finish and flicking your hand into the recovery of the stroke, because this can cause your arm to extend behind your back and potentially compromise the long-term health of the shoulder.

Completing the body rotation along the midline allows the arm to exit the water without obstruction. The elbow is the first part of the arm to exit the water, followed by the rest of the arm.

Fig. 6-6A Keep your arm relaxed as you lift your elbow.

Fig. 6-6B As your hand passes your shoulder, let it lead the rest of your arm to the entry point.

Recovery

The recovery is not propulsive; it is simply a movement that puts the hand back in position for the next power phase. Done correctly, there is a smooth transition from the finish of the power phase to the beginning of the recovery.

Lift your elbow so it comes out of the water first. Keep your elbow high throughout the recovery, but not so high that it causes stress on your shoulder. As you lift your elbow, keep your arm relaxed with your forearm hanging down **(Fig. 6-6A)**. Bring your arm around the side of your body in a relaxed motion, keeping your hand wider than your elbow. As your hand passes your shoulder, let it lead the rest of your arm and drive your hand forward to the entry point **(Fig. 6-6B)**. Allow your body to rotate throughout the recovery motion.

Kick

A **flutter kick** (a continuous, upward-and-downward kicking motion of the legs) is used in the front crawl. The size of the flutter kick (the distance the legs move up and down) varies with body type and flexibility. During a front crawl, most of the propulsion is generated from the arms, rather than from the kick. However, the kick is still an important part of this stroke. A forceful kick helps maintain proper body position high in the water and helps the body roll.

A flutter kick begins with the hips. As you kick, your thigh starts to move downward even though your calf and foot are still moving upward. As your thigh continues to move downward, the motion continues through your whole leg, and your calf and foot follow through. For most of the downbeat (the downward motion of the leg), your knee remains slightly flexed **(Fig. 6-7A)**. The propulsion occurs when your leg straightens. Snapping your foot downward (as though kicking a ball) completes the motion **(Fig. 6-7B)**. Because of this "snapping" motion, the flutter kick is most effective when the feet and ankles stay relaxed and "floppy." When the feet and ankles remain loose and relaxed, the kick will still be moderately effective even if other aspects of the kick need improvement. Flexing your feet during the flutter kick pulls your body downward and backward.

Fig. 6-7A Keep your knee slightly flexed during most of the downbeat.

Fig. 6-7B Keep your leg extended during the upbeat, allowing your heel to just break the surface.

Before you start the upbeat of the kick, extend your leg so that there is little or no bend in the knee. Keep your leg straight and raise it up until your heel just breaks the surface.

Swimmers use different cadences or "beats" for their kick. The **cadence** is the number of kicks in an arm cycle. (An **arm cycle** is the time it takes for one hand to enter the water, begin the pull and then return to that position.) Cadences for a front crawl are typically either a 2-beat kick or a 6-beat kick. Most swimmers use a 2-beat kick for longer distances and a 6-beat kick for shorter distances.

Back Crawl (Backstroke)

The back crawl is one of the four competitive strokes **(Fig. 6-8)**. It is the fastest stroke performed on the back.

The back crawl is performed on the back with the body horizontal. As with the front crawl, an effective back crawl depends on good body position and body roll with every stroke. Most of the propulsive movement of the back crawl comes from alternating arm strokes that move the body forward by pushing the water toward the feet. Additional propulsion is supplied by a flutter kick similar to that used in the front crawl. The back crawl kick is continuous, and the feet churn the surface of the water.

Fig. 6-8 The back crawl (referred to as the backstroke in competitive swimming) is the only competitive stroke performed on the back, but it is not just for competition. Many recreational swimmers enjoy doing the back crawl too.

Body Position and Motion

A horizontal and streamlined body position along with good body roll are the foundation for the back crawl.

Throughout the stroke, your head remains still and aligned with your spine. (Because your face is out of the water, it is not necessary to rotate your head to breathe.) The most efficient head position is tilted very slightly toward the feet. The water line typically runs from the middle of the top of your head to the

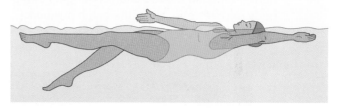

Fig. 6-9 To maintain good body position in the back crawl, keep your neck aligned with your spine. The rest of your body should be parallel to, and just underneath, the surface of the water.

tip of your chin, with your ears underwater. Your upper body is relaxed, but your shoulders are rolled forward so that your back curves slightly. Rounding of the back helps to keep your hips and legs horizontal and just below the surface of the water **(Fig. 6-9)**.

Evolution of the Back Crawl

Before 1900, swimming on the back was not used in competition. However, recreational swimmers were doing a variation of the popular breaststroke, performing it upside down on the back. This inverted breaststroke was a predecessor to the back crawl. Introduced in 1902, the back crawl developed from the inverted breaststroke and the trudgen. As the front crawl became more popular, swimmers tried the alternating overarm style on the back. Combined with a flutter kick, this created a fast and efficient way to swim on the back. In 1912, the back crawl became a competitive event. The continued effort to gain greater speed, along with studying and experimenting with the stroke, led to the back crawl as we know it today.

An effective back crawl depends on good body rotation with every arm stroke. In good body roll, your whole body, not just your shoulders, rotates around the midline while your head stays still. In the back crawl, your shoulders and torso rotate to the side about 30° from the surface of the water. Your legs kick from side to side naturally as your body rotates to each side. Rotating about 30° from the surface of the water allows the arms to achieve the strongest catch position at the optimal depth.

The timing of the body roll is also crucial in the back crawl. The body rotates toward the arm of the hand that is entering the water just before it enters the water. The body rotation is completed before the hand reaches the catch position. Avoid rotating in the middle of the arm's power phase.

Breathing and Timing

For the back crawl, use a regular breathing pattern during each stroke. Inhale when one arm recovers and exhale when the other arm recovers.

Arm Stroke

During the back crawl, your arms move continuously in constant opposition to each other—one arm recovers while the other arm pulls (**Fig. 6-10**). Your body stays streamlined and your head steady throughout the stroke. The shoulder of your stroking arm starts the body roll at the beginning of each arm stroke.

Fig. 6-10 During the back crawl, the arms move in constant opposition to each other. This is called "opposition rhythm."

Power Phase

The power phase of the arm stroke for the back crawl begins as your hand enters the water above your head, just outside the shoulder. Your arm is fully extended. The palm of your hand is facing out, so that your little finger enters the water first (**Fig. 6-11A**). Keep your wrist slightly bent, your hand relaxed and your fingers straight. Remember that it is important to complete the body roll before reaching the catch position.

—————— Back Crawl: Power Phase ——————

Fig. 6-11A Your hand enters the water with your arm fully extended and your palm facing out.

Fig. 6-11B To achieve the catch, bend your elbow so that your fingers are pointing away from your body. Your hand and forearm are horizontal, with your palm and forearm facing toward your feet.

Fig. 6-11C During the mid-pull, your hand follows a straight path toward your feet.

Fig. 6-11D The power phase ends with your arm straight and your hand below your hip.

Catch

The propulsive action starts with the catch. The hand slices downward 8–12 inches and at a slight outward angle and grabs the water. Bend your elbow so that your fingertips are pointing away from your body, toward the side of the pool (like swinging a tennis racquet). Your arm stays to the side of your body and your hand and forearm are horizontal once the catch position is achieved **(Fig. 6-11B)**. Be careful not to let your arm bend behind your back. This is a weak position that can make the shoulder vulnerable to injury.

Mid-pull

During the mid-pull, keep your palm and forearm facing toward your feet to push water backward most efficiently **(Fig. 6-11C)**. Your hand follows a straight path toward your feet while your fingertips continue to point toward the side. For the optimal pull, try to minimize up-and-down movement of your arm.

Finish

For the finish of the power phase, accelerate your hand as it follows through toward your feet. Keep your wrist extended and your palm pitched slightly downward. A strong finish (achieved by a quick push toward the bottom that maintains pressure on the water at the finish) helps your body rotate. The power phase ends with your arm straight and your hand below your hip **(Fig. 6-11D)**.

Recovery

Start the recovery from the shoulder, lifting your arm from the water, hand first with your wrist relaxed and your palm facing inward **(Fig. 6-12A)**. Your thumb leaves the water first. This arm position allows the large muscles on the back of your upper arm to relax. Keeping your arm straight but relaxed, move your arm almost perpendicular to the water **(Fig. 6-12B)**. Body roll helps to make this easier. Midway through the recovery, rotate your hand so that your little finger enters the water first **(Fig. 6-12C)**.

Back Crawl: Recovery

Fig. 6-12A Lift your arm from the water, leading with your thumb and with your palm facing inward.

Fig. 6-12B Move your arm alongside your head so that it is almost perpendicular to the water.

Fig. 6-12C Midway through the recovery, rotate your hand so that your little finger enters the water first.

Kick

The back crawl kick is similar to the flutter kick used in the front crawl. The kicking motion is a continuous, up-and-down movement that begins in the hips. The kick is very important for body position because it helps maintain stability as the body rolls. Throughout the kick, keep your knees relaxed and your ankles loose and floppy.

Fig. 6-13A At the end of the downbeat, bend your knee and then...

Keep your leg nearly straight in the downbeat. At the end of the downward motion, bend your knee in preparation for starting the upward kick. In the back crawl, most of the propulsive force generated by the legs comes from the upward kick. After bending your knee **(Fig. 6-13A)**, whip your foot upward (like kicking a ball) until your leg is straight and your toes reach the surface **(Fig. 6-13B)**. The size of the flutter kick (the distance the legs move up and down) depends on the length of the legs, the degree of hip and ankle flexibility and the pace of the

Fig. 6-13B Whip your foot upward until your leg is straight and your toes reach the surface.

stroke. A kick that is too large will create greater form drag and cancel out any added propulsion. The kicks should be forceful and steady. Most swimmers use a 6-beat kick for each full arm cycle; however, the cadence depends on the individual.

Breaststroke

The breaststroke is the oldest known swimming stroke used in competition. This stroke is also a good stroke to use for survival swimming because by adding an extended glide between strokes, the swimmer can rest briefly.

The breaststroke is performed at the surface of the water with the body horizontal and face-down. It relies on symmetrical movements of the arms and legs to propel the body forward **(Fig. 6-14)**. In the breaststroke and other strokes that use symmetrical movements (such as the elementary backstroke and butterfly), it is easier to keep the body aligned because the propulsive forces are naturally balanced when both arms move together and both legs move together, counteracting the forces that would push the body out

Fig. 6-14 In the breaststroke, symmetrical movements of the arms and legs propel the body forward.

of line. The arm stroke for the breaststroke is a sweeping "circular" motion with both arms. The kick (sometimes referred to anecdotally as a "frog kick") involves bringing both heels toward the buttocks, separating the knees, and then forcefully pressing the feet and knees backward until the legs are extended. The arm stroke and the kick alternate, so as the arms reach full extension, the legs kick. In the breaststroke, both the arms and the legs recover underwater.

The breaststroke includes a glide phase. To achieve optimal efficiency when performing the breaststroke, swimmers must find a balance between the propulsive forces created by the arm and leg actions and the effect they have on the glide. If the swimmer glides for too long, it requires more energy to resume stroking (law of inertia). If the swimmer begins stroking too soon, the propulsion generated by the previous arm and leg action is reduced.

In the past, the breaststroke was thought to be the best stroke to teach beginners because the stroke can be modified to keep the head up throughout, facilitating breathing and vision.

Evolution of the Breaststroke

Until the 1950s, the breaststroke was the only stroke with a defined style. Swimming research has helped the breaststroke evolve. Other strokes are faster (the underwater recovery of both arms and legs in the breaststroke is a natural barrier to speed), but the breaststroke is still used in competitive events.

However, keeping the head up lowers the legs, making for a more inefficient stroke. With more experience, swimmers learn to improve efficiency by submerging the head and lifting it to breathe at the end of the power phase of the arm stroke.

Body Position and Motion

The body position in this stroke is face-down, balanced and streamlined during the glide. Your arms stretch to the front with your palms face-down and below the surface. Your head is positioned between your arms and just below the surface, with your face down or slightly forward. Your back stays straight and your body is nearly horizontal. Your arms and legs move in the same motion, at the same time, on each side of the body. There is no body roll.

Breathing and Timing

Breathe during each arm stroke. As your arms and hands start to pull backward, your head and upper body lift naturally for a breath. As your arms recover, lean forward with your upper body and head to drive forward into the water, looking down or slightly forward as your head goes back in the water. Exhale in a slow, steady manner until just before the next breath.

The phrase, "Pull and breathe, kick and glide" can help you remember the timing for the breaststroke. From the glide position, start the power phase with your arms **(Fig. 6-15A)**. Near the end of the arm pull, take a breath and start to bend your legs to prepare for the kick **(Fig. 6-15B)**. Without pause, start to recover your arms and drive forward with your upper body. As soon as your arms reach full extension and just before you lower your head into the water between your arms, start the power phase of the kick by pressing backward with your feet **(Fig. 6-15C)**. Your upper body and arms will be in the glide position just before the kick ends **(Fig. 6-15D)**. Glide only briefly until your legs come together and then start the next stroke before losing forward momentum.

Breaststroke: Breathing and Timing

Fig. 6-15A From the glide position, start the power phase with your arms.

Fig. 6-15B Near the end of the arm pull, take a breath and start to bend your legs to prepare for the kick.

Fig. 6-15C Start the power phase of the kick as soon as your arms reach full extension.

Fig. 6-15D As the kick ends, your upper body and arms move into the glide position.

Arm Stroke

The arm stroke for the breaststroke is a sweeping and scooping circular motion.

— Breaststroke: Power Phase (Arms) —

Fig. 6-16A The catch begins with the arms extended in the glide position and the palms turned out at about a 45° angle to the surface of the water.

Fig. 6-16B During the mid-pull, keep your elbows near the surface, bend your arms and sweep your hands downward and inward.

Fig. 6-16C Finish by sweeping your hands inward and upward so that they are in front of your chest.

Power Phase

Catch

Start the catch in the glide position, with your arms extended forward. Turn your palms outward at about a 45° angle to the surface of the water **(Fig. 6-16A)**. With your arms slightly bent, press your palms outward until your hands are spread wider than your shoulders. (If you think of a clock face, your hands should be at about the 11:00 and 1:00 positions.)

Mid-pull

Bend your elbows and sweep your hands down and in **(Fig. 6-16B)**. Your hands should be relaxed with your fingers straight and together. Keep your elbows near the surface as your hands pass under your elbows so that your forearms are almost vertical. Elbow position is important for good propulsion. Throughout the power phase, keep your elbows higher than your hands and lower than your shoulders.

Finish

During the finish, accelerate your hands and bring your elbows to your sides. Sweep your hands inward and upward until your hands are in front of your chest. Your hands should be pitched slightly upward and almost touching each other **(Fig. 6-16C)**.

Recovery

The arm recovery is a continuous motion from the end of the power phase. After sweeping your hands together in front of your chest so your elbows are inside the width of your shoulders, push forward with your elbows so that your hands start moving forward with your palms angled slightly upward, rounding out the power phase. As you stretch your arms forward, rotate your wrists so that your palms are facing down and below the surface at full extension in the glide position.

Kick

When done correctly, the **breaststroke kick** is the only kick that generates more power than the arm stroke. The pressing action of the breaststroke kick generates backward thrust. Propulsion results from the reactive pressure of the water against the insides of the feet and lower legs.

The breaststroke kick starts from the glide position. Recover by bringing your heels toward your buttocks as much as possible without impacting body position and losing balance in the water. Allow your knees to drop toward the bottom of the pool **(Fig. 6-17A)**. As your legs recover, gradually separate your knees and heels until your knees are about hip-width apart and your feet are outside of the knees. At the end of recovery, flex your ankles and rotate your feet so that your toes point outward **(Fig. 6-17B)**. Forcefully press your feet and knees backward **(Fig. 6-17C)** until your legs are extended, your feet and ankles touch and your toes are pointed **(Fig. 6-17D)**.

Breaststroke: Kick

Fig. 6-17A Bring your heels toward your buttocks, allowing your knees to drop toward the bottom of the pool.

Fig. 6-17B Flex your ankles and rotate your feet so that your toes point outward.

Fig. 6-17C Forcefully press your feet and knees backward until…

Fig. 6-17D Your legs are fully extended with your feet and ankles touching and toes pointed.

Butterfly

Many people think of the butterfly as a difficult stroke that is useful only for competition. As a result, many swimmers, even those who are good at other strokes, do not try to learn it. However, even beginning swimmers can learn the butterfly **(Fig. 6-18)**. The key to this stroke is to stay relaxed and use your whole body in a flowing forward motion. The time and effort spent learning this stroke is well spent—swimming the butterfly offers a rewarding feeling of power and grace.

The butterfly is performed with the body horizontal and face-down in the water. The body and arms drive forward together, powered by the fluid motion of the abdominals, hips and legs. The arm stroke for the butterfly is similar to the front crawl, except that both arms move together. The arms pull underwater and recover over the surface of the water as the legs kick in unison upward and downward. The kick, sometimes called a "dolphin kick," is similar to the flutter kick used in the front crawl, except that the legs stay together and the kick originates in the upper abdominals and hips. To perform the butterfly effectively, the movements of the torso, hips and legs must be in harmony with each other while also working with the arms to achieve forward progress. If the swimmer does not use this combined movement well, the stroke becomes awkward or does not work at all.

Fig. 6-18 By learning the correct timing and technique, even a beginner can master the powerful butterfly stroke.

Evolution of the Butterfly

A stroke that featured simultaneous overarm recovery out of the water and an early form of the dolphin kick was developed at the University of Iowa in the 1930s. University of Iowa swimmer Jack Sieg swam 100 yards in 1:00.2 using this early form of the butterfly stroke. However, the butterfly breaststroke, as it was called, was declared a violation of competitive rules. In the 1950s, the butterfly stroke with the dolphin kick was legalized and has been a mainstay of competitive swimming ever since.

Body Position and Motion

The body position of the butterfly is face-down, horizontal and streamlined. The butterfly is characterized by the interplay of the up-and-down movements of the legs and the under-and-over arm action. The body moves forward and upward, and then forward and downward. This continuous motion, combined with good timing, drives the body forward through the water.

Breathing and Timing

The kick, breath and pull work in delicate harmony with one another to create efficient form. The butterfly uses two kicks at specific moments during each arm stroke. The timing of these movements is critical. With good timing, this stroke is graceful. With poor timing, the stroke is awkward and very difficult.

The timing of the butterfly depends on the relationship of the kicks to the entry and finish of the arm stroke. During the arm recovery, bend your knees to prepare for first kick. As your hands enter the water, press forward and downward with your chin and chest and extend your legs for the downbeat of the first kick **(Fig. 6-19A)**. Because your upper body angles slightly downward at this point, it will appear to bend or "pivot" at the waist. ("As the chest goes down, the hips go up.") During the catch, your upper body begins to rise toward the surface and continues to rise during the mid-pull while your knees bend to prepare for the second kick **(Fig. 6-19B)**. The downbeat of the second kick starts during the mid-pull **(Fig. 6-19C)** End the second kick just as the pull finishes and just prior to your hands exiting into the recovery **(Fig. 6-19D)**.

Breathing is timed to occur when the upper body reaches its highest point, at the finish of the arm stroke and the end of the second kick. Exhale fully during the underwater pull as your body is rising up. Thrust your chin forward (not upward) just as your face clears the water. There should be very little distance between your chin and the surface of the water. Be careful not to lift your head up too much, otherwise your hips will sink. Inhale just as your arms begin the recovery **(Fig. 6-19E)**. After taking a breath, press forward and down with your chin and chest to return your face under water and start the arm recovery **(Fig. 6-19F)**. Some swimmers learn to breathe every two or more strokes to gain efficiency.

Butterfly: Breathing and Timing

Fig. 6-19A As your hands enter the water, press downward with your chin and chest and extend your legs for the downbeat of the first kick.

Fig. 6-19B As your upper body comes up during the mid-pull phase, your legs prepare for the second kick.

Fig. 6-19C The downbeat of the second kick starts during the mid-pull.

Fig. 6-19D The second kick ends as the pull finishes and just before your hands exit the water for the recovery.

Fig. 6-19E Inhale when your face clears the water, at the finish of the arm stroke and the end of the second kick.

Fig. 6-19F Press down with your chin and chest to return your face underwater throughout the arm recovery.

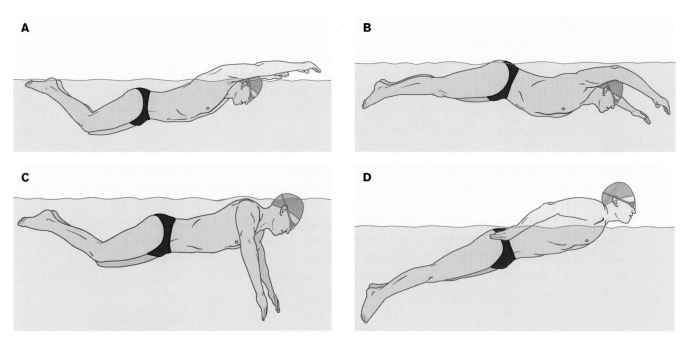

Fig. 6-20 The butterfly relies on a pivoting movement around the hips. (**A**) During the arm recovery, bend your knees to prepare for the first kick. (**B**) The downbeat of the first kick, which occurs as your hands enter the water, causes your hips to rise and your upper body to go deeper. (**C**) During the mid-pull, your upper body rises and your legs recover to prepare for the second kick. (**D**) Your upper body rises throughout the arm pull, reaching its highest point at the finish of the arm stroke and the end of the second kick.

The butterfly relies on a pivoting movement around the hips. The legs stabilize the hips so that the upper body and arms can do their job in the stroke. In the downbeat of the first kick, your hips go up and stabilize, while your upper body drives forward just under the surface (**Fig. 6-20A, B**). As your upper body comes up during the mid-pull phase, your legs recover (**Fig. 6-20C**). There is a tendency for your hips to drop at this point— try to keep them as high as possible. As the second kick finishes, your hips will remain high near the surface of the water while your upper body is at its high point along the surface of the water during the arm recovery (**Fig. 6-20D**).

Arm Stroke

Power Phase

During the power phase of the butterfly, the arms pull simultaneously with the objective of pushing water backward toward the feet. Because the arms are moving together, the catch starts wider than in the front crawl. The wide catch helps lift your upper body in preparation for the breath and the next stroke. Your hands come closer together as the arm stroke progresses (**Fig. 6-21**).

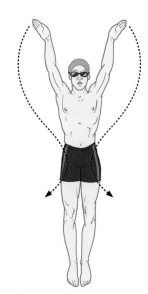

Fig. 6-21 In the butterfly stroke, your hands move from a wide position at the end of the catch to a narrow position at the finish.

Catch

The catch starts with your arms extended in front of your shoulders **(Fig. 6-22A)**. Begin to bend your elbows so that your palms and forearms start to face your feet. Keep your elbows high and your fingertips pointing down and slightly outward. Keep your hands relaxed with your fingers straight. Flex your wrists so as to not let your palms face outward too much. In order to achieve this position, your elbows and hands must move wider than your shoulders, with your hands making a circular path **(Fig. 6-22B)**. The catch ends with your elbows to the side of your shoulders and slightly in front of your body. At this point, your hands are directly below your elbows with your fingers pointing down.

Mid-pull

In the mid-pull, continue pressing backward with your palms and forearms. Throughout the mid-pull, your arms extend toward your feet and your hands come closer to your body as a result. Your hands move from the wide position at the end of the catch to a point at your waist that is just inside the width of your body **(Fig. 6-22C)**. As your hands sweep together, keep your elbows higher than your hands.

Finish

During the finish, continue pressing your hands back past your hips **(Fig. 6-22D)** and then sweep your hands outward into the recovery. As in the front crawl, the arms accelerate throughout the arm stroke so that they are moving the fastest at the end of the stroke.

— **Butterfly: Power Phase** —

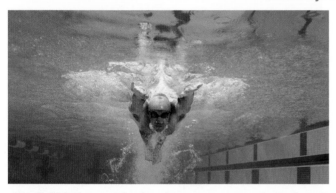

Fig. 6-22A The catch begins with your arms extended in front of your shoulders.

Fig. 6-22B Your elbows and hands move wider than your shoulders, with your hands making a circular path.

Fig. 6-22C In the mid-pull, your hands move to your waist, to a point just narrower than your body.

Fig. 6-22D In the finish, your hands press backward past your hips and then out of the water to start the recovery.

Recovery

The recovery takes more effort in the butterfly than in the front crawl, but relaxing the arms is still important. Unlike the front crawl, there is no body roll to help and your arms do not bend as much. To make the recovery easier, accelerate hard through the finish of the arm stroke and then push your face forward and down into the water as your arms recover.

The recovery starts as your hands finish their press toward your feet. Begin by sweeping your hands toward the side. During the sweep, your elbows should bend slightly and come out of the water first **(Fig. 6-23A)**. Then swing your arms wide to the sides with little or no bend in your elbows, making sure to lead this motion with your hands **(Fig. 6-23B)**. Move your arms just above the surface to enter the water in front of the shoulders **(Fig. 6-23C)**. Keep your wrists relaxed and your thumbs down throughout the recovery.

The recovery ends when your hands enter the water. Your hands enter the water thumbs first and palms down with your elbows remaining slightly flexed in front of or slightly outside of your shoulders. Reach forward with your hands and arms to maximize forward speed, being sure not to dive downward with your hands. After the entry, extend your elbows to prepare for the next arm stroke, and pitch your hands down and slightly outward for the catch.

Kick

The kick used in the butterfly is called the **dolphin kick**. Most of the power comes from the quick extension of the legs. However, the most effective dolphin kick involves the whole body, not just the legs. The timing of the kick includes kicking as the hands enter the water to help move the body forward and then kicking as the hands exit the water. ("Kick the hands in to help drive the body forward and then kick the hands out.")

Fig. 6-23A Your elbows bend slightly and come out of the water first.

Fig. 6-23B Your arms swing wide to the sides, with little to no bend in the elbows.

Fig. 6-23C Your hands enter the water in front of your shoulders.

Fig. 6-24A Bend your knees to start the downbeat.

Fig. 6-24B Extend your legs during the downbeat.

The kicking motion begins in the upper abdominals, hips and thighs. The same whip-like motion that is used in the flutter kick is used in the dolphin kick. Bend your knees to start the downbeat **(Fig. 6-24A)**. Extend your legs during the downbeat **(Fig. 6-24B)** and keep them straight during the upbeat **(Fig. 6-24C)**. Your heels should just break the surface at the end of the recovery. Although there appears to be a lot of up-and-down movement during a dolphin kick, the hips should only rise just above and return just below the surface during the kick.

Fig. 6-24C Keep your legs straight on the upbeat.

Elementary Backstroke

The elementary backstroke is used for recreation **(Fig. 6-25)**. It is also very useful in some survival swimming situations, because it is less strenuous than some other strokes and the face stays out of the water. In addition, in some lifesaving rescue techniques, the elementary backstroke kick is used when towing a victim.

The elementary backstroke is performed on the back with the body horizontal in the water. The stroke uses symmetrical and simultaneous movements of the arms and legs to propel the body forward. The arms move up the sides of the body and reach out to the sides at shoulder level, then press toward the feet simultaneously. The legs bend at the knee and make a circular kicking action. The arm stroke and the kick finish at the same time, allowing the swimmer to glide briefly in a streamlined position before initiating the next stroke.

Fig. 6-25 The elementary backstroke allows a swimmer to make slow but effective progress through the water.

Body Position and Motion

In the glide position, your back is straight, your legs are together and your arms are at your sides, with your palms facing and touching your thighs **(Fig. 6-26)**. Depending on your buoyancy, your hips and legs may be slightly lower than your head and shoulders, but your hips stay near the surface throughout the stroke. The water line usually covers your ears, but your face remains out of the water at all times.

Fig. 6-26 In the elementary backstroke glide, the body is horizontal and streamlined with the palms facing the thighs. The water line is at the ears.

Breathing and Timing

Because your face is always out of the water, breathing is easy when performing this stroke. Focus on developing a rhythmic, relaxed pattern of breathing during each stroke. Inhale as your arms recover up your sides, and exhale slowly as your arms press toward your feet during the power phase.

Your arms start their recovery just ahead of your legs **(Fig. 6-27A)**, but both move through their power phase simultaneously **(Fig. 6-27B)**. However, because your legs are stronger and travel a shorter distance than your arms, both finish their power phase at the same time **(Fig 6-27C)**. After this combined propulsion, briefly glide with your body streamlined until your momentum slows to minimize the drag of the arm and leg recovery.

Elementary Backstroke: Breathing and Timing

Fig. 6-27A The arms begin their recovery just before the legs.

Fig. 6-27B Both the arms and the legs move through the power phase simultaneously.

Fig. 6-27C Both the arms and the legs finish their thrust at the same time.

Arm Stroke

Move your arms continuously and smoothly from the start of the recovery to the completion of the power phase. Keep your arms and hands just below the surface throughout the stroke.

Recovery

From the glide position, recover your arms by bending your elbows so that your thumbs slide along your sides until they are near your armpits **(Fig. 6-28A)**. Keep your palms face down or facing in toward your body.

Power Phase

Point your fingers outward from your body so that your palms face your feet. Leading with your fingers, fully extend your arms out to the sides at or slightly above shoulder level **(Fig. 6-28B)**. (If you think of a clock face, your hands should extend no further than the 2:00 and 10:00 positions.) Without pausing, simultaneously press your palms and the insides of both arms in a broad sweeping motion toward your feet **(Fig. 6-28C)**.

Elementary Backstroke: Arm Stroke

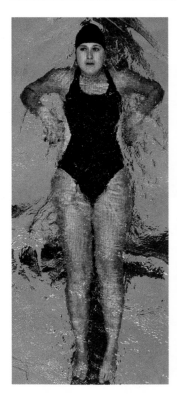

Fig. 6-28A Recover your arms by bending your elbows and sliding your hands along the sides of your body to a point just below your armpits.

Fig. 6-28B Extend your arms out to the sides.

Fig. 6-28C Press your arms in a broad sweeping motion toward your feet.

Kick

The kick for the elementary backstroke is similar to the kick used in the breaststroke. In both strokes, both legs bend at the knee and make a circular kicking action, and the legs remain underwater throughout the entire kick. The pressing action of this kick starts slowly and speeds up to completion. The kicking action is continuous and smooth, without a pause between the recovery and the power phase. The propulsion in the kick comes from flexing your feet during the kick. If you do not flex your feet, there will be no forward movement from the kick and your body position will suffer.

To start, your legs are together and extended, with your toes pointed during the glide. From this position, recover your legs by bending and slightly separating your knees, then dropping your heels downward to a point under and outside your knees **(Fig. 6-29A)**. Be careful not to drop your hips when you drop your heels. Your hips should stay in line with your thighs and near the surface. Your knees are spread hip-width or slightly wider (this position varies slightly among swimmers). At the end of the recovery, your knees rotate inward slightly while your ankles flex and your feet turn outward **(Fig. 6-29B)**. The movement of your knees and the position of your ankles creates leverage that is used for forward propulsion. Flex your feet and press them backward with a slightly rounded motion, ending with your legs in the glide position **(Fig. 6-29C)**. As your feet press backward, they move into a pointed position at the end of the kick. Your feet should be close together and may touch at the end of this motion.

Elementary Backstroke: Kick

Fig. 6-29A From the starting glide position, bend and slightly separate your knees, dropping your heels to a point under and outside your knees.

Fig. 6-29B Rotate your knees slightly inward, flex your ankles and rotate your feet outward.

Fig. 6-29C Push your feet out and around, ending in the glide position, toes pointed.

Sidestroke

The sidestroke is used for recreational swimming, as well as in some survival swimming situations **(Fig. 6-30)**.

The sidestroke is done on the side, with part of the head and one shoulder out of the water. The side-lying position creates a narrow body shape, reducing form drag and lessening the water's resistance to forward movement. In the sidestroke, one arm leads and the other trails. While the leading arm is in its power phase, the trailing arm is in recovery, and vice versa. The arms provide some propulsion and stabilize the body in the side-lying position, but most of the propulsion in this stroke comes from the scissors kick. In between strokes, the swimmer glides.

Fig. 6-30 Because the sidestroke is a resting stroke, it requires less energy and a swimmer can use it for long distances without tiring.

Body Position and Motion

Your body is nearly horizontal and side-lying during the glide. Your head, back and legs stay in a straight line, and your legs are together and fully extended **(Fig. 6-31)**. Your **leading arm** (or bottom arm) is extended forward, in line with the rest of your body, parallel to and 6 to 8 inches below the surface. Your palm is flat and faces down toward the bottom of the pool. Your **trailing arm** (or top arm) is fully extended toward your feet, with your hand above your thigh. Your lower ear rests in the water close to your shoulder. Your face is just high enough so that your mouth and nose remain above the water for easy breathing. Your gaze is focused across the surface of the water, but you may occasionally glance to the front to maintain direction. Keep your head and back aligned throughout the stroke.

Fig. 6-31 Body position for the sidestroke is nearly horizontal and on the side during the glide.

Breathing and Timing

Breathing is coordinated with the movement of the trailing arm. Inhale while your trailing arm recovers and exhale during your trailing arm's power phase.

To time the stroke correctly, start in the glide position. Begin the stroke by sweeping with your leading arm while your trailing arm and legs recover **(Fig. 6-32A)**. Then propel forward with the kick and stroke with your trailing arm while your leading arm recovers **(Fig. 6-32B)**. By the completion of the kick and the stroke of the trailing arm, your arms and legs should be fully extended **(Fig. 6-32C)**. Glide until your speed slows. Remember not to glide too long, because it takes more energy to start and stop than to keep moving.

——— Sidestroke: Breathing and Timing ———

Fig. 6-32A From the glide position, start the stroke with the sweep of your leading arm while your trailing arm and legs recover.

Fig. 6-32B Kick and stroke with your trailing arm while your leading arm recovers.

Fig. 6-32C When the kick and the stroke of your trailing arm are completed, your arms and legs are fully extended in the glide.

Arm Stroke

Leading Arm

The power phase of the leading arm begins in the glide position and uses a shallow pull. Begin by rotating your leading arm slightly so that your palm is down and angled slightly outward in the direction that you are facing **(Fig. 6-33A)**. This is the catch position. From the catch position, bend your elbow and sweep your hand downward slightly and then back toward your feet **(Fig. 6-33B)**, until your hand almost reaches your upper chest **(Fig. 6-33C)**. Without pausing, recover your leading arm by rotating your shoulder and dropping your elbow. Pass your hand under your ear until your fingers point forward **(Fig. 6-33D)**. Thrust your leading arm forward, rotating it so your palm is down for the glide position **(Fig. 6-33E)**.

Sidestroke: Arm Stroke (Leading Arm)

Fig. 6-33A From the catch position...

Fig. 6-33B bend your elbow and sweep your hand downward and back toward your feet until...

Fig. 6-33C Your hand almost reaches your upper chest.

Fig. 6-33D To recover the leading arm, rotate your shoulder, drop your elbow and pass your hand under your ear...

Fig. 6-33E Thrusting your arm forward and rotating it so your palm is down for the glide position.

Trailing Arm

During the power phase of the leading arm, recover your trailing arm from the glide position **(Fig. 6-34A)** by drawing your forearm along your body until your hand is nearly in front of the shoulder of the leading arm **(Fig. 6-34B)**. Keep your palm down and angled slightly backward. This position creates the necessary lift to help keep your face above water during the pull. Start the power phase by sweeping your trailing hand downward slightly **(Fig. 6-34C)** and then back toward your body and into the glide position **(Fig. 6-34D)**. Be sure that the palm of your trailing hand is always pitched toward your feet throughout the stroke. To do this, you will start the power phase of the trailing arm with your wrist flexed but finish with it extended.

Sidestroke: Arm Stroke (Trailing Arm)

Fig. 6-34A During the power phase of your leading arm, recover your trailing arm from the glide position by drawing your forearm along your body until...

Fig. 6-34B Your hand is nearly in front of the shoulder of the leading arm.

Fig. 6-34C Start the power phase by sweeping your trailing hand downward slightly and then...

Fig. 6-34D Back into the glide position.

Kick

The sidestroke uses a **scissors kick**. A scissors kick can also be used for treading water and the trudgen strokes. When done well, this kick provides enough propulsion for a short rest between strokes.

When doing a scissors kick, move your legs smoothly on a path that is nearly parallel to the surface of the water. Avoid rolling your hips forward or backward. To begin, recover your legs from the glide position by flexing your hips and knees and drawing your heels slowly toward your buttocks. Keep your knees close together during this movement **(Fig. 6-35A)**. Move your legs into their catch positions, top leg toward the front of your body with the foot flexed (as if taking a step while walking), bottom leg toward the back with the toes pointed **(Fig. 6-35B)**. When extended, your top leg should be nearly straight **(Fig. 6-35C)**. Without pausing, press your top leg backward while keeping it straight. At the same time, extend your bottom leg in a motion similar to kicking a ball until both legs are fully extended and together in the glide position **(Fig. 6-35D)**. Do not let your feet pass each other at the end of the kick, and keep your toes pointed to reduce drag during the glide.

During a scissors kick, you push the water with the bottom of your top foot and the top of your bottom foot. While moving your top foot backward, transition the ankle from a flexed position into a toes-pointed position. This allows the sole of your foot to press against the water with the greatest pressure.

The *inverted scissors kick* is identical to the scissors kick and has the same uses, except that it reverses the top and bottom leg actions. To attain the catch positions, move your top leg (with toes pointed) toward the rear of your body, while moving your bottom leg (with ankle flexed) toward the front of your body.

Sidestroke: Kick

Fig. 6-35A Recover your legs from the glide position by flexing your hips and knees and drawing your heels slowly toward your buttocks, keeping your knees close together.

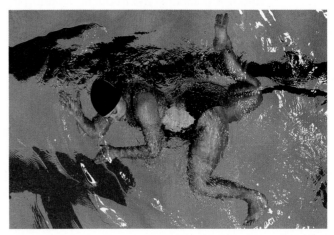

Fig. 6-35B Move your legs into their catch positions, top leg toward the front of your body, bottom leg toward the back.

Fig. 6-35C When extended, your top leg should be nearly straight.

Fig. 6-35D Press your top leg backward and extend your bottom leg forward until both legs are fully extended and together in the glide position.

Less Common Strokes

The six basic strokes form a good foundation for any swimmer. However, there are many more swimming strokes than just these six. Let us take a look at some less commonly used swimming strokes.

Trudgen Family

The trudgen family of strokes, which includes the trudgen, the trudgen crawl and the double trudgen, uses a shortened scissors kick by itself or combined with a flutter kick along with the breathing and arm pull of the front crawl **(Fig. 6-36)**. In this scissors kick, the knees do not recover as far as in the sidestroke. An alternative is a wider flutter kick, which also produces a greater body roll. **Table 6-1** compares the trudgen, the trudgen crawl and the double trudgen.

Fig. 6-36 The trudgen strokes were the forerunners of the front crawl.

Table 6-1 The Trudgen Family of Strokes

	Body Position	Breathing and Timing	Arm Stroke	Kick
Trudgen	Prone; accentuated roll to breathing side	Leg on breathing side kicks as arm on breathing side finishes power phase; inhalation at start of arm recovery	Similar to front crawl (more body roll to breathing side)	Scissors kick during final phase of arm stroke on breathing side; legs trail between kicks
Trudgen Crawl	Same as trudgen	Same as trudgen	Same as trudgen	Same as trudgen, with the addition of two or three flutter kicks between scissors kicks
Double Trudgen	Prone; greater body roll away from breathing side to accommodate second kick	Same as trudgen; may breathe to alternate sides	Catch-up stroke: each arm does a complete stroke and recovery before opposite arm strokes	Two scissors kicks for each arm cycle

Inverted Breaststroke

The inverted breaststroke, which evolved from the breaststroke and elementary backstroke and was a predecessor to the back crawl, is a relaxed style of swimming on the back. It is an especially good choice for those with good buoyancy.

Fig. 6-37A The inverted breaststroke features a glide with the arms extended beyond the head.

The glide position is streamlined, horizontal and on the back, with the arms extended beyond the head and the legs straight **(Fig. 6-37A)**. The arms, with the elbows slightly bent, press outward and back toward the feet until the palms are along the thighs. Without pause, the arms recover along the body to the armpits, where the palms turn up as the hands pass over the shoulders. Fingers first, the hands slide under the ears and extend to the glide position.

The swimmer inhales during arm recovery and exhales during the power phase. The kick is the same as in the elementary backstroke. The legs recover as the hands move under the ears **(Fig. 6-37B)**. The arms are two-thirds of the way through the recovery when the propulsive phase of the kick starts, and they reach the thighs just before the kick is finished.

Fig. 6-37B The legs recover for the kick (which is the same kick that is used in the elementary backstroke) as the arms recover alongside the ears.

Overarm Sidestroke

This stroke, which evolved from the sidestroke in 1871, differs from the sidestroke in that the trailing arm recovers out of the water **(Fig. 6-38)**. This reduces the drag of the water on the swimmer. Leisure swimmers often use this stroke.

Fig. 6-38 In the overarm sidestroke, the trailing arm recovers out of the water.

Body position, kick, leading arm action and breathing are the same as in the sidestroke. The trailing arm recovers out of the water with a "high" elbow, and the hand enters just in front of the face, similar to the front crawl. The trailing hand enters the water as the leading arm finishes its power phase and the legs recover. As the trailing hand starts its power phase, the legs extend and the leading arm recovers.

CHAPTER 7

Entries, Starts and Turns

Simple entries and starts are used to enter the water and start swimming, and basic turns are used to turn around in a pool. More advanced starts and turns are used to swim laps efficiently and in competitive swimming. With a little practice, you can learn these skills and improve your swimming efficiency.

Headfirst Entries

All advanced starts begin with a headfirst entry. In a headfirst entry, your arms are extended above your head so that your fingertips enter the water first. Your hands, arms, head and the rest of your body then follow.

A simple headfirst entry has three components:

1. **The starting position.** In this position, you are stationary and preparing to enter the water. For most swimmers, the starting position is at the side of the pool. For competitive swimmers, the starting position is on starting blocks.

2. **The takeoff.** This is the moment of propulsion, when you slightly push off with your feet.

3. **The entry.** A good entry involves entering the water at a low angle with your body aligned. To enter the water at the desired point of entry, focus on a target (either an imaginary point on the surface or a real or imagined target at the bottom of the pool) until your hands enter the water. Focusing attention on a target is a good way to maintain concentration and promote good alignment when learning this skill.

Fig. 7-1 Good body alignment and muscle control are needed for head-first entries.

Good body alignment is essential for proper, safe headfirst entry into the water as well as when you are in the water. Being mindful of head position during entry is important because it affects the position of your body in general. For example, lifting your head may cause your body to arch, resulting in a belly flop. Muscle control is also important for proper body alignment when entering the water. Use body tension to stay in a streamlined position during flight (the passage of the body through the air after takeoff). Good muscle control and alignment reduces drag and the risk of straining muscles or joints, and ensures a graceful entry **(Fig. 7-1)**. Once you enter the water, good body position allows you to steer back to the surface and begin to swim **(Fig. 7-2)**.

Fig. 7-2 Good body position after you enter the water makes it easier to steer back toward the surface and start swimming.

Safety Considerations

Whenever a person enters the water headfirst, there is some degree of risk. However, with proper training and by taking the necessary safety precautions, headfirst entries can be done safely. The following safety guidelines are recommended for headfirst entries:

- Take note of "No Diving" signs, which may be painted on the deck, embedded in the deck tile, or posted on walls, fences or stands in the pool area. Do not enter the water headfirst in areas where diving is not permitted.

- Be sure the water is at least 9 feet deep and free from obstructions. If you do not know how deep the water is, enter feetfirst the first time. Note that some regulating bodies (such as USA Swimming, the National Collegiate Athletic Association [NCAA], the Amateur Athletic Union [AAU], the National Federation of State High School Associations [NFHS], YMCA of the USA and the Fédération Internationale de Natation [FINA]) may permit headfirst entries in water that is less than 9 feet deep if the entry is performed with proper supervision.

- Never perform a headfirst entry into an aboveground pool, the shallow end of an inground pool or at a beach.

- Never perform a headfirst entry into cloudy or murky water.

- Check the shape of the pool bottom. Do not perform a headfirst entry if the pool bottom is hopper-shaped or spoon-shaped (see Chapter 2, Fig. 2-22).
- When performing a headfirst entry, make sure the area of entry is free of obstructions (such as lane lines, kickboards and other pool users) for at least 4 feet on both sides, with a clear, safe distance in front.
- Pools designed for competitive swimming are equipped with permanent or removable **starting blocks**. Competitive swimmers are trained to perform racing starts from blocks. Do not perform a headfirst entry from a starting block unless you are trained to do so and you are being properly supervised. Use of starting blocks is restricted to supervised competitive swimming.

Preparing to Learn Headfirst Entry Skills

Learning headfirst entry skills takes physical control, mental readiness and plenty of practice. With the help of an instructor or coach, you can learn to perform headfirst entries safely and correctly.

Assessing Readiness

First, you need to make sure that you are both physically and mentally ready to learn the skill.

Physical readiness

Basic swimming skills are necessary to do a headfirst entry. For example, you must be able to jump feetfirst into deep water, swim to the surface, turn around, level off and swim 10 feet.

Strength may also be a consideration. When entering the water headfirst, you must be able to keep your arms over your head and in line with your body as your body passes through the surface of the water. You can determine if you have the strength to do this by pushing forcefully off the side of the pool in a streamlined position and gliding. If you cannot keep your arms aligned during the glide you probably do not have the strength needed to perform a headfirst entry, and you should postpone learning this skill until your upper body strength increases.

Body alignment skills, such as torpedoing and porpoising (**Box 7-1**), are useful for practicing arm and head position in preparation for a headfirst entry.

Box 7-1
Body Alignment Skills

Torpedoing

1. In chest-deep water, push forcefully from the wall into a glide position, keeping your eyes open.

2. Maintain a streamlined body position: arms extended in front of you, pressed against your ears with your hands clasped together; legs together and extended behind you, with your toes pointed.

3. Hold this position until momentum is lost.

Porpoising

1. In chest-deep water, push forcefully from the wall into a glide position, keeping your eyes open.

2. Maintain a streamlined body position for a few seconds, then angle your head and arms down to submerge slightly toward the bottom, then position your head and arms straight ahead to move parallel to the surface, and then angle them up to glide to the surface.
   - Keep your head cradled between your extended arms at all times.
   - Note how raising and lowering your head and arms as a single unit changes the angle of your body as you descend and ascend.

3. As a variation, jump forward and slightly upward from a standing position before angling your head and arms to submerge.

Mental readiness

Although caution should be exercised when entering the water in a headfirst position, headfirst entries should be done with confidence. However, it is common for people who are learning to enter the water headfirst to feel fear or apprehension. Common fears include the following:

- **Fear of depth.** Some beginners are not comfortable in deep water or have a fear that they will not be able to swim back to the surface. As a result, when attempting a headfirst entry, they might lift the head in an effort to stay near the surface, resulting in a belly flop. If you are uncomfortable in deep water or afraid that you will not be able to swim back to the surface, work on improving your comfort level in deep water before learning headfirst entries. Surface diving and underwater swimming (see Chapter 5) can increase comfort in deep water and help you gain the necessary confidence to begin learning headfirst entry skills.

- **Fear of injury.** Beginners may be fearful of injury as a result of a headfirst entry either because they were hurt in the past when attempting to enter the water headfirst, or because they know someone who was injured while diving. Although minor pain can result from a poor landing, with proper safety precautions, headfirst entries can be practiced and learned with very little chance of injury. Learning these skills in a safe, step-by-step manner lowers the risk for injury and can help you overcome this fear.

- **Fear of heights.** This fear is quite common. In fact, nearly everyone has a height at which he or she will begin to feel afraid. But for some, even the relatively short distance from the pool deck to the surface of the water can cause anxiety. Additionally, being able to see the bottom of the pool can make the height seem greater. Progressions for a headfirst entry are ideal for beginners with this fear, because the entries start the swimmer close to the surface of the water, such as from a sitting or a kneeling position.

A progressive, step-wise approach to learning headfirst entries can help overcome anxiety. If you are nervous or hesitant, do not proceed to the next step until you feel more confident. Remember: A swimmer who is so afraid that he or she cannot concentrate on the skill is at a greater risk for injury while attempting the skill.

Progression for Learning Headfirst Entries

Swimmers who go through the progression of steps for learning a headfirst entry gain self-confidence and a feeling of success, along with knowledge of proper form. Move through these steps under the guidance of an instructor or coach at your own pace—some steps may require plenty of practice, while others may not. You should be able to enter the water with confidence and control at each step before moving on to the next. Once you are comfortable with performing each of the steps of the headfirst entry progression from the deck, you will be ready to move on to learning competitive racing starts, the progression for diving from a diving board or both.

The progression for learning headfirst entries is sitting position, kneeling position, compact position, stride position and shallow-angle dive. From each of these positions, you want to try to enter the water at roughly a 45° angle. This angle allows your head, torso and legs to slide into the water following a safe path. In addition, it allows you to be parallel to the surface of the water upon entry and puts you in the best position to steer up and start stroking.

Sitting Position

1. Sit on the edge of the pool with your feet on the edge of the gutter or against the side of the pool.

2. Extend your arms over your head **(Fig. 7-3)**.

3. Focus on a target that will allow you to enter the water at roughly a 45° angle.

4. Lean forward, try to touch the water and push with your legs.

5. Straighten your body and extend both legs upon entering the water.

6. Angle your hands toward the surface of the water to steer up.

Fig. 7-3 Headfirst entry from sitting position.

Kneeling Position

1. Kneel on the pool deck with one leg while gripping the pool edge with the toes of your other foot. The foot of your kneeling leg should be in a position to help push from the deck.

2. Extend your arms over your head **(Fig. 7-4)**.

3. Focus on a target that will allow you to enter the water at roughly a 45° angle.

4. Lean forward, try to touch the water and push with your legs.

5. Straighten your body and extend both legs upon entering the water.

6. Angle your hands toward the surface of the water to steer up.

Fig. 7-4 Headfirst entry from kneeling position.

Compact Position

1. Starting from the kneeling position, lift up so that both knees are flexed and off the deck. The toes of your leading foot grip the edge of the pool and your back foot is in a position to help push from the deck. Keep your knees bent so that you stay close to the water.

2. Extend your arms over your head **(Fig. 7-5)**.

3. Focus on a target that will allow you to enter the water at roughly a 45° angle.

4. Lean forward as though you are trying to touch the surface of the water and use your legs to push off the deck.

5. Straighten your legs and bring them together so that your body is in a straight line as you enter the water.

6. Angle your hands toward the surface of the water to steer up.

Fig. 7-5 Headfirst entry from compact position.

Stride Position

1. Stand upright with one leg forward and one leg back, with the toes of your leading foot gripping the edge of the pool.

2. Extend your arms above your head.

3. Focus on a target that will allow you to enter the water at roughly a 45° angle.

4. Bend your legs only slightly while also bending at the waist toward the water **(Fig. 7-6)**.

5. Lift your back leg until it is in a straight line with the rest of your body. Keep your forward leg as straight as possible as you lean forward.

6. Bring your legs together as you enter the water.

7. Angle your hands toward the surface of the water to steer up.

Shallow-angle Dive

1. Stand on the edge of the pool with your feet about shoulder-width apart and your toes gripping the edge of the pool.

2. Flex your hips and knees and bend forward until your upper back is nearly parallel to the pool deck.

3. Focus on a target that will allow you to enter the water at roughly a 45° angle.

4. To gain momentum for the dive, swing your arms backward and upward, letting your heels rise and your body start to move forward **(Fig. 7-7A)**.

5. When your arms reach their maximum backward extension, immediately swing them forward. Forcefully extend your hips, knees, ankles and toes, one after another, to drive your body forward in a line of flight over and nearly parallel to the surface of the water.

6. Keep your body stretched, with your arms angled slightly down and your hands interlocked in front.

7. Before entering the water, drop your head slightly between your outstretched arms.

8. Enter the water at an angle no greater than 45° to the surface of the water **(Fig. 7-7B)**.

9. Once underwater, use your hands and head to steer your body upward toward the surface. Keep your body fully extended and streamlined while gliding underwater. Before losing too much speed, start your leg kick to rise to the surface and start swimming.

Fig. 7-6 Headfirst entry from stride position.

Shallow-angle Dive

Fig. 7-7A To gain momentum for the dive, swing your arms backward and upward, letting your heels rise as your body begins to move forward.

Fig. 7-7B Enter the water at an angle no greater than 45°.

Competitive Racing Starts

Proficiency in headfirst entries leads naturally into competitive racing starts. Training and supervision are necessary when learning or practicing competitive racing starts. Before attempting any competitive racing start, you must be able to safely perform a shallow-angle dive from the deck. There are two competitive starts for strokes performed on the front—the grab start and track start—and one start for the backstroke—the backstroke start.

Grab Start

The **grab start** is the simplest start for all competitive strokes performed on the front.

1. To position for the start, curl your toes around the starting block with your feet about shoulder-width apart.

2. On the command "Take your mark," grasp the front edge of the starting block. Put your hands either inside or outside your feet, whichever feels more comfortable. Look straight down and bend your knees slightly **(Fig. 7-8A)**.

3. On the starting signal, pull against the starting block and bend your knees more, so that your body starts moving forward. Look toward the entry point, release the block and quickly extend your arms forward. As your hands let go of the block, bend your knees further and then push off by driving your feet against the block and forcefully extending your hips, knees and ankles **(Fig. 7-8B)**.

4. As your feet leave the block, focus on your target and aim your arms and hands at the entry point to lead your body's flight **(Fig. 7-8C)**.

5. Just before entering the water, lock your head between your arms **(Fig. 7-8D)** and enter smoothly, as if going through an imaginary hole in the water **(Fig. 7-8E)**.

6. Once in the water, angle your hands toward the surface. Glide up in a streamlined position, hands out in front **(Fig. 7-8F)**. When you reach your swimming speed, start a flutter or dolphin kick followed by your first arm pull, unless you are swimming the breaststroke. (In the breaststroke, kicking does not start until after the underwater arm pull.)

Grab Start

Fig. 7-8A Grasp the front edge of the starting block with your hands either inside or outside your feet. Look straight down and bend your knees slightly.

Fig. 7-8B As your hands let go of the block, bend your knees further, forcefully push off the block and extend your hips, knees and ankles.

Fig. 7-8C Keep your focus on your target to lead the body during flight.

Fig. 7-8D Just before entering the water, lock your head between your arms.

Fig. 7-8E Enter as if passing through a hole in the water.

Fig. 7-8F Once in the water, angle your hands toward the surface and glide.

Track Start

In the **track start**, the feet are staggered on the block, and the push of the rear leg enables the body to move forward very quickly.

1. To position for the start, stand with one foot forward and one foot back. Your rear foot should be placed further back than your hip. Curl the toes of your leading foot around the starting block.

2. On the command "Take your mark," grasp the front edge of the starting block. Look straight down and bend your knees slightly **(Fig. 7-9A)**.

3. On the starting signal, pull against the starting block, push with your rear leg and bend your knees so that your body starts to move forward. Look toward the entry point, release the block and quickly extend your arms forward. As your hands let go of the block, bend your knees further and then push off by driving your feet against the block and forcefully extending your hips, knees and ankles **(Fig. 7-9B)**.

Fig. 7-9A Stand with one foot forward and one foot back. Grasp the front edge of the starting block. Look straight down and bend your knees slightly.

Fig. 7-9B As your hands let go of the block, bend your knees further, forcefully push off the block and extend your hips, knees and ankles.

Continued on next page

Fig. 7-9C Keep your focus on your target to lead the body during flight.

Fig. 7-9D Just before entering the water, lock your head between your arms.

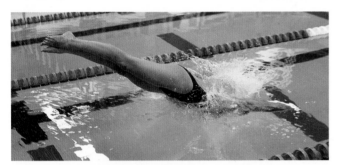

Fig. 7-9E Enter as if passing through a hole in the water.

Fig. 7-9F Once in the water, angle your hands toward the surface and glide.

4. As your feet leave the block, focus on your target and aim your arms and hands at the entry point to lead your body's flight **(Fig. 7-9C)**.

5. Just before entering the water, lock your head between your arms **(Fig. 7-9D)** and enter smoothly, as if going through an imaginary hole in the water **(Fig. 7-9E)**.

6. Once in the water, angle your hands toward the surface. Glide up in a streamlined position, hands out in front **(Fig. 7-9F)**. When you reach your swimming speed, start your kick followed by your first arm pull, unless you are swimming the breaststroke. (In the breaststroke, kicking does not start until after the underwater arm pull.)

Backstroke Start

1. To get in position for the backstroke start, grasp the starting block with both hands and place your feet parallel on the wall. (Note that current USA Swimming, NCAA and FINA rules do not allow swimmers to curl their toes over the lip of the gutter.) Move your feet a comfortable distance apart. It is acceptable to stagger your feet, placing one foot slightly higher than the other, to help maintain a stable position on the wall.

2. On the command "Take your mark," bend your arms and legs to pull your body up slightly and closer to the wall. Adjust the angle of your back so that it is perpendicular to the water, or slightly leaning back. To do this, bend your legs more to bring the hips closer to the wall or bend your arms less. Keep your back straight **(Fig. 7-10A)**.

Backstroke Start

Fig. 7-10A Grasp the starting block with both hands and place your feet against the wall. Adjust the bend in your arms and knees so that your back is perpendicular to the water, or leaning slightly back.

Fig. 7-10B Throw your head back, push your arms away from the block and over your head, and push away from the wall with your feet.

Fig. 7-10C Arch your back and drive your body up and out over the water.

Fig. 7-10D Tip your head back to achieve a streamlined position as your body enters the water.

Fig. 7-10E Enter as if passing through a hole in the water.

3. On the starting signal, throw your head back **(Fig. 7-10B)**. Release your hands from the block and over your head. Push forcefully with your legs while arching your back and driving your body, hands first, up and out over the water **(Fig. 7-10C)**.

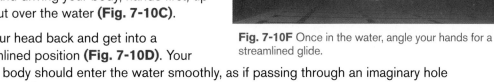

Fig. 7-10F Once in the water, angle your hands for a streamlined glide.

4. Tip your head back and get into a streamlined position **(Fig. 7-10D)**. Your whole body should enter the water smoothly, as if passing through an imaginary hole **(Fig. 7-10E)**.

5. Once in the water, adjust the angle of your hands for a streamlined glide **(Fig. 7-10F)**. When you reach your swimming speed, start your kick and use your first arm pull to come to the surface and begin swimming.

Many swimmers prefer to do several quick dolphin kicks after the start (and after each turn) instead of the flutter kick **(Fig. 7-11)**. Current rules for competitive backstroke state that the swimmer's head must break the surface of the water within 15 meters after a start or turn.

Fig. 7-11 Swimmers may use a dolphin kick instead of a flutter kick following the backstroke start and after each turn.

Turns

Swimming often takes place in pools, so being able to turn effectively and efficiently at the wall is important. To avoid injury, training and supervision are necessary when learning and practicing turns. Common beginner mistakes include misjudging the distance from the wall (putting the swimmer at risk for hitting the head or heels against the wall) and pushing off at the wrong angle (especially dangerous in shallow water).

Front Crawl (Freestyle) Open Turn

1. As you approach the wall, keep your leading arm extended until your hand touches the wall **(Fig. 7-12A)**.

2. Bend the elbow of your leading arm and drop your shoulder slightly as you rotate your body to move toward the wall.

3. Tuck your body at the hips and knees **(Fig. 7-12B)**, turn and spin away from your leading arm. During the spin, lift your face out of the water and take a breath.

4. Swing your feet under your body and place them against the wall sideways, with one foot above the other (if your right hand is leading, your right foot will be on top). Extend your other arm toward the opposite end of the pool. Return your face to the water as your leading arm recovers over the surface **(Fig. 7-12C)**.

5. As you push off the wall with your legs, extend both arms in front. Keep your body in a streamlined position on one side, rotating in the glide until you are face-down.

6. When you reach your swimming speed, start a flutter or dolphin kick to rise up to the surface and resume your arm stroke.

Front Crawl (Freestyle) Open Turn

Fig. 7-12A As you approach the wall, keep your leading arm extended.

Fig. 7-12B Bend your elbow and drop your shoulder slightly as you rotate toward the wall. Tuck your body at the hips and knees.

Sidestroke Open Turn

A sidestroke open turn is similar to a front crawl open turn.

1. Approach the wall with your leading arm extended.

2. After touching the wall with your hand, bend your elbow and drop your shoulder.

Fig. 7-12C After pushing off from the wall, return your face to the water as your leading arm recovers.

3. Tuck your body at the hips and knees, swing your feet under your body and place them against the wall sideways, one foot above the other.

4. Take a breath and extend your trailing arm, so that your trailing arm becomes your leading arm.

5. Keep your new trailing arm against your thigh as you push off the wall into the glide position.

6. Once in the glide position, stay on your side and resume swimming.

Back Crawl (Backstroke) Open Turn

This open turn is used for recreational swimming. When swimming back crawl, you must gauge your distance as you approach the wall. To do so, use a marker (such as the backstroke flags or the color change of the lane line) or glance backward if there are not any markers. When using a marker, count the number of strokes it takes you to swim from the marker to the wall.

1. When you are one stroke short of touching the wall (about two arm lengths; **Fig. 7-13A**), start to rotate to the side by turning your head and looking toward your pulling arm **(Fig. 7-13B)**.

2. Continue the arm pull underwater as you complete the rotation onto your front. Extend your arm until it touches the wall **(Fig. 7-13C)**.

3. Bend the elbow of your leading arm and drop your shoulder slightly.

4. Tuck your hips and knees as your body continues to move toward the wall **(Fig. 7-13D)**.

5. Turn and spin away from your leading hand. As you spin, take a breath. Press your feet against the wall, one foot above the other.

6. Extend both arms as you push off, keeping your body in a streamlined position on your back **(Fig. 7-13E)**.

7. When you reach your swimming speed, start kicking to rise to the surface and resume your arm stroke.

—— Back Crawl (Backstroke) Open Turn ——

Fig. 7-13A When you are one stroke short of touching the wall ...

Fig. 7-13B Start to rotate to the side by turning your head and looking toward the pulling arm.

Fig. 7-13C Continue the arm pull underwater as you complete the rotation onto your front. Extend your arm until it touches the wall.

Fig. 7-13D Bend the elbow of your leading arm, drop your shoulder and tuck your hips and knees as your body continues to move toward the wall. Press your feet against the wall, one foot above the other.

Fig. 7-13E Extend both arms as you push off, keeping your body in a streamlined position on your back.

Front Flip Turn

The front flip turn is a fast and efficient turn for the front crawl. Use the bottom markings to help judge your distance from the wall.

1. When you are one stroke-length away from the wall (about two arm lengths), keep your trailing arm at your side while taking the last stroke with your leading arm **(Fig. 7-14A)**. Both hands will end up at your thighs.

2. Perform a half-somersault by tucking your chin to your chest and bending at the waist while using a single dolphin kick to push your hips forward and upward **(Fig. 7-14B)**.

3. Turn your palms down and push your hands toward your head to help flip your legs over. As you turn, bend your legs to prepare to touch the wall **(Fig. 7-14C)**. Your hands will have reached your ears, helping to complete the forward flip.

4. Plant your feet on the wall with your toes pointed up or slightly to the side and your knees bent **(Fig. 7-14D)**. Some swimmers prefer to rotate into a side-lying position as they plant their feet on the wall, but the push-off on the back is generally considered the faster method of turning.

5. Extend your arms into a streamlined position above your head, push off while facing up or diagonally to the side **(Fig. 7-14E),** and then rotate into a face-down position during the glide.

6. When you reach your swimming speed, start a steady kick and resume your arm stroke **(Fig. 7-14F)**.

Front Flip Turn

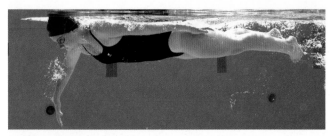

Fig. 7-14A When you are one stroke-length away from the wall, keep your trailing arm at your side while taking the last stroke with your leading arm.

Fig. 7-14B Tuck your chin to your chest and bend at the waist while using a single dolphin kick to push your hips forward and upward.

Fig. 7-14C As you turn, bend your legs.

Fig. 7-14D Plant your feet on the wall with your toes pointed up or slightly to the side and your knees bent.

Fig. 7-14E Extend your arms into a streamlined position above your head and push off.

Fig. 7-14F Rotate into a face-down position during the glide and then start to kick.

Breaststroke Turn

1. Time your last stroke so that your body is fully stretched as you reach the wall **(Fig. 7-15A)**.

2. Place both hands on the wall at the same time, then dip your shoulder and turn your head in the direction of the turn. For example, dip your left shoulder and turn your head to the left if you are turning to the left.

3. Bend your elbow and move your arm backward, keeping it as close as possible to your body. Tuck your hips and legs in tightly so that they are directly underneath your body as they continue to move toward the wall **(Fig. 7-15B)**.

4. When your legs pass under your body, move the opposite arm over your head, keeping it close to your head. Plant both feet on the wall with your toes pointing toward the side and your knees bent **(Fig. 7-15C)**.

5. Take a deep breath before submerging your head. Extend your arms into a streamlined position and push off with your body angled toward the side **(Fig. 7-15D)**.

6. Rotate into a face-down position while gliding below the surface **(Fig. 7-15E)**.

7. When you reach your swimming speed, take a complete underwater breaststroke pull (called a "pullout") to the thighs, glide again and then kick upward as your hands recover close to your body. Return to the surface to resume stroking.

Breaststroke Turn

Fig. 7-15A Fully extend your body, placing both hands against the wall.

Fig. 7-15B Dip your shoulder and turn your head in the direction of the turn. Bend your elbow and move the arm backward as you tuck your hips and legs in tightly.

Fig. 7-15C When your legs pass under your body, move the opposite arm over your head. Plant both feet on the wall with your toes pointing toward the side and your knees bent.

Fig. 7-15D Extend your arms into a streamlined position and push off with your body angled toward the side.

Fig. 7-15E Rotate into a face-down position and glide before starting the underwater breaststroke pull.

The pullout used for the breaststroke turn differs from the arm pull used in the stroke. In the pullout, your hands move from a wide position to a narrow position, finishing along your thighs, and then recover along the sides of your body **(Fig. 7-16A–D)**. In competition, one pullout is allowed at the beginning of each length, and then the swimmer's head must surface. Current rules also allow for a single dolphin kick after the underwater pull has started. The downward action of the dolphin kick cannot take place before the hands separate for the pull.

Underwater Breaststroke Pull ("Pullout")

Fig. 7-16A Start with your hands wide. Pull back and down, bringing your hands close to your body so that they …

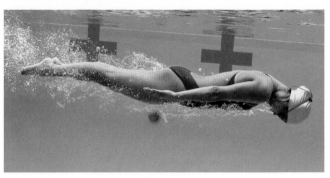

Fig. 7-16B Finish near the thighs.

Fig. 7-16C Recover your hands along the sides of your body …

Fig. 7-16D Extending them out in front.

Butterfly Turn

The mechanics of the butterfly turn are the same as for the breaststroke turn, except that following the butterfly turn, there is no pullout. Instead, you dolphin kick to get to the surface and then resume stroking.

1. Time your last stroke so that your body is fully extended when you reach the wall.

2. When both hands touch the wall, dip your shoulder and turn your head in the direction of the turn.

3. Bend your elbow and move your arm back, keeping it as close as possible to your body. Tuck your hips and legs in tightly so that they are directly underneath your body as they continue to move toward the wall.

4. When your legs pass under your body, move the opposite arm over your head, keeping it close to your head. Plant both of your feet on the wall with your toes pointing toward the side and your knees bent.

5. Take a deep breath before submerging your head. Extend your arms into a streamlined position and push off with your body angled toward the side.

6. Rotate into a face-down position while gliding a short distance, then dolphin kick to the surface and start stroking.

Backstroke Flip Turn

1. After you pass the backstroke flags, accelerate toward the wall **(Fig. 7-17A)**.

2. Start the flip by turning your head and looking toward your pulling arm during the catch **(Fig. 7-17B)**.

3. While pulling, rotate onto your stomach, drive your head downward and stop the pulling hand at your hips **(Fig. 7-17C)**. At the same time, the other arm recovers across the body, enters the water in the same position as in the front crawl and pulls to the hips.

4. Drive your head down and start somersaulting while tucking your knees tightly to your chest **(Fig. 7-17D)**. During the somersault, turn both palms down and push your hands toward your head to complete the flip. Keep your legs tucked until your feet contact the wall, toes pointed upward **(Fig. 7-17E)**.

5. While you are still on your back, forcefully push straight off the wall in a streamlined position **(Fig. 7-17F)**.

6. When you reach your swimming speed, kick to rise to the surface and resume your arm stroke.

During competition, the turn must be continuous. Any hesitation, dolphin kicks or extra strokes after turning onto the front may lead to disqualification. The shoulders may turn past vertical as long as the motion is part of a continuous turning action. The swimmer is also required to touch the wall with some part of the body, and to return to a position on the back before the feet leave the wall.

Backstroke Flip Turn

Fig. 7-17A As you approach the wall, accelerate.

Fig. 7-17B Start the flip one stroke cycle from the wall by turning your head and looking toward the pulling arm during the catch.

Fig. 7-17C While pulling, rotate onto your stomach, drive your head downward and stop the pulling hand at your hips. Recover your other arm across your body, then do a front crawl pull to the hips.

Fig. 7-17D Drive your head down, tuck your knees tightly to your chest, and somersault.

Fig. 7-17E Keep your legs tucked until your feet contact the wall, toes pointed upward.

Fig. 7-17F Forcefully push straight off the wall in a streamlined position.

CHAPTER 8
Diving

Diving is a sport that involves entering the water from a springboard or platform. In competitive diving, the diver performs acrobatic moves such as somersaults or twists during the flight through the air. However, even for non-competitive divers who are only interested in diving headfirst from a springboard at the local pool or swim club, learning proper technique is important. This chapter explains the principles of safe diving and the progressions for learning how to dive from poolside and from a springboard.

Diving Equipment

Diving Facilities and Commercial Pools

Diving is performed from a springboard or platform. Well-equipped facilities may have 1-meter and 3-meter springboards as well as 5-meter, 7.5-meter and 10-meter platforms **(Fig. 8-1)**. An elevated structure with diving platforms at several heights is called a **diving tower**.

A **springboard** is a flexible plank that extends horizontally over the water at a height of 1 meter or 3 meters. The **fulcrum** (a pivot near the center of the springboard) lets the board bend and spring. Advanced dives should only be learned and practiced on equipment that meets the standards for competitive diving. Springboards used for competitive diving are made of aluminum and coated with a nonslip surface. Guardrails on each side of the springboard and stairs made of a nonslip material help to prevent falls. The fulcrum is usually moveable so that it can be adjusted according to the individual diver's strength, weight, timing and ability **(Fig. 8-2)**. The springboard should stay level when the fulcrum is moved. A level board helps the diver reach the proper distance from the board in flight and entry.

A **diving platform** is a rigid structure that extends horizontally over the water at a height of 5 meters, 7.5 meters or 10 meters. A properly constructed platform includes a solid foundation and a nonslip surface. Diving platforms should only be used under the direct supervision of a qualified diving coach or instructor.

Some diving facilities may be equipped with an **air sparging system (Box 8-1)**. The air sparging system creates a cushion of aerated water on the surface of the pool, allowing divers to practice new dives while reducing the risk of severe injury as a result of a poor landing.

Fig. 8-1 Diving facilities may have 1- and 3-meter springboards, as well as 5-, 7.5- and 10-meter platforms.

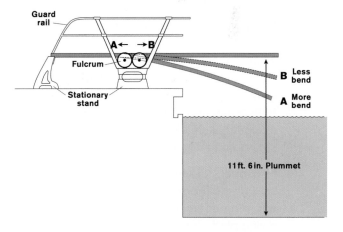

Fig. 8-2 Equipment for competitive diving has evolved into an advanced system of stationary stand, movable fulcrum and springboard.

Residential Pools

Residential pools may be equipped with a **diving board** (a flexible board on a rigid stand with a stationary fulcrum) or a **jump board** (a flexible board on a flexible stand that includes a coiled spring). Diving boards and jump boards are usually narrower and shorter than the springboards used for competitive diving, and they are also usually mounted closer to the surface of the water (20 inches is the most common height). For safety considerations related to the use of diving equipment in residential pools, see Chapter 2.

Box 8-1
Air Sparging Systems

Facilities where competitive divers train may be equipped with an air sparging system ("bubble machine"). Located on the pool bottom, the air sparger shoots air at high velocity into the pool, creating a uniform mixture of air and water in the area where divers enter the pool. The bubbles form a "cushion" above the normal surface level of the water to soften divers' entries. This protection allows divers to concentrate on technique, rather than on the landing, while learning new dives. Coaches control the system with a handheld remote that starts and stops the instant air release. They can start the system before the diver leaves the tower or board and stop it as soon as the diver enters the water.

Photo: Courtesy of Pulsair Systems.

If a diver lands horizontally on the water from a height of 10 meters, the force of the impact is measured in thousands of pounds. Such an impact can be quite painful and can cause severe injury, including ruptured organs and detached retinas. Sparging systems can reduce the force of impact by as much as 80%. This means that landing flat from 10 meters on bubbles has almost the same impact as landing flat from 2 meters on "solid" water.

Although the sparging system can reduce the force of impact, proper alignment is still important. When a diver's body is not "tight" on entry, the force of impact can knock the wind out of the diver and may cause severe tissue injury. Sparging systems are not a substitute for proper skills and should not be used as a crutch, but they can help divers gain the confidence and skills they need to perform dives into "solid" water.

Diving Safety

With proper training, equipment and supervision, diving is a safe activity. However, when safety guidelines are not followed, diving can be dangerous. Injuries can occur as a result of collisions with other pool users or underwater hazards, from the dives themselves or from falls from diving equipment or the poolside. Whether you are learning how to dive for fun or for competition, it is important to learn from a qualified instructor and adhere to the principles of safe diving (**Box 8-2**).

Pool operators must ensure that their pools and diving facilities meet minimum standards for safe diving. For example, the depth of the water for springboard diving must meet standard depth requirements. Public and private facilities with 1-meter or 3-meter springboards, diving platforms or both that are suitable for competition must meet stringent pool design standards set by the National Collegiate Athletic Association (NCAA), the Fédération Internationale de Natation (FINA), USA Diving and other organizations that sponsor diving competition. Facilities should adhere to standards set by these organizations before permitting diving. In diving facilities not built to minimum standards, variations in equipment (such as differences in board length, board resiliency, placement of the fulcrum and the height of the board over the water) can be dangerous because a diver cannot tell if the equipment is reliable.

Box 8-2
Safety Guidelines for Diving from a Springboard or Platform

- Learn how to dive safely from a qualified instructor. A self-taught diver is at a higher risk for injury than a diver who is properly trained.
- Follow safety rules at all times—never make exceptions.
- Check that springboard diving equipment meets the same standards set for competition. For dives from a 1-meter springboard, there should be 10 feet of clearance to the side of the pool.
- Be aware that the presence of diving equipment does not necessarily mean the pool is safe for diving. Many pools at homes, motels and hotels do not have a safe diving envelope. (See Chapter 2 for more information on diving safety for residential pools.)
- Do not dive from a height greater than 1 meter unless you have been trained to do so.
- Do not run on a springboard.
- Do not attempt to dive a long way forward through the air. The water might be too shallow at the point of entry.
- Do not bounce more than once on the end of a springboard unless you are being supervised by a coach. Bouncing more than once might result in missing the edge or slipping off the board.
- Dive only off the end of a springboard. Diving off the side of a springboard might result in striking the side of the pool or entering water that is too shallow.
- When performing dives with headfirst entries, your hands should enter the water first.
- Swim away from the springboard after entering the water. Do not be a hazard for the next diver.
- Do not wear earplugs or goggles; pressure changes experienced when diving make them dangerous.
- Never use drugs or alcohol when diving.

Some swimming pools have underwater ledges (sometimes called safety ledges) that may present a diving hazard **(Fig. 8-3)**. If the ledge is hard to see, it is possible to dive into what seems to be deep water, hit the ledge and injure your head, neck or spine. To reduce this risk, diving facilities should use color-contrasting tile or paint to clearly mark both the horizontal and vertical borders of the ledge.

All swimming pools with springboards, platforms or both should display their diving rules near the springboard or tower and strictly enforce them **(Fig. 8-4)**. Such rules may include the following:

- Use the ladder to climb onto the springboard or tower. Climbing in any other way is prohibited.
- Only one person on the springboard at a time.
- No other swimmers are permitted in the diving area when the springboard or tower is in use.
- Look before diving or jumping to make sure no one is in the diving area.
- Only one bounce on the end of the springboard, unless supervised by a coach.

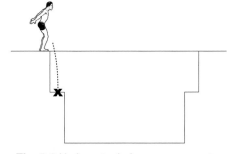

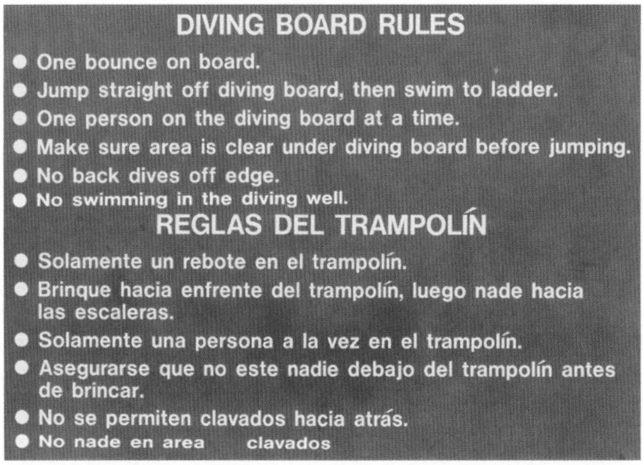

Fig. 8-3 Underwater ledges may present a diving hazard.

DIVING BOARD RULES
- One bounce on board.
- Jump straight off diving board, then swim to ladder.
- One person on the diving board at a time.
- Make sure area is clear under diving board before jumping.
- No back dives off edge.
- No swimming in the diving well.

REGLAS DEL TRAMPOLÍN
- Solamente un rebote en el trampolín.
- Brinque hacia enfrente del trampolín, luego nade hacia las escaleras.
- Solamente una persona a la vez en el trampolín.
- Asegurarse que no este nadie debajo del trampolín antes de brincar.
- No se permiten clavados hacia atrás.
- No nade en area   clavados

Fig. 8-4 The facility's rules for diving should be displayed near the springboard or tower.

- Only dive or jump straight out from the end of the springboard or platform.
- Swim to the closest ladder or wall immediately after entering the water.
- The tower can be used only with supervision from a qualified instructor or coach.
- Twisting, somersaulting, and inward and reverse dives may only be learned or practiced under the close supervision of a qualified instructor or coach.

Hydrodynamics of Diving

Many hydrodynamic principles are at work in diving. One of these principles is the law of action and reaction. When the diver's feet push down and back against the deck or springboard with sufficient force during the takeoff (the action), the diver's body is propelled upward and outward through the air (the reaction). The law of inertia is also at work. Once in the air, the only external force acting on the diver is the diver's weight (gravity force). Because gravity exerts a downward force, it slows, stops and reverses the upward momentum the diver generated during the takeoff and the diver then falls back toward the water after reaching the highest point of the dive. As the diver submerges, gravity tends to increase the diver's downward momentum. However, gravity is largely counteracted by the buoyant force that acts upward. As a result, the diver's descent underwater slows and then stops, and the diver begins to rise slowly to the surface once the diver's specific gravity is less than that of water. If the diver's specific gravity is greater than that of water, as is the case for some individuals, the buoyant force will be less than the diver's weight and the diver will continue toward the bottom. In any case, it is necessary for the diver to assist the buoyant force and swim upward toward the surface.

Preparing to Learn Diving Skills

Visual and Kinesthetic Awareness

Visual and kinesthetic awareness are very important when learning diving skills. Visual awareness is the ability to keep the eyes focused on a reference point to determine and control the body's position in space, such as during flight from a springboard. Kinesthetic awareness is the ability to perceive what the body or parts of the body are doing at any given moment, such as being aware of the position of the arms and legs during rotation. Divers use both visual and kinesthetic awareness when performing both simple and complex dives. These skills help them maintain awareness of their body position in relation to the water, achieve good body alignment for entry and maintain muscular control.

Body Position for Diving

In Chapter 7, you learned about physical readiness factors (such as strength and muscular control) that a person must possess before learning headfirst entries. These same factors apply when you are learning diving skills. Keeping your body aligned in an extended position is crucial for a safe and graceful dive **(Fig. 8-5)**. Proper

Fig. 8-5 In a headfirst dive, the diver's body is tensed and straight from the hands to the pointed toes.

alignment when entering the water reduces both form drag and the risk of straining muscles or joints. Keeping your head aligned between your upper arms is also very important because your head affects the position of the rest of your body. Moving your head back or up may cause your body to arch, resulting in a painful belly flop, while tucking in your chin too much may cause your body to bend at the waist. Bending at the waist can cause parts of the body to be stung by the impact with the water. In addition, a body that is not in alignment causes a big splash, resulting in an unattractive dive. Muscular control is important for proper body alignment and the body tension needed for a safe, effective dive.

To learn correct body position, start on dry land and practice proper body alignment in a standing position:

- **Hands.** Place the palm of one hand on top of the back of your other hand and grip your bottom hand with the fingers of your top hand. Interlock your thumbs. Hyperextend both wrists so the palm of your bottom hand hits flat on the surface. This helps protect your head, neck and back and helps reduces splash upon entry **(Fig. 8-6A)**.

- **Arms.** Raise your arms overhead with your hands in line with your shoulders and hips. Lock your elbows. Press your upper arms tightly against your ears and head. Keeping your arms, wrists and fingers in line with your head helps control the angle of entry, reducing the impact of the water on the top of your head and helping to protect against injury.

Fig. 8-6 Body position for diving. **(A)** Hand position. **(B)** Upper body position.

- **Head.** Keep your head erect and tilted back very slightly to maintain alignment between your arms and with your torso. Tilting your head back or forward too far may reduce the streamlined body alignment, produce too much or too little muscular tension and possibly cause neck or spinal injury.

- **Upper body.** Lift your ribs up and align your back in a straight line **(Fig. 8-6B)**.

- **Hips.** Tilt the top of your pelvis (your hips) backward to help reduce excess curvature or sway in your lower back. Such sway creates tension in the lower back and spine and could lead to injury.

- **Legs and feet.** Keep your legs straight at your hips and knees, and your toes pointed.

Maintaining proper body position is important for all dives, but it is particularly important when diving from a springboard because of the height and speed with which the body makes contact with the water. The diver must maintain streamlined body alignment and sufficient muscular tension and enter the water as close to vertical as possible. Mastering body position from poolside will give you the foundation you need to move on to performing a basic dive from the deck, and then to diving from a springboard.

Body position is also important after entering the water. In diving, the goal is to dive straight down into the pool and create as little splash as possible. Learning to surface dive will help you to understand body position for diving straight down. To practice surface diving:

1. Start at the wall in deep water. Push off the wall into a glide to gain forward momentum, extending your arms forward (**Fig. 8-7A**).

2. Take a breath, tuck your chin and sweep your arms back toward your thighs while flexing sharply at the hips (pike position). Once your hands reach your thighs, extend your arms overhead and then sweep your hands back to your thighs to move toward the bottom (**Fig. 8-7B**).

3. As you move toward the bottom of the pool, lift your legs upward, keeping your knees straight and together so that the weight of your legs helps your downward descent.

Learning a Basic Dive from the Pool Deck

Fig. 8-7 Surface diving. (**A**) Push off the wall and glide, extending your arms forward. (**B**) Sweep your hands back to your thighs to move toward the bottom.

After you are skilled in performing a shallow-angle headfirst entry for swimming (that is, a shallow-angle dive; see Chapter 7), you may move on to learning a basic dive from the pool deck and then to learning how to dive from a board. While the progressions for learning the basic dive are quite similar to the progressions for learning the shallow-angle dive, there are important differences in the angles of takeoff and entry, as well as the resulting underwater swimming path. Basic dives have a more vertical takeoff and entry than shallow-angle dives.

A basic dive has four parts:

1. **The starting position.** In this position, you are stationary and preparing to enter the water. You can begin a basic dive from different starting positions, which are discussed later in this chapter.

2. **The takeoff.** This is the moment of propulsion. The takeoff for a basic dive is quite easy, usually a slight push with one or both feet.

3. **The flight or trajectory.** This is the passage of your body through the air. To maintain control and make the dive more graceful, try to stay in a streamlined position in flight. To maintain concentration and dive into the water at a correct point of entry, focus on a target (either an imaginary point on the surface or a real or imagined target on the bottom of the pool) until your hands enter the water. You may close your eyes at that point and open them again after entering the water. Focusing on a target helps you enter the water at the right place and at an appropriate angle, avoiding a belly flop.

4. **The entry.** A good entry involves entering the water at an appropriate angle while keeping the body aligned.

Divers who go through the following progression of steps for learning the basic dive from the poolside gain self-confidence and a feeling of success, along with knowledge of proper form. Move through these steps under the guidance of an instructor or coach at your own pace—some steps may require plenty of practice, while others may not. Practice each step until you are able to do it comfortably and enter the water smoothly each time. Remember that the water depth should be at least 9 feet for practicing headfirst entries from poolside. (Some regulating bodies may permit headfirst entries in water that is less than 9 feet deep if the entry is performed with proper supervision.)

Kneeling Position from Poolside

1. Kneel on one knee on the pool edge. The leg in front should be bent with the toes of the forward foot gripping the pool edge. The other leg should be bent at the knee and the foot bent at the ankle with the toes tucked under to help push off from the deck. (Be very careful when practicing dives from poolsides with gutters. Not only can the gutter be slippery when wet, but it can also create a hazard if you do not dive far enough away from the edge.)

2. Extend your arms over your head with your upper arms pressing together against your ears **(Fig. 8-8)**.

3. Focus on a target on the surface of the water about 2 feet from poolside.

4. Lean forward, keeping your chin tucked against your chest. Try to touch the water with your hands. When you start to lose your balance, push with your feet and legs. The objective is to dive downward, not outward.

Fig. 8-8 Kneeling position from poolside.

5. As you enter the water, straighten your body at the hips and extend both legs.

Forward Dive Fall-in from Poolside

1. Stand with your feet together or shoulder-width apart, with the toes of both feet on the edge of the deck. (Whether you start with your feet together or further apart depends on how flexible you are, as well as your level of confidence. As you gain confidence and your flexibility improves, move your feet closer together.)

2. Extend your arms overhead with your upper arms pressing together against your ears.

3. Bend forward at the waist so your upper body is at approximately a 45°–90° angle to your legs in the pike position **(Fig. 8-9)**.

4. Focus on a target on the surface of the water about 2 feet from poolside and tuck your chin to your chest.

5. Rise up onto the balls of your feet and fall forward toward the water, keeping your knees straight.

6. As you fall forward, lift your hips and extend your legs upward so they are in line with your torso.

Fig. 8-9 Forward dive fall-in from poolside.

Standing Dive from Poolside

1. Stand with your feet together or shoulder-width apart, with your toes gripping the edge of the deck.

2. Extend your arms overhead with your upper arms pressing together against your ears.

3. Focus on a target on the surface of the water about 3 feet from poolside.

4. Bend at your knees and begin to angle your hands down toward the target.

5. Push off the deck, lifting your hips and extending your legs so they are in line with your torso. Angle your hands down toward the target and keep your chin tucked toward your chest.

Learning Forward Dives from a Springboard

A forward dive from a springboard adds several features to the elements of a basic dive from poolside:

- There is a moving start, involving a one- or two-part approach.

- There is the interaction between the diver and the springboard.

- There is a height component, because the springboard is higher above the water than the pool deck.

- As compared with a basic dive, a springboard dive has an entry that is even more perpendicular to the surface of the water as a result of the more powerful downward thrust achieved during the takeoff.

- The additional height and the propulsive lifting action of the springboard provide time for a diver to add somersaults and twists to the dive. Depending on the type of dive, the entry is either feetfirst or headfirst.

The interaction between the diver and the springboard involves the downward press and upward lift. The **press** is the diver's final downward push on the springboard assisted by the landing from the approach **(Fig. 8-10A)**. The **lift** is the force of the springboard pushing the diver into the air **(Fig. 8-10B)**. The strength of the leg extension, the efficiency

Fig. 8-10 The interaction between diver and springboard. (**A**) The diver presses downward on the springboard. (**B**) The springboard lifts the diver into the air.

of the takeoff and the angle of the diver's body at the last instant of contact with the board determine the height and distance of the diver's flight. During the takeoff, the diver gains energy from the board as it recoils. The diver's vertical velocity at the end of the takeoff determines how high the dive will go and how long the diver will be in the air while the horizontal velocity determines how far out the dive will go. Gravity (an external force acting downward) continuously reduces the diver's vertical velocity. As a result, the upward motion from the board becomes progressively slower until the diver reaches the peak of the flight and begins to fall back toward the water. The downward motion becomes progressively faster until contact is made with the water. Since there is no horizontal external force to change the diver's horizontal velocity during the flight, the diver will continue to move away from the board at a constant speed. The vertical and horizontal velocity along with gravity cause the diver's center of gravity (or center of mass) to follow a parabolic (cone-shaped) path during the flight of the dive. Nothing the diver does while in the air can change this path.

When diving from a springboard, the diver may assume one of three basic positions during flight:

- **Tuck position**. To assume the tuck position, bend at the hips and knees, pulling your knees close to your chest and your heels up to your buttocks. Grasp both legs at the shins midway between your ankles and knees to keep your body in a tight ball **(Fig. 8-11A)**. Point your toes. Because of its compact position, it is easiest to do somersaults in the tuck position.

- **Pike position**. To assume the pike position, bend your body at the hips while keeping your legs straight **(Fig. 8-11B)**. Reach your arms and hands toward your toes, or grasp your calves midway between your ankles and knees. Bring your thighs close to your chest.

- **Straight position**. In the straight position, your torso is straight or arched slightly backward with your legs together and straight. There is no bend at the hips or knees **(Fig. 8-11C)**.

Competitive divers may also use the free position while performing twisting dives **(Box 8-3)**.

Fig. 8-11 Three basic positions for diving. **(A)** Tuck position. **(B)** Pike position. **(C)** Straight position.

Box 8-3
Competitive Diving

Competitive dives have grown in variety and difficulty over the past several decades. Divers continue to prepare new combinations of skills to be used in competition. All dives, however, involve some combination of the following elements, although not all combinations are approved for competition—or are even possible.

- **Takeoff.** The diver may leave the apparatus facing forward (e.g., using an approach and hurdle from a springboard or a standing jump from a platform) or facing backward (e.g., using a backward press).
- **Somersaults.** Regardless of the takeoff direction, somersaults may be forward (with rotation in the direction the diver is facing) or backward (with rotation in the opposite direction).
- **Body position.** The body may be in tuck, pike, straight or free positions. The free position gives the diver an option to use any of the three basic positions, or combinations of the positions, when performing a twisting dive.
- **Twists.** A twist is a rotation along the midline of the body, which is held straight during the twist. Twisting may be combined with somersaults in some dives.
- **Entry.** The water entry may be headfirst or feetfirst.

Depending on the combination of elements, each dive is assigned a degree of difficulty. Judges' evaluations are based on the approach, the height (whether the diver reaches an appropriate height), the execution and the entry (whether the diver creates a "ripped" entry or whether there is excessive splash). A diver's score in competition is based on both the degree of difficulty of the dive and the judges' scores.

Before learning how to dive from a springboard, you must be able to do a standing dive from poolside with confidence. Springboard diving should only be learned and practiced under the supervision of a qualified instructor or coach in water depths of at least 11½ feet (deeper if state or local regulations require). The information that follows is for use in Red Cross Learn-to-Swim courses using a 1-meter springboard. Those interested in the sport of competitive diving should seek instruction from a qualified diving instructor or coach.

Progression for Learning a Basic Dive from the Springboard

Learning to dive from the springboard begins with the kneeling dive. Once you are able to perform the kneeling dive, you can move on to learning the forward dive fall-in and standing dive from a springboard. Practice each step in the progression until you can enter the water in a streamlined body position, creating a minimal splash.

Kneeling Position from the Springboard

To practice the kneeling dive, move the fulcrum (if it is moveable) all the way forward to make the springboard more stable. Because the surface of the springboard may be rough, consider putting a nonslip chamois or a wet towel on the end of the board when using the kneeling position.

1. Kneel on one knee at the end of the springboard. The leg in front should be bent with the forward foot flat on the board. The other leg should be bent at the knee with the foot bent at the ankle and the toes tucked under to help push off from the board.

2. Extend your arms overhead with your upper arms pressing together against your ears.

3. Focus on a target on the surface of the water about 4 feet from the end of the springboard.

4. Reach toward the water, dropping your hands and head. Try to touch the water with your hands. When you start to lose your balance, push with your feet and legs **(Fig. 8-12)**.

5. Straighten your body, extend both legs and point your toes immediately upon leaving the board. Enter the water in a vertical, streamlined position.

Fig. 8-12 Kneeling position from springboard.

Forward Dive Fall-in from the Springboard

The forward dive fall-in provides an opportunity to work on streamlined body alignment and appropriate muscular tension for the entry without being concerned with the takeoff or flight. Practice proper body position first on dry land. Because the springboard is 1 meter (more than 3 feet) above the water surface, the forward fall-in dive provides plenty of time for the body to rotate forward enough to produce a streamlined entry, even for most beginners.

Fig. 8-13 Forward dive fall-in from springboard.

1. Stand with your feet together and your toes at the end of the springboard.

2. Extend your arms overhead with your upper arms pressing together against your ears.

3. Bend forward at the waist so your upper body is at a 90° angle to your legs. Focus on a target on the surface of the water about 4 feet from the end of the springboard **(Fig. 8-13)**.

4. Rise up slightly onto the balls of your feet and fall forward toward the water, keeping focused on the target.

5. Squeeze your upper arms against your ears while falling toward the water. Your head should remain aligned between your arms.

6. Extend your body to a streamlined position for the entry.

Standing Dive from the Springboard

1. Stand with your feet together and your toes at the end of the springboard.

2. Extend your arms overhead with your upper arms pressing together against your ears **(Fig. 8-14A)**.

3. Focus on a target on the surface of the water about 4 feet from the end of the springboard.

4. Bend your knees slightly and begin to angle your hands down toward the target.

5. Push off the board, lift your hips and extend your legs so they are in line with your torso **(Fig. 8-14B)**. Enter the water in a streamlined body position.

Fig. 8-14A Extend your arms overhead with your upper arms pressing against your ears.

Fig. 8-14B Push off the board, lift your hips and extend your legs so they are in line with your torso.

Progression for Learning Takeoffs

Once you have mastered the standing dive from the springboard, you can begin learning springboard diving skills, starting with takeoffs. Start by practicing standing takeoffs on dry land. When you are comfortable with the one-part and two-part takeoffs from dry land, you can move on to poolside practice and then springboard practice.

One-part Takeoff on the Deck

The standing takeoff uses coordination of both the arms and legs to gain greater height for the flight. Start by standing upright with your arms at your sides. Then move your body up–down–up into a jump as follows:

One-part Takeoff on Deck

Fig. 8-15A Slowly raise your heels as you lift your arms overhead into a "Y" position.

Fig. 8-15B With your feet flat on the ground, continue to bend your knees into a squat.

1. Slowly raise your heels up as you lift your arms overhead into a "Y" position (Fig. 8-15A).

2. Circle your arms slowly back and down behind your hips as you begin to bend your knees.

3. With your feet flat on the ground, continue to bend your knees into a squat (Fig. 8-15B). Swing your arms forward and upward, extending into a straight jump.

Two-part Takeoff on the Deck

The two-part takeoff is similar to the one-part takeoff, but it includes a jump forward before the straight jump. You move your body up–down–up, jump forward and land with both feet, rebound and simulate a straight jump into the water as follows:

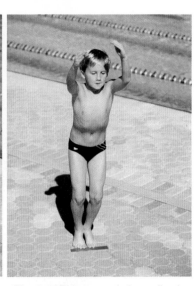

1. Slowly raise your heels up as you lift your arms overhead into a "Y" position.
2. Circle your arms slowly back and down behind your hips as you begin to bend your knees.
3. With your feet flat on the ground, continue to bend your knees into a squat. Swing your arms forward and upward, extending into a straight jump and traveling forward about 2 foot lengths **(Fig. 8-16A)**.
4. Jump again immediately after touching down, circling your arms back and down while jumping high and traveling forward **(Fig. 8-16B)**.

Two-part Takeoff on Deck

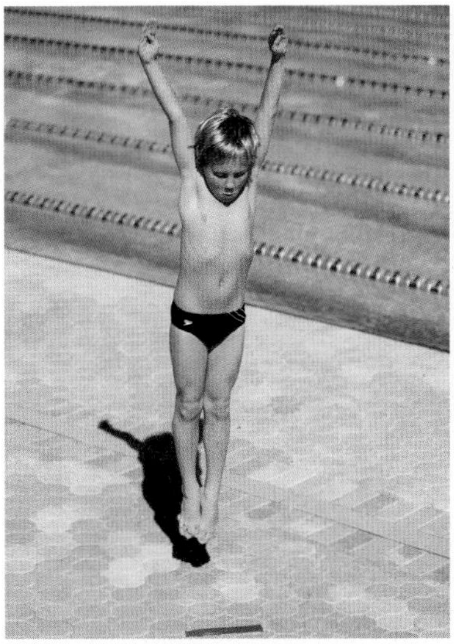

Fig. 8-16A Swing your arms forward and upward, extending into a straight jump that travels about 2 foot lengths forward.

Fig. 8-16B Jump again immediately, circling your arms back and down.

One-part Takeoff from Poolside

Once you are comfortable practicing takeoffs on the deck, you can move on to practicing the one-part takeoff from poolside. (Two-part takeoffs are not practiced from poolside.) To practice the one-part takeoff from poolside:

1. Slowly raise your heels up as you lift your arms overhead into a "Y" position.
2. Circle your arms slowly back and down behind your hips as you begin to bend your knees **(Fig. 8-17A)**.
3. With your feet flat on the ground, continue to bend your knees into a squat. Swing your arms forward and upward, extending into a straight jump and landing feetfirst in the water **(Fig. 8-17B)**.

One-part Takeoff from Poolside

Fig. 8-17A Circle your arms back and down as you bend your knees.

Fig. 8-17B Swing your arms forward and upward, extending into a straight jump and landing feetfirst in the water.

One-part Takeoff from the Springboard

When beginning to dive from the springboard with takeoffs, always start with the fulcrum as far forward as possible for better stability. Once you are comfortable with the takeoff motion, you can adjust the fulcrum.

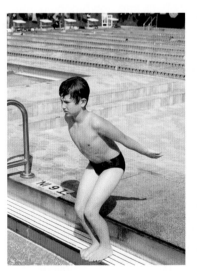

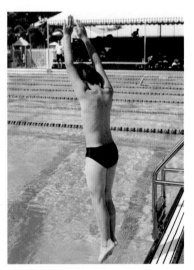

Fig. 8-18A With your feet flat on the board, bend your knees into a squat.

Fig. 8-18B Swing your arms forward and upward, extending into a straight jump and landing feetfirst in the water.

1. Stand upright with your feet together and your toes at the end of the springboard. Focus on a point in the middle of the pool to help keep your head in the proper position.

2. Slowly raise your heels up as you lift your arms overhead into a "Y" position.

3. Circle your arms slowly back and down behind your hips as you begin to bend your knees **(Fig. 8-18A)**.

4. With your feet flat on the board, continue to bend your knees into a squat. Swing your arms forward and upward, extending into a straight jump **(Fig. 8-18B)** and landing feetfirst in the water.

Two-part Takeoff from the Springboard

As you gain confidence, move to a starting point 2 foot lengths back from the end of the board and practice the two-part takeoff from the springboard:

1. Measure 2 foot lengths back from the end of the board. Focus on a point in the middle of the pool to help keep your head in the proper position.

2. Slowly raise your heels up as you lift your arms overhead into a "Y" position.

3. Circle your arms slowly back and down behind your hips as you begin to bend your knees.

4. With your feet flat on the board, continue to bend your knees into a squat. Swing your arms forward and upward, extending into a straight jump and traveling forward about 2 foot lengths **(Fig. 8-19)**.

5. Jump again immediately after touching down, circling your arms back and down while jumping high and traveling forward into a straight jump, landing feetfirst in the water.

Fig. 8-19 Two-part takeoff from springboard.

Progression for Learning Dives in the Tuck Position

After mastering basic dive progressions, springboard progressions, and one- and two-part takeoffs, you can begin to incorporate different positions into your dives. You can begin with the tuck position. A simple dry-land exercise can help you get used to the tuck position:

1. Sit or lie on the deck and pull your knees up to your chest.

2. Grab both legs at your shins midway between your ankles and knees, pulling your knees tight to your chest to form a tight ball shape.

To learn forward dives in the tuck position, first you will practice jumping in the tuck position from the poolside and then the board, and then you will move on to practicing diving in the tuck position, first from the poolside and then from the board. Practice each step in the progression until you can enter the water in a streamlined body position, creating a minimal splash.

Forward Jump, Tuck Position

The forward jump tuck lets you experience the feeling of the tuck position during flight. It also helps you develop the ability to maintain upright body position control. Start with a jump from poolside and then progress to practicing the forward jump, tuck position from the springboard.

One-part takeoff with forward jump tuck from poolside

After practicing the tuck position sitting or lying on the deck, try the jump tuck from poolside in the following way:

1. Stand with your feet together on the edge of the deck.

2. Perform a one-part takeoff, jumping as high as possible and moving into a straight jump position.

3. While in flight, pull your knees up to your chest and grab them briefly **(Fig. 8-20)**.

4. Kick your legs and straighten them toward the water. Enter feetfirst in a streamlined position.

One-part takeoff with forward jump tuck from the springboard

The standing jump tuck from the springboard is done in the same manner as from poolside. Jump as high as possible, briefly grab your knees, and then quickly straighten your legs and point your toes for a smooth entry.

Two-part takeoff with forward jump tuck from the springboard

Fig. 8-20 One-part takeoff with forward jump tuck from poolside.

As you gain confidence, move to a starting point 2 foot lengths back from the end of the board and combine the two-part takeoff with a tuck jump and kick out into deep water. Although the two-part takeoff gives greater height for doing the jump tuck, you still perform the tuck on the ascent and stretch into a straight line as you pass the board on the descent.

Forward Dive, Tuck Position

Once you have mastered the forward jump tuck from the board, you are ready to rotate into a headfirst position. Begin with a forward dive tuck from poolside.

One-part takeoff with forward dive tuck from poolside

1. Stand at the edge of the deck with your arms overhead. Focus on a target at a 45° angle across the pool. This will help keep your head in the proper position at the start of the dive and help your body rotate forward for the headfirst entry.

2. Start by using the one-part takeoff. Just before you push your legs against the deck to begin the dive, throw your arms overhead to propel your upper body, arms and head into a tuck position. The motion of the arms is similar to the one used to throw a ball overhead using two hands **(Fig. 8-21A)**.

3. As your body rotates forward, assume the tuck position by grasping the middle of your shins, pulling your thighs to your chest and your heels to your buttocks **(Fig. 8-21B)**.

4. Kick your legs out on the way up.

5. While coming out of the tuck, bend your elbows, move your hands up the midline and grab your hands overhead to prepare for entry. Swinging your arms straight out in front can cause your legs to go past vertical.

6. Align your body in a streamlined position and reach for the entry with your hands **(Fig. 8-21C)**.

One-part Takeoff with Forward Dive Tuck from Poolside

Fig. 8-21A Throw your arms overhead to propel your upper body, arms and head into the tuck position.

Fig. 8-21B Assume the tuck position.

Fig. 8-21C Enter the water in a streamlined position.

Fig. 8-22A Throw your arms overhead to propel your upper body, arms and head into the tuck position.

Fig. 8-22B Assume the tuck position.

Fig. 8-22C Enter the water in a streamlined position.

Dropping your head too much before takeoff or pushing your hips over your head increases rotation. This rotation can be controlled in a number of ways. If you feel as if the dive is going past vertical, come out of the tuck position and reach for the entry. If you feel as if the dive is short of vertical, stay in the tuck position slightly longer. With practice, you will learn to rotate the right amount and when to come out of the tuck.

One-part takeoff with forward dive tuck from the springboard

With your toes on the end of the board, repeat the forward dive tuck on the springboard using a one-part takeoff.

Two-part takeoff with forward dive tuck from the springboard

Start 2 foot lengths back from the end of the springboard. Perform the two-part takeoff and combine it with a forward dive tuck **(Fig. 8-22A-C)**.

Progression for Learning Dives in the Pike Position

Practice the forward dive pike using the following progression. Note that the pike position is not practiced poolside:

1. The pike position (on the deck)
2. One-part takeoff with forward jump pike from springboard
3. Two-part takeoff with forward jump pike from springboard
4. One-part takeoff with forward dive pike from springboard
5. Two-part takeoff with forward dive pike from springboard

Fig. 8-23A After your body leaves the board, allow your hips to rise up while reaching for your toes.

Fig. 8-23B After touching your toes, extend your arms overhead.

Fig. 8-23C Enter the water in a streamlined position.

To perform the forward dive in the pike position, follow these steps. When your body is in the air, allow your hips to rise up while reaching for your toes after your body has left the board **(Fig. 8-23A)**. Keep your legs straight at the knees and bend only at the hips. After touching your toes with your fingers, extend your arms overhead **(Fig. 8-23B)**, squeezing your ears between your arms, in preparation for the entry **(Fig. 8-23C)**.

PART 3

Aquatics for Health and Fitness

CHAPTER 9

Aquatics for People with Disabilities or Health Conditions

For people with disabilities or health conditions such as asthma or heart disease, aquatic activities can provide enjoyment and health benefits. Increasingly, aquatics facilities and outdoor recreation areas are being designed or modified with accessibility in mind, and aquatics programs have been adapted to help all people participate in, and enjoy, aquatic activities. Similarly, national organizations for many water sports, such as canoeing, kayaking, rowing, sailing, scuba diving and waterskiing, are working to make these activities accessible to people with disabilities.

Benefits of Aquatic Activities for People with Disabilities or Health Conditions

Participating in aquatic activities offers physical, psychological and social benefits. For a person with a disability or health condition, these benefits can be especially valuable.

Physical Benefits

Aquatic activities, such as swimming, enhance overall physical fitness, including cardiovascular endurance (the ability of the heart and lungs to sustain vigorous activity), muscular strength and flexibility. In addition, aquatic activities can help with weight management. The physical benefits of regular participation in aquatic activities may be particularly important for a person with a disability or health condition **(Box 9-1)**. Because of its unique physical properties, water enables many people with physical limitations to move more freely than they are otherwise able to on land, offering them the opportunity to improve or maintain physical fitness **(Fig. 9-1)**. In addition, the resistance offered by moving through water can help to strengthen weak muscles and regain or maintain range of motion in the joints. Finally, exercises that are used to practice breath control (such as blowing bubbles) can improve respiratory muscle function and the ability to control the muscles of the mouth (such as those used for speech).

Aquatic activities can also help to improve motor proficiency (the brain's ability to direct reflexive and voluntary movement). Motor proficiency encompasses areas such as speed, agility (the ability to change direction while moving) and perceptual motor skills (that is, the ability to integrate perception with action). Participating in aquatic activities can help a person develop or maintain perceptual motor skills by improving balance, hand–eye coordination, body–eye coordination and spatial orientation (that is, the ability to sense the body's position in relation to space and other objects).

Psychological Benefits

Engaging in swimming and other aquatic activities can also have many psychological benefits. Participation in aquatic activities allows a person to set goals and achieve them **(Fig. 9-2)**. The sense of accomplishment that comes from achieving a new goal, whether it is small (entering

Fig. 9-1 The buoyant property of water allows people with mobility issues to move more freely, helping them to maintain or regain physical fitness. *Photo credit: Design Pics/Steve Nagy.*

Fig. 9-2 Participating in aquatic activities can help to meet the human need for self-actualization (i.e., the sense of developing one's full potential). This swimmer qualified to represent team Louisiana at the National Special Olympics in 2014. *© Casey Gisclair/Tri-Parish Times.*

Box 9-1
Aquatic Physical Therapy

Aquatic physical therapy is a type of physical therapy prescribed by a health care provider and usually performed in a warm-water pool. Aquatic physical therapists are licensed physical therapists who design aquatic therapy programs to help maintain or restore function in people of all ages who have acute or chronic impairments or disabilities. The therapy program is then carried out by the aquatic physical therapist or by an aquatic physical therapist assistant.

Photo: Getty Images/Adrian Peacock

Aquatic therapy can be useful for treating many different conditions, including:

- Pain
- Weakness
- Limited range of motion
- Balance deficits
- Heart disease
- Obesity
- Orthopedic injuries
- Arthritis
- Neurologic disorders

The water has several properties that make it a good environment for therapy. The buoyancy of water helps support the person's weight during exercise without placing stress on the joints. The resistance of the water can help people who need to strengthen their muscles. The hydrostatic pressure of the water helps reduce swelling and improve awareness of joint position. Aquatic therapy in warm water can help relax muscles and improve blood flow.

During aquatic therapy, people perform weight-bearing exercises and activities in the water, such as walking and jogging, that may be difficult for them to do on dry land. The exercises can help them achieve new functional goals and enhance their quality of life. For example, aquatic therapy can help maintain or improve:

- Balance and coordination.
- Agility.
- Endurance and aerobic capacity.
- Flexibility.
- Muscle strength and endurance.
- Body mechanics and posture.
- Gait.
- Self-esteem.

the water, letting go of the side of the pool) or large (mastering a new skill, swimming an entire length) is important for building self-esteem. Additionally, participation in aquatic activities provides opportunities for acceptance by peers and can improve body image, both of which help to build self-esteem. For example, the aquatic environment often allows people with mobility issues to move more independently and freely, giving them a renewed sense of what their bodies are capable of. Finally, time spent engaging in an enjoyable hobby or activity provides distraction and escape from the stresses of everyday life, and is important for mental health **(Box 9-2)**.

Social Benefits

Being comfortable in the water and developing aquatic and water safety skills enables people with disabilities or health conditions to participate with family and friends in activities that take place in, on or around the water. Participation in organized aquatic activities also provides the opportunity to meet new people and make new friends. For people with disabilities that affect social skills, swim lessons or other group aquatic activities can provide a valuable opportunity for practicing social behaviors, such as sharing and taking turns.

Box 9-2
Opportunities in Aquatics for People with Disabilities or Health Conditions

Being comfortable in a pool setting and learning how to swim opens the door to many opportunities in aquatics, including recreational activities (such as snorkeling, scuba diving, boating, adventure recreation, water sports and visiting waterparks) and competition.

Recreation

Participating in aquatic recreational activities provides an opportunity to develop additional aquatic skills. If you have a disability or health condition and are interested in participating in a new aquatic recreational activity, you should:

- Check with your health care provider before starting a new recreational activity, especially one that involves adventure or risk.
- Determine what swimming skills you need to begin the activity and learn those skills first.
- Take any needed lessons from a qualified or certified instructor.
- Advise the instructor, program coordinator and lifeguard of any limitations so that they are better able to provide a safe environment.
- Participate with an able-bodied companion. This can make learning more fun and ensures that someone is there to help if needed.

Competition

People with disabilities have opportunities in two types of competitive programs—with able-bodied peers and through organizations geared to those with specific disabilities. Swim teams and swim clubs should be open to any person who makes the qualifying standards, despite any impairment. Special Olympics is an organization that offers athletes with intellectual disabilities the opportunity to train and compete in a variety of sports, including swimming. Competition is also available at the elite level for athletes with disabilities, including the Paralympic Games (held in the same year and at the same venues as the Olympic Games) and the Fédération Internationale de Natation Amateur (FINA) World Swimming Championships. For more information on Special Olympics and United States Paralympics, see Appendix A, Opportunities in Aquatics.

Accessibility of Aquatic Activities for People with Disabilities or Health Conditions

For people with disabilities or health conditions, it is becoming easier to access aquatics facilities and settings (such as waterfronts) and enjoy the benefits of aquatic activities. If you have a disability or health condition (or if you are accompanying someone with a disability or health condition), contact the facility you are planning to visit ahead of time to be sure the location, planned activity or both will be safe and accessible. Being an informed consumer can help you decide which facilities to patronize based on the facility's ability to meet your needs **(Box 9-3)**.

Box 9-3
Features of Aquatic Facilities That Seek to Accommodate Patrons with Disabilities or Health Conditions

- Accessible routes that make it easy to enter and access different areas in the facility, including the pool area, restrooms and locker rooms, concession stands and other amenities
- Accessibility features, such as:
  - Designated parking near the entrance to the facility
  - Doorways that are wide enough for wheelchairs (32 inches, minimum)
  - Bathrooms with private dressing rooms and dressing tables or areas designated for people who need to dress or be helped to dress lying down
  - Handheld or low-level showerheads and shower chairs or benches
  - Hair dryers mounted at various heights
  - Safety signs that include pictures and Braille as well as words

©AP Photos: Chris Carlson

- Facility staff who are knowledgeable about the needs of people with disabilities and who strive to provide quality customer service
- A willingness to make accommodations to meet disability-related needs, such as the need for adaptive equipment, assistive devices or service animals
- Varied programming that provides opportunities for physical activity and socialization with others
- A willingness to adjust programming to make accommodations and modifications as needed to allow people with disabilities or health conditions to participate in the program
- Availability of equipment to improve accessibility (e.g., water chairs, modified life jackets)

Environmental Adaptations

Pools can be built or equipped with features such as sloped entries, chair lifts and transfer systems that make it easier for a person with a disability to get in and out of the water **(Fig. 9-3)**. In 2010, the Department of Justice published updated regulations under the Americans with Disabilities Act (ADA). These regulations adopted the 2010 Standards for Accessible Design (2010 Standards), which contain specific accessibility requirements for recreational facilities that serve the public, including swimming pools, wading pools and spas. Highlights of these new requirements, which apply to public swimming pools (such as those found in hotels, motels, health clubs and community centers), include the following:

- Continuous, unobstructed paths connecting the pool area with other areas in the facility, including restrooms, locker rooms, concession stands, telephones and the first aid station, should be provided.

- There should be a primary means of entry into the swimming pool (either a sloped entry or a pool lift that a person with a disability can operate independently). Pool lifts may be permanently or temporarily installed.

- If the pool has more than 300 linear feet of pool wall, a secondary means of entry should be provided as well. The secondary means of entry can include a sloped entry, independently operated pool lift, transfer wall, transfer system or stairs. Ideally, the second means of entry is different from the primary means of entry.

In addition, the ADA requires public facilities to provide equipment such as water chairs (aquatic wheelchairs) to promote accessibility.

For more information on the legislation related to accessibility guidelines for aquatic facilities that serve the public, consult *Accessible Swimming Pools & Spas: A Summary of Accessibility Guidelines for Recreation Facilities*, published by the United States Access Board (http://www.access-board.gov).

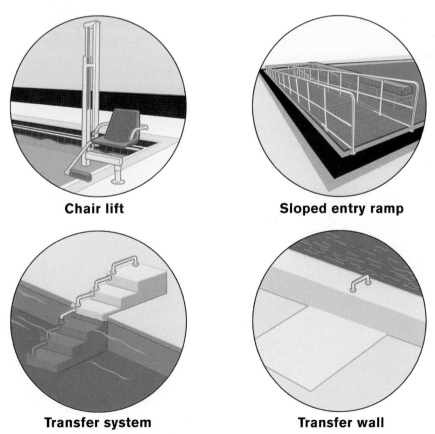

Chair lift

Sloped entry ramp

Transfer system

Transfer wall

Fig. 9-3 Examples of accessible means of entering and exiting the water include chair lifts, sloped entry ramps, transfer systems and transfer walls.

Programming Options

Community pools, recreation centers and swim clubs offer a variety of aquatics classes and activities, ranging from swimming lessons to team sports to fitness classes to scuba diving.

People with disabilities or health conditions should be welcomed and encouraged to join these programs. Participating in water safety education and learn-to-swim classes enables a person with a disability or other health condition to more safely participate in activities in, on or around the water with family and friends **(Fig. 9-4)**, and joining a sports team or participating in an aquatic fitness class provides physical, social and psychological benefits. Facility staff should work to include people with disabilities or health conditions in regular programming as much as possible, making accommodations or modifications as necessary to meet the individual's needs. The American Red Cross Swimming and Water Safety program strives to integrate participants with disabilities or health conditions into conventional programming whenever possible. In some cases, the person's needs may be better met through modified programming.

Fig. 9-4 Participating in aquatics programming can help people with disabilities develop skills they will use in and out of the pool, and also enables them to enjoy aquatic activities with friends and family. © iStockphoto.com/jarenwicklund

Aquatics programming options range from participation in regular programming (mainstreaming, integration or inclusive programming) to one-on-one instruction in an adapted aquatics program given by an instructor specifically trained to teach people with disabilities or health conditions **(Fig. 9-5)**. Between these extremes are many possibilities. Accommodations or modifications can often be made to help people with disabilities or health conditions participate in regular programming. Accommodation means adjusting the way a program or class is run, without changing the objectives, in order to help a participant succeed. For example, an instructor may need to use more visual cues in class, or a program may need to create a smaller class so that the instructor can spend more time

Fig. 9-5 Options for people with disabilities or health conditions who wish to learn how to swim range from (**A**) inclusion in a regular class (mainstreaming) to (**B**) specialized one-on-one instruction in an adapted aquatics program.

with the participant who has special needs **(Fig. 9-6)**. Modification means adjusting the way the person participates in a class or program. Making accommodations for the individual, modifications to the learning environment or both can allow many people with disabilities or health conditions to participate in most aquatics programs.

Meeting with the program coordinator, instructor or both ahead of time facilitates matching the person with a class or group that best meets the person's specific needs and capitalizes on his or her abilities **(Fig. 9-7)**. Many factors affect a person's readiness to participate in an aquatics program. Evaluating these factors and matching the person to the right class or group has a direct impact on the person's ability to be successful. When a person with a disability or other health condition is interested in participating in an aquatics program, the program coordinator should be able to provide information about the program and guidance regarding which class or group is most appropriate for the person. In order to do this, the program coordinator needs to gather basic information that will help him or her to better understand the person's specific needs. If you are seeking entry into an aquatics program for yourself or for someone else who has a disability or health condition, expect to answer questions about:

Fig. 9-6 Keeping the class size small, adding an additional instructor or instructor aide, or including the participant's parent or caregiver in the class are steps that can be taken to modify regular programming to accommodate a person with disabilities.

Fig. 9-7 Meeting with facility staff to share information about the person's abilities and limitations helps them to tailor instruction to best meet the person's needs.

- The specific nature of the disability or health condition.
- Conditions that may pose a risk to the person's safety or the safety of others, such as seizures, bowel incontinence and neurologic conditions that might be made worse by immersion or affect the person's safety in the water (e.g., tonic neck reflex, seizures).
- Abilities, such as the ability to sit or stand independently and hold the head up.
- Medications that might affect the person's ability to safely participate in the program.
- Social skills and the ability to function in a group setting.

Just as with any exercise program, anyone interested in participating in an aquatics program should first check with a health care provider to get approval to participate, especially those who have not exercised in a while. It is also important for anyone with specific concerns about limitations caused by a specific disability or health condition to consult a health care provider before entering any aquatics program.

All potential participants in an aquatics program should be fairly and consistently screened, and any age or skill requirements should apply to all participants **(Box 9-4)**. Some conditions

Box 9-4

Rights and Responsibilities of People with Disabilities or Health Conditions when Applying for Entry to an Aquatics Program

Rights

- The right to general information about the aquatics program, so they can determine if it suits their needs
- The right to apply for entry into the program
- The right to a specific explanation if the program coordinator or instructor believes the program is not suitable for the person

Responsibilities

- The responsibility to give the program coordinator and instructor any pertinent information concerning their condition
- The responsibility to comply with a program coordinator's or instructor's request for a pretest or trial lesson if needed
- The responsibility to provide one's own assistance, if needed, for dressing and for pool entry and exit

preclude participation in aquatic activities, due to safety concerns for the person or for others in the water. These include uncontrolled seizures, communicable disease, diarrhea and an elevated body temperature. Other conditions may limit participation in an aquatics program. These include uncontrolled diabetes, active joint inflammation, severe respiratory compromise, skin infections, bowel incontinence, or a history of fluid aspiration, chlorine sensitivity or latex allergies. Some pediatricians keep children who have had tympanotomy tubes inserted in the ear canal from participating in aquatics programs. Because medical professionals disagree about swimming, ear infections and tympanotomy tubes, you should follow your health care provider's instructions.

Safety Considerations for People with Disabilities or Health Conditions

Hazards exist in any aquatic environment, but these hazards may present an even greater risk for people with disabilities or health conditions. Sensory impairments (such as hearing impairment, vision impairment or tactile impairment), impaired proprioception (a decreased ability to sense the body's position in space and in relation to other objects), problems with balance and impaired muscular control are examples of conditions that can increase a person's risk for injury in an aquatic environment. Take steps to lower these risks by taking a water safety course, such as Basic Water Rescue or other water safety courses offered by the American Red Cross. Ensure that everyone in the family knows personal water safety skills (such as how to wear a life jacket) and land-based rescue skills that are consistent with their abilities. Chapters 2 and 3 of this book contain information about preventing and responding to aquatic emergencies, respectively.

In addition to taking general water safety precautions any time you are in, on or around water, it is important to be aware of specific precautions that you should take based on the specific disability or health condition (Table 9-1). Safety precautions for specific medical

Table 9-1 Participation in Aquatic Activities for People with Specific Conditions

Condition	Benefits of Participating in Aquatic Activities	Special Considerations
Arthritis	• May help maintain joint function and mobility by decreasing pain and increasing range of motion in affected joints	• Warmer water temperatures promote comfort. • Participation in aquatic activities should not increase the pain. If pain results and does not subside within 2 hours, shorten future workouts or modify the painful activity.
Asthma	• May help improve respiratory symptoms (breath control exercises)	• Take activities slowly and allow for rest breaks. • Keep your inhaler at poolside.
Autism spectrum disorder	• Can help improve social skills, motor skills, speech and self-esteem	• Provide vigilant supervision because some people with autism may not be able to fully appreciate the dangers associated with water. • Provide time to adjust to being around the water. • The pool environment (loud noises, physical contact, bright lights) may be upsetting or confusing for some people with autism. • Share information with facility staff about the person's specific needs and how best to interact with the person.
Bone disorders (e.g., osteoporosis, osteogenesis imperfecta)	• Builds muscle mass and aids in maintaining flexibility	• Avoid sources of physical trauma, such as turbulent water, collisions with other swimmers, and diving or jumping into the water. • Use less strenuous strokes, such as sidestroke or elementary backstroke.
Cerebral palsy	• Helps to relieve body stiffness and joint stress • Helps to increase and maintain joint range of motion and muscle flexibility	• People with cerebral palsy who have severe impairments may require specialized aquatics instruction. • A collar or other buoyant support around the neck may be needed if tonic neck reflex is present.
Cystic fibrosis	• Can strengthen muscles used for breathing, making breathing easier	• As the disease progresses, aquatic activity may become too physically stressful. Physical comfort and the desire to continue are the key factors in deciding how long to stay in a program. • Because engaging in aquatic activities can help to clear mucus from the lungs, keep a towel poolside to contain secretions produced by coughing.

Continued on next page

Table 9-1 Participation in Aquatic Activities for People with Specific Conditions (Continued)

Condition	Benefits of Participating in Aquatic Activities	Special Considerations
Degenerative neuromuscular conditions (e.g., multiple sclerosis, amyotrophic lateral sclerosis)	• Can play an important part in rehabilitation	• A person who is experiencing problems breathing, maintaining head control, recovering balance or staying in a safe position in the water may need specialized instruction and assistance. • Abilities will likely decrease over time. What is a safe activity one day may not be safe the next day.
Diabetes	• Aids in weight management and better control of blood glucose levels	• Because a diabetic emergency can result in loss of consciousness, never swim alone.
Down syndrome	• Provides physical, psychological and social benefits	• Headfirst entries and the butterfly stroke are prohibited for people with Down syndrome who also have atlantoaxial instability. Cervical x-rays are needed to determine if this condition exists.
Epilepsy	• Provides physical, psychological and social benefits	• Always swim with a companion who knows about your seizures. • Always swim in a lifeguarded area and notify the lifeguards of your condition. • If the epilepsy is poorly controlled, wear a U.S. Coast Guard–approved Type I life jacket or a specially designed head float. • Avoid getting too tired or too cold while in the water. • Do not swim if you have not taken your seizure medication.
Hearing impairment	• Provides physical, psychological and social benefits	• Wearing goggles while swimming can help improve kinesthetic awareness.
Heart disease	• Improves and maintains cardiovascular endurance • Aids in weight management	• Follow exercise guidelines set by your health care provider. • Swimming in water that is too warm or too cold can put excess stress on the heart.
Vision impairment	• Provides physical, psychological and social benefits	• Glasses with plastic frames and lenses are best for the water. An elastic strap or swim cap can help to keep glasses in place. • Do not jump or dive into the water with glasses on. • Do not wear contact lenses in the water. • As an alternative to glasses or contact lenses, corrective goggles and masks are available.

conditions should be followed carefully. When in doubt, check with your health care provider for recommendations.

Mobility, Balance or Motor-control Impairment

People with mobility, balance or motor-control impairments may need help moving on wet decks and ramps. Because crutches, braces and canes may slip, even on decks that are kept as dry as possible, consider using a wheelchair or walker when moving about the deck. People who normally use wheelchairs should continue to use them in the pool area. This includes children, because it is unsafe to carry anyone, even small children, on wet, slippery decks. If the disorder is associated with limited control of the legs, feetfirst entries from a diving board or other height should be avoided because this may cause twisting of the spine and injury to the muscles. Feetfirst entries from the deck are preferred for people with limited control of the legs.

For people with disorders that affect balance, consider taking additional safety measures such as extra supervision, having the person wear a U.S. Coast Guard–approved life jacket or both.

Special considerations for people with paralysis (the loss of voluntary movement, sensation or both) include the following:

- Take steps to avoid cuts or abrasions caused by scraping the hands and feet, especially if sensation is reduced. For example, use transfer mats to reduce the risk for abrasions caused by dragging body parts across the deck, and wear water shoes to reduce abrasions from the bottom of the pool.
- Wear thermal gear if you are prone to chilling, and watch for signs of hypothermia.
- If you have a pressure ulcer, do not participate in aquatic activities until the pressure ulcer has healed.
- If the paralysis affects the ability to control the bowel or bladder, wear containment briefs that are especially designed for swimmers with incontinence. These briefs are meant to be worn under a regular bathing suit. If you have a colostomy or urostomy, empty the ostomy bag immediately prior to entering the pool.

Seizure Disorders

Anyone with a seizure disorder is at a higher risk for drowning and must take care when near the water. No one should ever swim alone, but this is especially true for people with a seizure disorder. A seizure that occurs in the water is a medical emergency. The person may go underwater without warning or a call for help. A person who is having (or just had) a seizure may not be breathing or may try to breathe while underwater. Both conditions can cause life-threatening problems.

Most people with a seizure disorder can join an aquatics program, as long as they are closely supervised. People with poorly controlled seizures need close supervision and should wear a U.S. Coast Guard–approved Type I life jacket or a specially designed head float to help support the head in the event of a seizure. For some people with poorly controlled seizures, an adapted aquatics program staffed by specially trained personnel is recommended.

Safety measures for a person with a seizure disorder include the following:

- Never swim alone. When in the water, make sure that someone is present at all times who knows what to do if a seizure occurs.
- Wear a U.S. Coast Guard–approved Type I life jacket or a specially designed head float when you are in, on or around the water if the seizure disorder is poorly controlled.
- Inform lifeguards and other facility staff of the seizure disorder, and describe to them what the seizure looks like when it is occurring.

- Avoid getting over-tired or too cold while in the water.
- Some seizures can be brought on by flashing light. Wearing polarized sunglasses or dark goggles reduces the flicker effect of sunlight on the water and other reflective surfaces and may prevent a seizure from occurring.
- Take seizure medication before swimming. Do not swim if you have not taken your seizure medication. Store seizure medications in a dry place; exposure to water can cause many seizure medications to lose effectiveness.
- If a family member has a seizure disorder, it is important to know how to respond if the person experiences a seizure in the water. Support the person to keep the head and face above the water so that the person can breathe. Call the lifeguard for help and make sure that emergency medical services (EMS) personnel are called. Do not remove the person from the water until the seizure is over. When the seizure is over, place the person on his or her side on a padded area of the deck and keep the person warm (for example, by covering the person with towels) until EMS personnel arrive. Monitor the person's airway to make sure that the person is breathing.

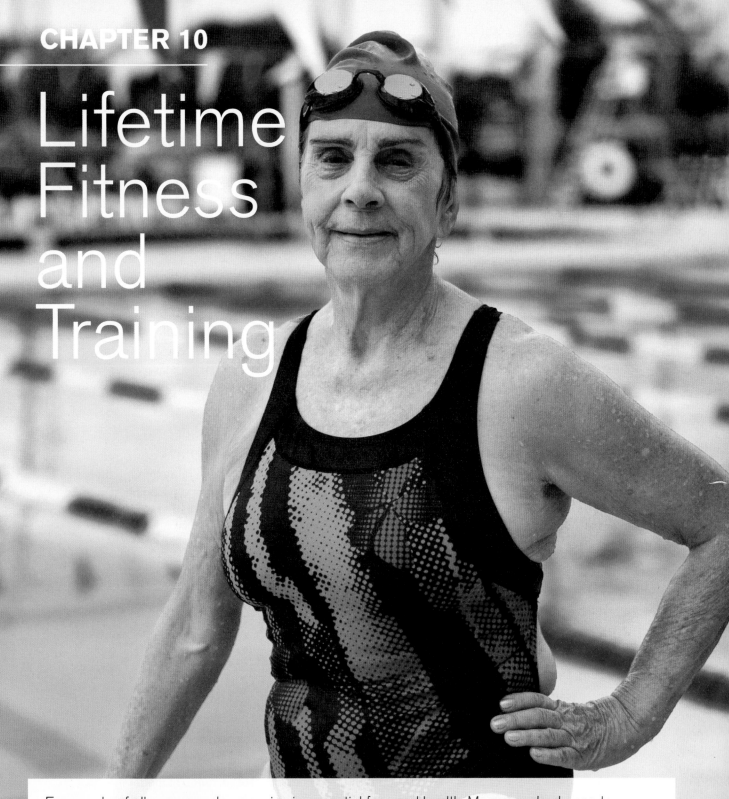

CHAPTER 10

Lifetime Fitness and Training

For people of all ages, regular exercise is essential for good health. Many people choose to incorporate aquatic activities (such as fitness swimming or participating in an aquatic exercise class) into their exercise routines as a way of maintaining or improving their health. Others train with the goal of participating in competitive events, such as swim meets or triathlons. No matter what your fitness or training goal, aquatics offers a way to help you achieve it. In this chapter, you will learn about two basic types of aquatic fitness programs that can benefit people of varying ages and fitness levels—fitness swimming and aquatic exercise—as well as about training programs for serious or competitive swimmers.

Exercising for Fitness

Benefits of Exercise

Engaging in regular exercise can change your body in ways that improve your health. For optimum health benefits, an exercise program should incorporate **aerobic exercise** (rhythmic, physical exercise that is sustained for a continuous period and requires additional effort by the heart and lungs to meet the body's increased demand for oxygen, also known as "cardio"), muscular development exercises (resistance training) and flexibility exercises **(Fig. 10-1)**.

The benefits of regular exercise include:

- Improved cardiovascular endurance.
- Increased muscular strength and endurance.
- Enhanced flexibility.
- Better weight management.

Fig. 10-1 A well-balanced exercise program includes exercise that promotes (**A**) cardiovascular endurance, (**B**) muscle strength and endurance and (**C**) flexibility. *Photo A: © iStockphoto.com/ GlobalStock, Photo B: © iStockphoto.com/ebstock*

Cardiovascular Endurance

The cardiovascular (circulatory) system supplies oxygen and nutrients to the body through the blood. Maintaining and promoting cardiovascular health reduces your risk for developing serious health conditions such as hypertension, coronary artery disease (which can lead to a myocardial infarction or "heart attack") and stroke.

With the right exercise, your cardiovascular efficiency (also known as aerobic capacity) improves. Your heart becomes stronger and can pump more blood with each beat. Circulation improves and blood vessels stay healthy. Other benefits include:

- A lower heart rate at rest and in moderate exercise.
- A shorter recovery time (the time it takes for the heart to resume its regular rate after exercise).
- Improved blood circulation to the heart.
- Increased capacity of the blood to carry oxygen.
- Increased ability of the muscles to use oxygen.
- Decreased lactic acid, a byproduct of exercise that may cause muscle soreness and fatigue.
- A lower resting blood pressure (especially in people with high blood pressure).
- Increased "good" (HDL) cholesterol levels and decreased "bad" (LDL) cholesterol levels.

The American College of Sports Medicine (ACSM) recommends 150 minutes of moderate-intensity aerobic exercise per week. This may be met by exercising for 30 minutes per day, 5 days per week.

Muscular Strength and Endurance

Muscular performance involves both strength and endurance. **Muscular strength** is the ability of muscle to exert force. Muscular strength is an important factor for staying healthy and avoiding or correcting muscular imbalances. Muscle weakness can cause imbalances that can impair normal movement and cause pain. For instance, a weak core (muscles in the abdomen, back and pelvis) combined with poor flexibility in the lower back and hamstring muscles (at the back of the thigh) can lead to lower back pain. Aquatic activity is a popular, effective way to develop this strength.

Muscular strength also can improve **muscular endurance** (the ability of the muscle to contract repeatedly with the same force over an extended period). For many people who engage in athletic activities, muscular endurance, which helps to resist fatigue, is more important than muscular strength.

Muscular strength and endurance generally decrease as people get older or become less active. Over time, the loss of strength and endurance may reduce the ability to do everyday activities and enjoy recreation. For this reason, the ACSM recommends muscular-development exercises for each major muscle group two or three times per week.

Flexibility

Flexibility is the range of motion in a joint or group of joints. Flexibility varies from joint to joint in the same person. Sufficient flexibility helps prevent injuries to the bones, muscles, tendons (fibrous tissue bands that connect muscle to bone) and ligaments (strong elastic tissue that holds bones in place at the joints). Although flexibility is partly determined by heredity, you can improve your flexibility with stretching and activities such as yoga.

Weight Management

Almost 70% of adults in the United States are overweight, and about one third are obese. In addition, one out of three children in the United States is overweight or obese. According to the Centers for Disease Control and Prevention (CDC), people who are overweight or obese are at an increased risk for many health conditions, including high blood pressure, type 2 diabetes, stroke, coronary heart disease and some types of cancer. The health consequences associated with obesity are so great that encouraging people to achieve and maintain a healthy body weight has become a national health priority. **Box 10-1** describes methods used to determine whether a person is overweight or obese.

Box 10-1
Screening for Overweight and Obesity

Body mass index (BMI) is a calculation made based on a person's weight and height that is commonly used to screen for overweight and obesity, conditions that can put a person at risk for health problems. An overweight person has a BMI of 25–29.9. An obese person has a BMI of 30 or more. Although BMI correlates with body fat, it does not directly measure body fat. (In other words, BMI does not account for body composition—the percentage of fat, bone and muscle in the body.) As a result, very muscular people may have BMIs that classify them as being overweight (because muscle weighs more than fat) even though they do not have excess body fat.

Several methods can be used to measure body composition. In anthropometric tests, the circumference of different body parts is measured and then these measurements are used to calculate body composition. In skinfold tests, a caliper is used to measure fat under the skin at different places, then similar body composition calculations are made. Bioimpedance tests measure electric currents through the body. Because the electrical properties of fat differ from those of muscle, the measurements can be used to calculate body composition. Underwater weighing (hydrostatic weighing) is a very accurate way to measure body composition and is based on Archimedes' principle. Weighing a person in water provides the total body density (weight/volume). Because fat is less dense than bone and muscle, a person with a higher percentage of body fat will have a lower density. Thus, hydrostatic weighing can be used to determine the amount of body fat.

Regular exercise is an essential part of a healthy lifestyle and is important for long-term weight management. Exercise helps control body weight by:

- Increasing the basal metabolic rate (the amount of calories the body burns at rest).
- Decreasing body fat.
- Maintaining lean muscle tissue.
- Increasing the body's ability to use fat as fuel.

Getting Results from an Exercise Program

If you are trying to achieve and maintain a healthy level of fitness, you need to establish and follow an exercise program. Always obtain a general health assessment (such as a physical examination or an exercise stress test with blood testing) from a health care provider to evaluate your fitness level before beginning an exercise program. This is especially important for those who have not exercised in a long time and for those who have health conditions. The information obtained through the health assessment helps to determine an appropriate and safe level at which to begin exercising.

To reach or maintain a level of physical fitness, exercise must put sufficient stress on body systems so that they adapt beyond their current state. This is called **overload**. For example, in order to increase your muscular strength by lifting weights, you must gradually increase the amount of weight that you lift over time. Muscular endurance, on the other hand, improves by increasing the number of repetitions rather than the load—for example, lifting the same weight more times. The results you will see from your exercise program depend on the frequency, intensity, time and type of your workouts. An easy way to remember this is to think of the acronym FITT.

Frequency

Frequency refers to how often you do an exercise. The recommended frequency for aerobic exercise for most people is 3–5 days a week. The minimum recommended frequency for muscular-development exercises is 2 days a week. Individual fitness levels and goals help to determine frequency. For example, exercising too much, too soon, can lead to overuse injuries and burnout.

Intensity

Intensity refers to how hard you work when you exercise. You will achieve the best results when the intensity of your workouts stays within an optimum range. While very-low-intensity exercise does have some benefits, cardiovascular improvement is slower when you exercise at an intensity level below your optimum range. On the other hand, working out at an intensity above your optimum range can cause excessive fatigue and lead to injuries. Different methods can be used to evaluate the intensity of your workout, including target heart rate, rate of perceived exertion (RPE) and the talk test.

Target heart rate

One way to determine exercise intensity is by measuring your heart rate. The more intense the exercise, the higher your heart rate becomes. The heart rate range needed to achieve the greatest cardiovascular benefit is called the **target heart rate range**. For most people, the ACSM recommends that the target heart rate range while exercising be 50–85% of the maximum heart rate. To calculate your maximum heart rate, subtract your age from 220.

A moderate-intensity workout should raise your heart rate to between 50% and 70% of your maximum heart rate. A vigorous-intensity workout should raise your heart rate to between 70% and 85% of your maximum heart rate. To calculate your target heart rate, first subtract your age from 220 then multiply this figure by the percentage of the desired workout intensity.

For example, the target heart rate for a 40-year-old with a desired workout intensity of 50% is 90 beats per minute (bpm):

$$220 - 40 \text{ years} = 180$$

$$180 \times 0.50 \,(50\%) = 90$$

To measure your heart rate while exercising, briefly stop and find your pulse by pressing lightly with your index and middle finger at the radial artery in the wrist or the carotid artery in the neck **(Fig. 10-2)**. Because the pulse starts to slow down once exercise is stopped, the most accurate estimation of your heart rate while exercising can be obtained by counting the number of beats in 10 seconds and multiplying by 6. Alternatively, count the number of beats in 30 seconds and multiply by 2, or count for 1 full minute. If your heart rate is below the target range, increase the intensity of your workout. In aquatic exercise, making larger arm and leg motions or increasing water resistance helps raise the intensity of workouts. If your heart rate is above the target range, decrease the intensity of your workout by making smaller movements, slowing down or taking rest breaks more often.

Keep your heart rate within the target range for the type of exercise you are doing to achieve safe and consistent progress toward your fitness goals **(Box 10-2)**. The 50–85% range is appropriate for most people. However, a sedentary person's cardiovascular health may begin to improve with an intensity level as low as 40–50%. In contrast, very fit athletes might need to work out at a higher intensity level (for example, 90%) in order to achieve their training goals.

A

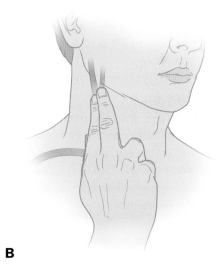

B

Fig. 10-2 (A) The radial artery is located on the inside of the wrist on the same side as the thumb. **(B)** The carotid artery is located in the neck, just below the angle of the jaw.

Box 10-2

Target Heart Rate Range for Aquatic Fitness Activities

When you are swimming, your target heart rate range should be 10–13 beats per minute lower than it would be when performing similar aerobic exercise on land. A swimmer's horizontal position along with the water pressure on the body prevents the heart rate from increasing as much as it does during vertical, dry-land exercise of the same intensity. The cooling effect of the water also helps with the task of cooling the body.

It is unclear whether the target heart rate range should be lower for aquatic exercise that takes place in a vertical position (such as when participating in a water aerobics class). Some research shows that heart rates from vertical aquatic exercise are lower than rates on dry land. Other studies report that heart rates are the same as rates in dry-land programs with similar intensity. Subtracting 10–13 beats from the target heart rate range when doing aquatic exercise may lead to underestimating the intensity and target heart rate range needed to reach exercise goals.

Rate of perceived exertion (RPE)

The target heart rate method of determining workout intensity might not work well for everyone. For example, some people may have a heart rate that is often above or below their target heart rate range even though they feel like they are working out at the right intensity. In this situation, **rate of perceived exertion (RPE)** may be a more effective way to evaluate exercise intensity.

RPE is a reliable method for determining the intensity of a workout based on how hard you feel you are working. Studies have shown that RPE correlates highly with other intensity indicators, such as heart rate and breathing rate. The RPE scale ranges from 6–20, with 6 being no exertion and 20 being maximum exertion **(Fig. 10-3)**. To use the RPE method to evaluate intensity, simply identify a number on the RPE scale that corresponds with the intensity at which you feel you are working. In the initial stages of an exercise program, it is often useful to select the RPE rating that best describes how you are feeling and then check your heart rate to see how the two numbers correspond. Once you establish the relationship between heart rate and RPE, rely less on heart rate and more on feeling.

Talk test

Like RPE, the talk-test method is a subjective and simple way to evaluate exercise intensity. As a general rule of thumb, if you are able to talk while exercising, you are working out at a low to moderate intensity. If you are breathless and unable to say more than a few words without pausing for breath, you are working out at a higher intensity.

Time

The time you spend during each exercise session also influences results. As with frequency, individual fitness levels and goals help to determine the duration of your workouts.

Type

Type refers to the kind of exercise you perform (for example, aerobic exercise or strength training). The principle of specificity is the most important factor in choosing what type of exercise to perform. This means that to improve performance, you must practice the particular exercise, activity or skill you want to improve. For example, if you wish to improve your level of cardiovascular fitness, you should engage in aerobic exercises.

Components of a Workout

A typical safe and effective workout includes:

- A warm-up.
- An aerobic set, a muscular-development set or both.
- A cool-down.
- Stretching.

Perceived Exertion

20-Maximum Exertion
19-Very, Very Hard
18
17-Very Hard
16
15-Hard
14
13-Somewhat Hard
12
11-Fairly Light
10
9-Very Light
8
7-Very, Very Light
6-No Exertion

Fig. 10-3 Rate of perceived exertion (RPE) is an easy, subjective way to gauge workout intensity.

Warm-up

The warm-up prepares your body for exercise. It increases blood flow and helps your body adjust to the workout environment. The warm-up should last 5–10 minutes and may consist of activities such as slow walking, jogging or low-intensity swimming. Because pool water is often several degrees cooler than skin temperature, aquatic exercisers should spend some time warming up on deck before entering the water.

Aerobic Set

To benefit from an aerobic workout, it is important to keep your heart rate in the target range for 20–60 minutes depending on the intensity of your workout and your current fitness level **(Fig. 10-4)**. The aerobic set should comprise 50–70% percent of your workout time and distance.

Muscular-development Set

The ACSM recommends that a fitness program include some exercise for muscular development. Strength training should be performed at least two times per week on nonconsecutive days and include 8–10 exercises to target the major muscle groups. Dry-land strength training using weights, machines or one's own body weight is one effective way of improving muscular strength and endurance. Exercising in water is another way **(Fig. 10-5)**. Strength development for fitness should be general in nature. For most people, it is best to perform one or two exercises for each muscle group, rather than focusing on one muscle group. Learn the proper way to do each exercise; proper form is important for seeing results and avoiding injury.

Fig. 10-4 To gain cardiovascular benefits from your workout, keep your heart rate in your target range during the aerobic set.

Dry-land strength training

A standard program for beginners is to perform 1–3 sets of 8–12 repetitions each. When using weights, select a weight that allows you to complete a set of repetitions using proper form without pausing. If you cannot complete the set using proper form, the weight is too heavy for that exercise. However, by the last repetition, the muscles should be fatigued. If you can perform all of the repetitions easily, the weight you are using is too light. As your strength improves, gradually increase the amount of weight that you lift. For more information on safe weight-training techniques, consult a coach or a trainer.

Fig. 10-5 Exercises using (**A**) one's own body weight or (**B**) the resistance of water are both very effective for building muscular strength and endurance. *Photo B: © iStockphoto.com/fotovampir*

Resistance training in water

Resistance training in water is another way to improve muscular strength and endurance. It is difficult to calculate the resistance the water provides, so performing only two or three sets might not provide the overload needed to increase strength and endurance. Increasing the speed of movement, the number of sets or the number of repetitions per set may be necessary. The best way to determine overload in aquatic exercise is through perception.

Cool-down

Like the warm-up, the cool-down should last 5–10 minutes. A proper cool-down helps return the blood from the working muscles to the brain, lungs and internal organs. It also helps the body recover from fatigue and may reduce muscle soreness later. During the cool-down, begin to taper off exercise so that your heart rate, blood pressure and metabolic rate return to their resting levels.

One way to cool-down is by simply slowing down. If you are swimming, you can change to a resting stroke to gradually slow down the workout and keep blood from collecting in the muscles. Static stretching toward the end of the cool-down, but not immediately after strenuous activity in the aerobic set or the muscular development set, is also a good idea.

Stretching

Stretching makes joints more flexible and improves range of motion **(Fig. 10-6)**. Stretching is more effective when muscles are warm. There are two types of stretches: dynamic and static. Dynamic stretches involve exaggerated movements that replicate specific sports or exercise movements. Dynamic stretches are often used during warm-ups or right after them. Static stretches involve slowly stretching the muscle and holding the position for 10–30 seconds. Static stretches should be done after exercise, for example, as part of the cool-down.

Fig. 10-6 Stretching should be incorporated into every workout.

Phases of an Exercise Program

As your fitness level improves, your body adapts and it takes less effort to complete the same workout that you have been doing. Gradually increase the workload to continue to benefit from your workouts. You can increase workload by increasing the frequency, intensity or duration of your workouts. In general, it is a good idea to increase the duration first, then the intensity or frequency.

The rate of improvement depends on your fitness level at the beginning of the program and other individual factors. For safe and effective exercise, it is usually best to increase workload gradually in three phases: the initial phase, the improvement phase and the maintenance phase. Remember, fitness levels will not improve unless workload increases. In fact, fitness levels may decline if the workload decreases or stops.

Initial Phase

This phase should include lower-intensity exercise. If you have not exercised in a long time, this phase helps increase workload slowly and comfortably. When you are able to comfortably maintain 60% intensity for at least 30 minutes, move on to the improvement phase. It is important to be patient during this phase. It may take up to 10 weeks to move from the initial phase to the improvement phase.

Improvement Phase

The improvement phase begins when you reach the minimum level of fitness needed to attain cardiovascular fitness. You have reached this threshold when you are exercising three times per week for at least 20 minutes at a level of at least 60% intensity. Fitness will improve by increasing frequency, intensity or duration. When increasing duration, be sure that your heart rate continues to stay within the target range throughout your workout. Expect to see improvements more rapidly in this phase, as compared with the initial phase.

Maintenance Phase

The maintenance phase begins after you have achieved your desired fitness level. The goal during this phase is to maintain that fitness level, rather than to increase the workload. At this stage, you can exercise at a comfortable level and set different goals.

The physical fitness gained from exercise can be lost. If you stop exercising regularly, your fitness level will decrease and gradually return to its pre-exercise program level. It is better to maintain your fitness level than to let it decline and try to regain it. Having once been physically fit does not make it any easier to get back into shape, except that it may not be necessary to learn specific workout skills again. For most people, the key to a successful fitness program is developing fitness habits they can use for a lifetime **(Fig. 10-7)**.

Fig. 10-7 Developing fitness habits you enjoy can help you to stay active and healthy throughout your life. © iStockphoto.com/Lisay

Fitness Swimming and Aquatic Exercise

Exercising in water has unique benefits. Buoyancy reduces stress on joints, while the resistance provided by the water helps improve muscular strength and endurance. Regardless of your age or fitness level, exercising in water can allow you to incorporate all areas of a well-balanced exercise program—aerobic exercise, muscular strength and endurance and flexibility—into your workouts **(Fig. 10-8)**.

Fitness Swimming

In **fitness swimming** workouts, swimming strokes are used to reach a specified level of intensity sustained for a set time **(Fig. 10-9)**. Fitness swimming is an excellent way to improve cardiovascular endurance and your overall physical fitness level.

Designing a Fitness Swimming Program

When beginning a fitness swimming program, it is important to start at the right level. If you are just starting a fitness swimming program, check your heart rate or monitor RPE at each break to make sure that you are exercising within your target range. Rest as often as needed (for example, by switching to a resting stroke, such as sidestroke or elementary backstroke). The goal is to slowly raise intensity levels by gradually increasing the time spent continuously swimming and decreasing

Fig. 10-8 Aquatic workouts can be designed to meet the needs of everyone, regardless of age and fitness level. © The Image Bank/Getty Images

Fig 10-9 Incorporating swimming workouts into your exercise routine is a great way to improve and maintain overall fitness. Image © Paul Atkinson, 2014. Used under license from Shutterstock.com

rest breaks. Bear in mind that if you are a novice swimmer, swimming one length of the pool can be exhausting. Because you are still working on mastering technique, you may use more energy, even at slow speeds, because you swim less efficiently.

When designing a fitness swimming program, always incorporate a warm-up, an aerobic set, a cool-down and stretching into each workout and be sure to check your heart rate before, during and after workouts to make sure that you are exercising at the proper intensity. Include a muscular-development set in two or three workouts each week.

There are several ways to track your progress as you work through your fitness swimming program. One way is to check your resting heart rate every 3–4 weeks. As your fitness level improves, your resting heart rate will drop. You may also notice that your heart rate returns to normal more quickly as your fitness level improves. This is another indication of progress. You can also use the Cooper 12-Minute Swimming Test **(Box 10-3)** to track your progress.

Box 10-3
Cooper 12-Minute Swimming Test

The 12-minute swimming test, devised by Kenneth Cooper, M.D., is an easy way to track progress as your fitness levels improve. This test is not recommended for people older than 35 years of age unless they have already developed good aerobic capacity. The best way to determine this, of course, is to consult a health care provider.

In this test, you swim to cover the greatest distance possible in 12 minutes, using whatever stroke is preferred, resting as necessary, but going as far as you can. The easiest way to take the test is to swim in a pool with known dimensions, and it helps to have someone there to time the test and record the number of lengths.

Distance (Yards) Swam in 12 Minutes

Fitness Category	Age (Years)					
	13–19	20–29	30–39	40–49	50–59	>60
I. Very poor						
Men	<500	<400	<350	<300	<250	<250
Women	<400	<300	<250	<200	<150	<150
II. Poor						
Men	500–599	400–499	350–449	300–399	250–349	250–299
Women	400–499	300–399	250–349	200–299	150–249	150–199
III. Fair						
Men	600–699	500–599	450–549	400–499	350–449	300–399
Women	500–599	400–499	350–449	300–399	250–349	200–299
IV. Good						
Men	700–799	600–699	550–649	500–599	450–549	400–499
Women	600–699	500–599	450–549	400–499	350–449	300–399
V. Excellent						
Men	>800	>700	>650	>600	>550	>500
Women	>700	>600	>550	>500	>450	>400

< means "less than"; > means "more than."

From Cooper K. H.: *The Aerobics Program for Total Well-Being,* New York: Bantam Books, 1982.

Initial phase

Box 10-4 describes a progression for the initial phase of a fitness swimming program that would be suitable for a beginner with an inactive lifestyle. For a beginner who is just starting an exercise program, this initial phase may take as long as 10 weeks to complete. However, if you are more fit to start, you may move through the initial phase quickly or even be able to skip it. Move at your

Box 10-4
Sample Progression for the Initial Phase of a Fitness Swimming Program

This sample progression assumes a pool that is 25 yards long (a common length for pools in the United States). You should be able to swim one length of the pool using any stroke. Complete a warm-up and dynamic stretching exercises before the aerobic set and a cool-down and stretching exercises afterwards. Between pool lengths, rest, walk or jog in the water for 15–30 seconds. Aim to complete the workout on three nonconsecutive days per week.

During the initial phase of this program, reaching 60% intensity is not necessary. If you have not exercised in a while, begin at 50% for the progression. Proceed with each step until you can do it easily, keeping your heart rate close to the lower limit of the target range.

To find a safe level to start, swim one pool length and check your heart rate. If it is above the target range, start with Step 1. If your heart rate is well within the target range, start with Step 3.

Step	Aerobic Set
Step 1	In chest-deep water, walk* 5 minutes and exercise the upper body with an underwater arm stroke, such as the breaststroke. Check your heart rate after each length. If, after walking 5 minutes, your heart rate does not rise above your target heart rate range, rest 15–30 seconds and do the 5-minute walk two more times. Gradually decrease the rest period until it is possible to walk and perform the underwater arm stroke for 15 minutes continuously, being sure your heart rate does not go past the upper limit of your target range.
Step 2	In chest-deep water, walk one length using the arm stroke as described in Step 1, then jog one length. Rest 15–20 seconds after the jogging length. Continue for 15 minutes. Check your heart rate at each break. Gradually decrease the rest breaks until it is possible to walk or jog 15 minutes continuously. Check your heart rate every 5 minutes during the workout.
Step 3	Swim one length at a pace that takes more effort than jogging, and then rest by walking or jogging one length. Continue for 5 minutes. Check your heart rate to be sure it is not too high. If it is, rest another minute. If your heart rate is within your target range, continue alternating swimming lengths with walking or jogging lengths. Check your heart rate every 5 minutes. Gradually decrease the rest breaks until it is possible to swim or jog continuously for 15 minutes.
Step 4	Swim one length with effort, rest 15–30 seconds, and swim another length. Use a resting stroke on the second length or swim slower. Check your heart rate after three lengths. Continue this sequence for 15 minutes. Gradually decrease the rest break to 10 seconds.
Step 5	When it is possible to swim 15 minutes continuously or with minimum rest as in Step 4, recalculate your target heart rate at 60% intensity and repeat Step 4. When it is possible to swim continuously for 15 minutes at an intensity of 60%, you have completed the initial phase. Move on to the improvement phase.

* If the water is too deep for walking or jogging, use a life jacket. Using a life jacket does not substitute for knowing how to swim.

Box 10-5
Sample Progression for the Improvement Phase of a Fitness Swimming Program

This sample progression assumes a pool that is 25 yards long. You should be able to swim continuously for 15 minutes at an intensity of 60%. Complete a warm-up and dynamic stretching exercises before the aerobic set and a cool-down and stretching exercises afterwards.

These steps move in 2-week increments. Proceed with each step until you can do it easily, keeping your heart rate close to the lower limit of the target range. You may not need the full 2 weeks to complete each step.

Step	Aerobic Set
Step 1 (Weeks 1–2)	Swim two lengths. Rest 15–30 seconds. Repeat for 15 minutes. Every few minutes, check your heart rate during your rest break.
Step 2 (Weeks 3–4)	Swim three lengths followed by a slow length or resting stroke. Rest 15–30 seconds. Check your heart rate periodically. Continue for 20 minutes. With each successive workout, gradually decrease the rest breaks to 10 seconds.
Step 3 (Weeks 5–6)	Swim five lengths followed by a slow length or resting stroke. Rest 15–30 seconds. Check your heart rate periodically. Continue for 20 minutes. With each successive workout, gradually decrease the rest breaks to 10 seconds.
Step 4 (Weeks 7–8)	Swim continuously for 20 minutes. Rest only when needed but not longer than 10 seconds. If possible, use resting strokes instead of breaks. Check your heart rate every 10 minutes during the workout.
Step 5 (Weeks 9–10)	Swim continuously for 20 minutes. With each successive workout, add one or two lengths until it is possible to swim continuously for 30 minutes.
Step 6 (Weeks 11–12)	Swim 30 minutes continuously without rest. In the last week of this progression, test your progress by swimming a timed 12-minute swim **(see Box 10-3)**.

own pace and avoid rushing. Remember, the success of a program depends on a comfortable, practical plan that can be sustained long-term.

Improvement phase

Box 10-5 describes a progression for the improvement phase of a fitness swimming program. Progress during the improvement phase varies greatly. Those who start out with a low level of fitness can expect to progress more slowly than those who are more fit.

When you are able to swim continuously for 30 minutes without rest, continue to increase overload by increasing the frequency, intensity or duration of your workouts. Change only one variable at a time to keep the progression gradual.

Maintenance phase

Once you achieve your initial fitness goals, set new ones. For example, consider working on learning a new stroke or using the training techniques described later in this chapter

(see Table 10-1) to add variety and challenge to your workouts. This will help keep your workouts interesting and challenge your body in new ways.

Swimming Etiquette

Fitness swimmers rarely get a lane to themselves. Proper swimming etiquette helps to ensure that everyone has a safe, enjoyable workout.

Select a lane based on your swimming speed. Sharing a lane works best when all of the swimmers are doing similar types of workouts (pulls, kicks, repeat short distances, long continuous swims) at similar speeds. Although many pools have lanes for fast, medium and slow swimmers, the speed within a lane can still vary.

Circle swimming is a technique that allows multiple swimmers to swim in the same lane simultaneously. Swimmers swim in a counterclockwise pattern around the center of the pool lane **(Fig. 10-10)**. Leaving the wall at intervals of 5 seconds helps to maintain a safe distance between swimmers. A faster swimmer who overtakes a slower swimmer in the lane signals to pass by tapping the lead swimmer's foot. The lead swimmer should stop at the wall or pull over to the right to let the faster swimmer pass. It is common courtesy to allow the new lead swimmer at least a 5-second lead before following. Although this may seem to disrupt the workout, these short breaks will not affect the intensity.

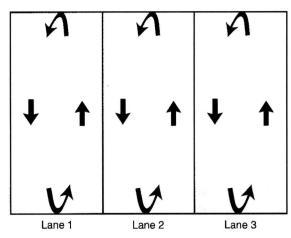

Lane 1   Lane 2   Lane 3

Fig. 10-10 Circle swimming allows multiple swimmers to share the same lane safely.

Aquatic Exercise

Aquatic exercise is an in-water fitness activity generally performed in a vertical position with the face out of the water **(Fig. 10-11)**. Aquatic exercise workouts involve walking, jogging and jumping in shallow water or running in deeper water, sometimes using a flotation device. Some aquatic exercise programs focus on cardiovascular fitness; others emphasize muscular strength and flexibility. Many aquatic exercise programs do not require that participants know how to swim, making this form of exercise accessible to most people. Because of the special properties of the aquatic environment, aquatic exercise can be especially beneficial for those with health conditions or disabilities that might limit movement, and those who are recovering from an injury.

Fig. 10-11 Aquatic exercise does not always involve swimming. © *Getty Images*

Factors that Affect the Workout

The intensity of an aquatic workout depends on body position and movement. The following factors have the greatest effect on the intensity of aquatic workouts:

- Buoyancy and water depth.
- The resistance the working muscles must overcome.
- The speed of movement.
- The type of movement.

Buoyancy and water depth

Buoyancy is the upward force that water exerts on an object or a body less dense than itself; it reduces the apparent pull of gravity on the limbs and trunk and enables flotation. The closer the depth of the water is to your standing height, the more support the water gives. Exercising in water that is only ankle or knee deep does little to reduce the impact of the feet landing when jogging or jumping. Yet, in neck-deep water, you have to work harder to stay balanced and in control because the body has more buoyancy. Exercising in chest-deep water allows the arms to stay submerged, which helps maintain balance and proper body alignment. In addition, the effort of pushing the water improves upper body strength and endurance. Arm work underwater also strengthens the muscles that stabilize the trunk.

People who are obese may need to adjust their workouts if their center of buoyancy is lower (due to weight carried in the hips and thighs). Their legs will tend to rise toward the surface, making it hard to stay balanced. Those who are obese may need to exercise in shallower water, but it should still be deep enough to support and protect the body from hard landings.

Buoyancy also affects the intensity of the workout. With bouncing and bounding movements (such as those commonly associated with aerobic exercise done out of the water), the heart rate might not reach the target range because the body has a short rest while it drifts back to the bottom. However, movements involving walking or jogging in the water can be of value for progressing toward workouts of higher intensity. People who do these exercises in the water typically avoid problems and injuries that are associated with the impact of landing.

Resistance

The amount of surface area that you present as you move through the water greatly impacts resistance **(Fig. 10-12)**. Exercise intensity is greater when the surface area of the body is larger because more drag is created. (Drag is the resistance of water on a body moving through it.) When you exercise in the water, you can choose to move specific limbs in certain ways to adjust the resistance your body experiences when pushing against the water. For example, you can increase resistance by cupping your hands and decrease resistance by slicing your hands through the water. Similarly, a biceps curl uses more effort with an open hand than with a fist. Moving a longer body segment, such as a straight arm from shoulder to hand, uses more effort than moving a shorter body segment, such as just the forearm. Another way to adjust resistance is to use equipment designed for aquatic resistance training.

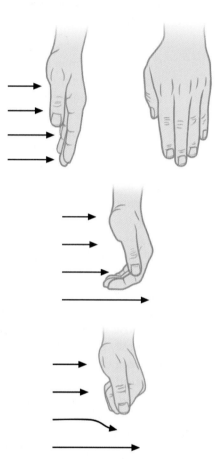

Fig. 10-12 You can adjust resistance during an aquatic workout by adjusting the amount of surface area the water encounters. For example, doing a biceps curl with a flat hand offers the most surface area and the most resistance. If you cup your hand, surface area is slightly decreased and so is resistance. If you make a fist, surface area is minimized and so is resistance.

Speed of movement

The speed of movement also affects the intensity of your workout. Faster movements result in greater resistance and require more effort. In aquatic exercise, this principle applies both to the speed of moving individual limbs and to the speed of moving your whole body from one point in the pool to another.

Type of movement

When your limbs move through the water in aquatic exercise, the water is set in motion and stays in motion. If you continue moving with the water, you encounter less resistance. You can maintain resistance by accelerating your limbs (moving them faster and faster) or changing direction to move against the flow of water.

Bouncing, leaping, running and walking forward, backward and sideways are some of the movements that use the lower body. Scooping, lifting, punching and squeezing water are types of upper body movements. Arm movements can be used in combination with leg movements to increase intensity. For instance, while jogging in shallow water, bursts of quick, short arm movements can increase workout intensity.

Aquatic Exercise for Muscular Development

Muscular development is an important part of any fitness program and when done in the water can be fun and effective. The intensity of resistance training increases as the size of the surface area and the speed of movement increase. You effectively lift more weight when your movements are faster and the surface area meeting resistance is larger.

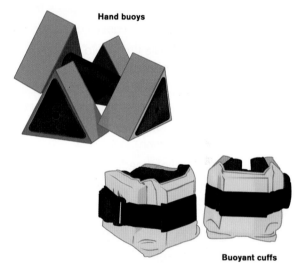

For most people, the water alone provides adequate overload for improvements in strength and muscular endurance. However, more advanced exercisers may need to use equipment to help maintain the proper intensity for their workouts. Several products are available that provide greater overload during resistance training **(Fig. 10-13)**. Wearing buoyant cuffs on wrists or ankles means that greater force must be used to move limbs deeper. Hand buoys and handheld paddles increase resistance when you are exercising your arms. Other devices increase the surface area of the limbs to provide resistance.

Fig. 10-13 Equipment designed for aquatic exercise, such as buoyant cuffs and hand buoys, increase the effort needed to move through the water.

Equipment for aquatic resistance training is not recommended for beginners. In addition, anyone who has a history of joint problems should check with a health care provider before using resistance equipment. Additional safety precautions to take during aquatic exercise are given in **Box 10-6**.

Box 10-6
Safety Precautions for Aquatic Exercise

- Never exercise alone in a pool.
- Use the right equipment. It is important to use equipment specifically designed for aquatic exercise. Improvised equipment may cause injury. Once a piece of equipment is in motion, it may continue to move, striking your body. If you do not have enough strength to stop and reverse the motion or to stabilize your body during the movement, your safety may be jeopardized.

© iStockphoto.com/CEFutcher

- Keep your body centered. Body alignment is especially important when using equipment for resistance training. Choose exercises in which the movement is toward and away from the center of the body. Movements with limbs fully extended, such as leg or arm circles, may cause injury.

- When performing lifting motions, keep your back flat, your abdominal muscles tight, your knees slightly bent and your feet flat on the pool bottom to stabilize your trunk. The greater the surface area of what you are lifting, the more trunk stability is required for safe lifting technique. Stability throughout the lift is affected by the inertia of the equipment and, to a limited degree, by buoyancy.

- Isolate and work one muscle group at a time. Be sure to exercise opposing muscle groups equally.

- Work major muscle groups first. Working the smaller, assisting muscle groups first causes these muscles to fatigue early and limits the work you are able to do with the major muscle groups.

- Plan movements. First imagine where the piece of equipment will be at the end of the movement, and then perform the action. Use exercises that involve a full range of motion and return fully to the starting position. Make sure the equipment stays in the water. Passing the equipment into or out of the water can cause injuries to the joints and muscles.

- Exhale during the work phase and inhale during the recovery phase. Avoid holding your breath; doing so increases blood pressure and makes the exercise feel more difficult.

- Stop any exercise that causes sharp pain. Report any recurring pain to a health care provider.

- Be aware of signals that could indicate a serious health condition. Stop the workout and seek immediate help if you experience:
  - Persistent pain or pressure in the chest, arm or throat (pain or pressure that does not go away within 3–5 minutes and is not relieved by resting or changing position).
  - Cardiac abnormalities (such as a heart rate that stays high for some time after completing the exercise session).
  - Dizziness, lightheadedness or confusion.
  - Breathlessness or wheezing.

Designing an Aquatic Exercise Program

An aquatic exercise workout should have the same components as a fitness swimming workout. The warm-up lasts 5–10 minutes and consists of walking, slow jogging and slow aerobic activities. Warm-ups can be done in the water or on deck if the water is not warm enough. The aerobic set should be rhythmic and continuous and use both the arms and the legs. Monitor your heart rate several times during this set to be sure it stays in the target range. Two or three times each week, include a muscular-development set in your workout to promote flexibility, range of motion, strength and muscular endurance. The cool-down in an aquatic workout should consist of slow, rhythmic activities. A good format for the cool-down is simply to reverse the warm-up activities. Finish by stretching, either as part of the cool-down or as a stand-alone activity.

In aquatic exercise programs, the key to progressively overloading the system and maintaining target heart rates is to control how surface area, speed and type of movement interact (**Fig. 10-14**). These

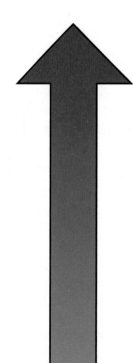

- **Maintain speed**
- **Incorporate periods of longer levers and more angular motion**

- **Greater speed**
- **Short levers**
- **Curvilinear motion**

- **Medium speed**
- **Incorporate periods of longer levers and more angular motion**

- **Medium speed**
- **Short levers**
- **Curvilinear motion**

- **Slow speed**
- **Incorporate periods of longer levers (more surface area)**
- **Alternate curvilinear and angular motion**

- **Slow speed**
- **Short levers (small surface area)**
- **Curvilinear motion**

Fig. 10-14 Progression in an aquatic exercise program relies on changing how surface area, speed and type of movement interact to affect intensity. (Courtesy of Terri Lees)

three factors influence the intensity of the workout. People who are less fit should begin with slow, rhythmic curvilinear movements that minimize surface area, such as walking in chest-deep water or slow jogging in waist-deep water. People who are more fit can use faster, angular movements and larger surface areas. It is possible to stay at the same intensity with a smaller surface area (for example, moving from chest-deep to waist-deep water) by increasing the speed of movement (such as walking or jogging faster). You also can change from angular motions to curved motions without losing intensity by increasing the surface area or the speed. Once you are able to adjust the intensity of your workouts, you can participate in classes with others who are exercising at different intensities.

Training for Competitive Events

Training refers to a physical improvement program designed to prepare a person for competition in sports **(Fig. 10-15)**. If you are going to undertake a training program, you should already have a good level of fitness before you begin.

Training differs from fitness exercise in several ways. The first difference is the intensity of workouts. The goal of fitness exercise is to stay within the target heart rate range, usually at the lower end for those just starting a fitness program. Athletes who are training are often at the upper end of the target heart rate range and may even be above it for brief periods. The second difference is the amount of time spent in muscular-development. In training programs, improved strength and endurance are critical goals. Therefore, muscular-development sets are usually more frequent and more extensive in a training program.

Fig. 10-15 Training helps athletes and serious swimmers prepare for competition.
© Image Source/Getty Images

Training to increase the strength or endurance of specific muscle groups and to improve skills helps swimmers prepare for competition. Competitive swimmers train nearly every day and often complete more than one training session per day. They may also use special equipment to enhance their training **(Box 10-7)**.

Box 10-7
Equipment Used for Training

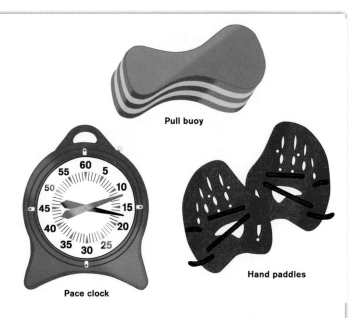

- **Kickboards**. Experienced swimmers may use kickboards to increase their workload during the aerobic or strengthening portions of their workouts.

- **Pull buoys**. A pull buoy is a figure-eight–shaped piece of foam that is held between the thighs or legs to prevent kicking. Pull buoys help swimmers isolate their arm action and strengthen their upper body.

- **Hand paddles**. Hand paddles increase the resistance the arms feel when pushing the water. Hand paddles require greater strength, so they are not suitable for use with young children.

- **Fins.** Accomplished swimmers may use fins to build their leg muscles and improve the flexibility of their ankles.

- **Drag devices**. Competitive swimmers often use devices that create drag or resistance to improve their performance, such as stationary trainers, drag boards, drag suits, training tubes and stretching tethers.
- **Pace clock**. A pace clock is a large device on the pool deck that works like a stop watch. It helps competitive swimmers maintain the appropriate pace during the different phases of their training programs.
- **Dry-land resistance equipment**. Swimmers use resistance equipment (such as free weights, barbells, dumbbells and stretch cords) out of the water to improve their strength and endurance. In addition, mini-gyms and isokinetic swim benches designed specifically for swimmers allow them to duplicate swimming motions on land. These isokinetic devices automatically adjust resistance based on the force applied by the muscles. The swim bench also measures the force of the pull as the swimmer simulates swimming movements.

Training Principles

When planning a training program, following the principles of specificity, overload and progression increases the effectiveness of the training.

Specificity

The principle of specificity states that the benefits of exercise relate directly to the activity performed. Put another way, beyond the general benefits of exercise, there is very little transfer of effects from one kind of activity to another. For example, a runner who trains on the track will not have much improvement in swimming performance. Running uses specific leg muscles, whereas specific arm muscles do most of the work in swimming. Still, both activities improve aerobic capacity.

The principle of specificity applies to training in two areas: the muscles exercised in a given activity, and the energy system used. Two major energy systems supply fuel to the muscles: aerobic ("oxygen-using") and anaerobic ("without oxygen"). The aerobic energy system breaks down carbohydrates, fats and protein for energy, fueling the muscles during longer-lasting exercise, such as during aerobic exercise. The anaerobic energy system uses the most rapidly available source of energy—sugars and carbohydrates stored in the body—for muscular activity. This system is the primary source of energy for **anaerobic exercise** (short-lasting, high-intensity activity, where the muscles' demand for oxygen exceeds the available supply). People who are fit usually exercise anaerobically when their heart rate is above the 85% level of intensity. For those who are not as physically fit, exercise may be anaerobic at an intensity level of much less than 85%.

The specific energy system the body uses in an activity depends on the duration and intensity of the activity **(Box 10-8)**. The benefits of training depend on which energy system is being used. Continuous, low- to moderate-intensity training leads to improvements in the aerobic energy system. Short-duration, high-intensity training leads to improvements in the anaerobic energy system. So, for example, if you are training to improve your sprint performance, using swimming workouts that focus on repeated distances at high intensity will not be effective.

Overload

The principle of overload states that a body system improves only if the system is regularly worked at loads greater than normal. As discussed earlier in this chapter, frequency, intensity and duration are variables that can be adjusted to overload the whole body or specific body systems or muscle groups.

Progression

The body gradually adapts to the workload imposed on it. Improvement will not occur unless the workload is progressively increased.

Box 10-8
Energy Systems Used in Different Types of Activities

Mostly aerobic (low to moderate intensity, long duration)

- Swimming
- Aerobics or aquatic exercise
- Distance running or walking
- Distance cycling
- Cross-country skiing
- Rowing
- Workouts on exercise equipment, such as bikes and treadmills

Mixture of aerobic and anaerobic

- Water polo
- Recreational basketball
- Racquetball
- Resistance training
- Baseball or softball
- Football
- Tennis

Anaerobic (high intensity, short duration)

- Sprints of any kind (running, swimming, cycling)
- Field events in track competition
- Heavy weight lifting
- Jumping rope
- Hill climbing
- Isometric exercises (exercises that involve contracting the muscle without moving the joint)

Training Goals

An obvious training goal for competitive swimmers is to improve their speed. To do this, consider two concepts: stroke length and stroke frequency. **Stroke length** is the distance traveled in one complete cycle of the arms (from the time the hand enters the water, through the pull phase, to exit and reentry). To determine stroke length, count the cycles you take when swimming a known distance and then divide that distance by the number of strokes. **Stroke frequency** is the number of complete arm cycles in a specified length of time. To determine stroke frequency, count the cycles you swam in a known amount of time, and then divide the number of cycles by the number of seconds. For example, if you cover 50 meters in 25 seconds with 25 arm strokes, your stroke length is 2 meters/cycle and your stroke frequency is 1 cycle/second:

Stroke Length = distance stroked/number of cycles = 50 meters/25 cycles = 2 meters/cycle

Stroke Frequency = number of cycles/time = 25 cycles/25 seconds = 1 cycle/second

Speed is the product of stroke length and stroke frequency. In the above example, your speed would be 2 meters/second:

Speed = stroke length × stroke frequency = 2 meters/cycle × 1 cycle/second = 2 meters/second

To increase speed, you must make a corresponding increase in stroke length or stroke frequency. One way to increase speed efficiently is to gain greater distance from each stroke without increasing the number of cycles per second.

Training Techniques

The training techniques described in **Table 10-1** can be used either alone or in combination in workouts to meet specific fitness and training goals. Using different techniques adds variety to workouts. Swimming distances and speeds, as well as the duration of rest periods, depend on various factors, such as the time allotted for training, training goals and the input of coaches or trainers who are present.

Table 10-1 Training Techniques

Technique	Description
Over-distance training	• Swimming long distances with moderate exertion (the heart rate stays in the low- to mid-target range for the whole swim) with short or no rest periods • Useful for improving endurance and as a warm-up activity
Fartlek method	• Swims are broken into slow and fast lengths of the pool, using the same stroke • Can make long swims more interesting and is good for developing speed and endurance simultaneously
Interval set	• A series of repeat swims of the same distance and time, with specific rest periods in between the times spent swimming—e.g., "8 × 100 on 1:30," where the first number (8) represents the number of times to repeat the distance, the second number (100) is the distance of each swim in yards or meters, and the last number (1:30) is the total amount of time for the swim and rest (e.g., if the swimmer swims the 100 meters in 1:15, he or she would have 15 seconds available for rest before swimming the next 100 meters) • The short break prevents the heart from returning to its resting rate between swims • Best all-around method for developing both speed and endurance; used primarily in the main set of a workout
Repetition	• Swim sets of the same distance done at close to maximum effort (up to 90% effort) with rest periods as long as or longer than the swim time • Used after the swimmer develops a good aerobic base to develop speed and anaerobic capacity; often incorporated into the workout after the aerobic set as a muscular-development set
Sprints	• Short, fast swims (100% effort) to simulate race conditions; the rest between sprints is usually long enough to let the heart return to its resting rate • Used to improve anaerobic capacity
Straight sets	• A steady speed is maintained throughout the set; the swimmer monitors his or her time to keep an even pace • Often used by distance swimmers
Negative split sets	• Swimming the second half of each swim period faster than the first half (e.g., if swimming 200 yards four times, the second 100 yards should be faster than the first 100 yards in each repetition)

Table 10-1 Training Techniques (continued)

Technique	Description
Descending sets	• Decreasing the time on successive swims (e.g., if swimming 200 yards four times, each 200 yards would be faster than the 200 yards preceding it)
Ladders	• Swims with regular increases or decreases in distance (e.g., a swim of 25 yards, then 50 yards, then 75 yards) • Can be varied by increasing the number of times the distance is repeated as the distances get shorter (e.g., swimming one 500, then two 400s, then three 300s, then four 200s and five 100s)
Pyramids	• Swims with regular increases and decreases in distance (e.g., a swim of 25 yards, then 50 yards, then 75 yards, then 50 yards, then 25 yards) • Can be varied by increasing the number of times the distance is repeated as the distances get shorter (e.g., swimming one 500, then two 400s, then three 300s, then four 200s and five 100s)
Broken swims	• Swims that divide a target distance into shorter intervals with a short rest in between (e.g., 10 seconds); the goal is to perform each segment at a faster pace than can be maintained over the entire distance • Swimming pace is determined by timing each segment and then subtracting the total time for rest from the total time • A highly motivating method of training because it simulates the stress conditions of competition but yields swimming times that may be faster than the racing time for an actual event • Often combined with other training methods, such as negative splits and descending swims
Dry-land training	• Uses out-of-water training techniques to develop flexibility and strength to improve swimming skills • A half-hour of strength training 3 days a week combined with 15 minutes of stretching can produce favorable results • When possible, dry-land strength training should be done after water training so that training in the pool is not affected by fatigue from the dry-land training
Cross-training	• A method of exercising so that the effects of training in one sport enhance the effects in another; strengthens different muscle groups and can diminish the risk for injury

Training Phases

In general, there are two competitive swimming seasons. The short-course season for 25-yard pools usually runs from September to May; the long-course season for 50-meter pools usually runs from June to August.

For either season, training should follow three phases to culminate at the competitive event. These phases are individually set based on personal goals. The phase of training determines the type of workouts. A sample training workout for each phase of the training season is shown in **Box 10-9** and includes samples of over-distance, Fartlek, interval and sprint training techniques.

Early Season Phase

The early season phase lasts about 6–8 weeks and focuses on general conditioning to build a foundation for the whole season. Long, easy swims using various strokes help build endurance. Swim at a slower rate and make needed changes to stroke technique, flip turns and breathing patterns. Supplement swimming with dry-land training to help improve strength, flexibility and cardiovascular conditioning.

Mid-season Phase

In the mid-season phase, which is about 8–12 weeks long, start to tailor your individual training based on specific goals. Workouts can increase in distance so you can pay more attention to fine-tuning strokes. Quality is the emphasis of the workout. Use dry-land training at a maintenance level during this time.

Taper Phase

The taper phase is the last and shortest part of training, usually lasting 1–3 weeks. As the set date for peak performance draws near, decrease the distances to swim but increase the intensity almost to racing speed. Do this by resting more between sets and by using broken swims and descending sets. Practice starts and turns to improve technique. The specifics of the taper

---

Box 10-9
Sample Workouts for Each Phase of the Training Season

Early Season Phase	Mid-Season Phase	Taper Phase
Warm-up	**Warm-up**	**Warm-up**
4 × 200 swim/pull/kick/swim	8 × 100 alternating between swimming and kicking	300 easy swim
Main set	**Main set**	**Main set**
800 maintain even pace at 100s	5 × 200 broken swims on 4:00 with 10 seconds' rest at each break	6 × 50 descending set on 2:00
1650 broken swim with 15 seconds' rest after each interval	1 × 100	4 × 100 broken swims on 3:00 with 20 seconds' rest at each break
1 × 500	2 × 50	2 × 50
1 × 400	5 × 300, swim first 200, kick last 100; rest 15 seconds between swims	**Cool-down**
1 × 300	**Cool-down**	200 easy swim
1 × 200	12 × 50 on 1:00	starts and turns
1 × 100		
1 × 75		
1 × 50		
1 × 25		
Cool-down		
200 easy swim		

---

phase depend on the individual and the length and time of training in the earlier phases. For example, sprinters usually taper longer than distance swimmers, and older athletes taper longer than younger athletes do.

Specific Competitive Events

Competitive events for swimmers can include swim meets held at pools, open-water meets and triathlons.

Swim Meets

To find out about local meets, contact the local pool or swim team or get in touch with USA Swimming or US Masters Swimming (see Appendix A). They can help you find a local organization that sponsors meets. Work with them to get a meet information sheet with lists of events, deadlines and other information, such as club membership. Joining a club or swim team is a good way to get involved in competitive swimming and participate in meets.

Once you know which meet you will be participating in, look over information about the meet carefully, complete the entry form and include any entry fees. It is important to pay attention to deadlines. For a club or team, the coach may send in all the registrations together. With the assistance of your coach, choose which events you feel comfortable entering and check that they are spaced far enough apart to allow for rest in between. It is helpful to make a list of the events you have entered and when they occur in the meet. If you need more rest during the meet, you can change plans even after entering by letting the officials know that you will not be entering an event. This is called a **scratch**.

Box 10-10 lists items that are useful to have on hand when you are attending a swim meet. Before the meet, you may feel nervous. This is perfectly normal. Think positively, and remember all

Box 10-10
Items to Bring to a Swim Meet

- **Extra swimwear.** Sitting around in a wet suit is uncomfortable so bring more than one. Change into a dry suit after warm-ups and your events.
- **Sun protection.** Bring a hat, sunscreen and sunglasses.
- **Swim cap (if you wear one).** An extra one is handy in case of rips.
- **Goggles.** A spare pair or strap is a good idea.
- **Towels.** Bring at least two, the larger the better.
- **Extra clothes.** Dry clothes prevent you from getting chilled and can offer an extra layer of protection from the sun. Bring a T-shirt, a sweatshirt, sweatpants and socks and shoes.

- **Toiletries.** Bring shampoo, soap and other personal care items for showering after the meet. For safety, use plastic bottles only.
- **A lock.** Keep belongings safe in a locker.
- **Water and snacks.** Swim meets last for several hours. Consider packing a cooler.
- **Medicines.** Bring any necessary medications. Make sure they have been approved for use during swimming by your health care provider and the swim competition rules and regulations committee.
- **Miscellaneous items.** Many people also like to bring along something to keep notes and records with, a stopwatch, a camera and a beach chair. It is also a good idea to have some cash on hand.

of the training you have done to reach this point. You can help your body perform by "rehearsing" the meet events in your mind. Remembering all of the things you have done well in the past can help to bolster your confidence.

When you arrive at the pool, check in with the meet organizers and verify the events that you have entered. This information is listed on the heat sheet, which is usually posted in a window, on a bulletin board or on a table.

Some events are divided into **heats**. This is done when there are more competitors than there are lanes in the pool. When heats are used, entrants are organized into several groupings (for example, eight competitors at a time if the pool has eight lanes). Depending on the organization of the meet, the winners may be those who swim the fastest time in their heats or the fastest swimmers from several heats may face each other in a final heat that determines the winner.

After checking in, warm up. Look for published warm-up rules and safety procedures. Find a lane with people who swim about the same speed as you do. Ease into the pool from the edge or jump in feetfirst. Do not dive into the warm-up pool. Pay attention to others in the lane. While swimming a few laps, you can loosen up and practice the strokes you will swim to safely raise your heart rate. Also use the warm-up time to orient yourself to the pool. For example, you can get used to the targets on the wall and find out if the wall is slippery. If you are swimming the backstroke, you can check to see if the flags are the same number of strokes from the wall that you are accustomed to. Use starting blocks only under the supervision of a coach.

During the race, swim at a constant pace. Use the first few strokes to establish a pace and stroke rhythm. Stay mentally alert during the race by focusing on whatever actions—such as turns—require hard work to master. If you can get someone to time splits (segments of a race) during the race, you can use this information to analyze your race performance and set future goals.

After the race, keep moving until your body cools down and your heart rate returns to its resting rate. If there is a cool-down area, you can stay in the water and do some easy laps, bob, scull or float. If there is no cool-down area, walk around the pool area until your body recovers.

You can review the race later. You may feel proud if your time improved, even slightly; or if your time was not as good as you hoped, you can look ahead to a future chance. Evaluating your performance at the meet is a great aid in setting new goals for training for the next season or meet.

Open-water Events

In competitive **open-water swimming**, the event can be a single event (for example, a 5K or 10K swim) or part of another event, such as a triathlon. Open-water swimming events can take place in the ocean or in a lake or river **(Fig. 10-16)**. The event may involve swimming parallel to shore; to or around a fixed point or landmark (such as a rock, island or pier); around a closed course marked by buoys; or point-to-point.

Risks associated with open-water swimming include environmental illnesses (such as hypothermia and heat-related illness) and hazards related to being in open water (such as aquatic life, currents, choppy water, murky water and submerged objects). Open-water swimmers are also at risk for exhaustion because there are no turns and no lane ropes to use for support. Training properly for the event, knowing your personal limits,

Fig. 10-16 Open-water events challenge participants in new ways. *Photo: Image © ChameleonsEye, 2013. Used under license from Shutterstock.*

familiarizing yourself with the open-water environment in which you will be swimming and attending the pre-race briefing are steps you can take to minimize risk. You should also check to see that race organizers have taken steps to ensure safety. Adequate numbers of lifeguards and first responders should be on site, and rescue personnel in small boats should accompany swimmers during open-water events. A system should be in place to account for every participant who enters and exits the water.

Training

Training for open water is much like training for long-distance swims. When you are training in a swimming pool, train in the longest pool available or swim around the perimeter of the pool. The fewer turns taken, the more carryover there will be for the long-distance event. Practice taking your goggles off and putting them on in the deep end without the support of the pool bottom or sides. If possible, practice in moderately cold water. Repeated exposure to cold water helps your body acclimate to it.

The best way to train for open-water swimming, however, is by swimming in open water. Always swim with a training partner and notify the lifeguard of your plans. Open water is rarely as calm as the roughest, most crowded pool. To manage the rougher water, raise your elbows higher and roll your shoulders more to keep from catching them on the waves. Getting off course can be a problem in open water. To swim in a straight line, every few strokes, lift your head and look ahead while taking a breath. Practice this in the pool before venturing out into open water. Alternating breathing (breathing on each side) or having a friend paddle alongside in a boat can also help you maintain a straight line.

At the event

Dress appropriately. At some open-water events, you may be required to wear a wetsuit to reduce your risk for hypothermia.

Races with many swimmers often use staggered starts with swimmers positioning themselves. Be honest and smart. If you are unsure of your time, start among swimmers of moderate ability. Avoid being an obstacle that better swimmers need to climb over and go around. Staying to the side of the pack may mean swimming slightly farther to get on course, but you will avoid the crowd of swimmers in a mass start. For safety, many meet organizers provide color-coded caps to swimmers based on age or ability. If you are unsure of your ability, request a cap color that puts you in a category with swimmers of moderate ability. If you need to leave the race for any reason, signal for help using the method described in the pre-race briefing.

Triathlons

A **triathlon** is a race combining any three sports done consecutively **(Fig. 10-17)**. The most common configuration is swimming, cycling and running (in that order), but other sports combinations exist as well (for example, instead of swimming, the first leg could be kayaking). Participants may compete individually or as a team, depending on the race. In a relay competition, each member of the team completes one leg of the race. A triathlon can also be organized as a stage-event triathlon, in which each sport has a set start and finish time, possibly on different days.

Fig. 10-17 Swimming is usually the first leg of a triathlon. Here, triathletes have completed the swim course and are about to begin the bike course. *Image © Martin Good, 2014. Used under license from Shutterstock.com*

The best-known triathlon is the Ironman Triathlon World Championship held in Kona, Hawaii. This race consists of a 2.4-mile swim, a 112-mile bike ride and a 26.2-mile run in which contestants complete each event individually. Worldwide, it is considered the premier endurance event.

Opportunities in Aquatics

If you love being in, on or around the water, there are many ways to build on that passion, ranging from participating in a sport to taking up a new hobby to working in an aquatic environment. This appendix provides resources for more information for those interested in pursuing specialized interests related to the world of aquatics.

Competition and Fitness

Swimming

USA Swimming

USA Swimming (www.usaswimming.org) is the national governing body for amateur competitive swimming in the United States. Founded in 1980, USA Swimming makes rules, implements policies and procedures, conducts national championships, gives out safety and sports medicine information and selects athletes to represent the United States in international competition.

USA Swimming is involved with competitive swimming at the international, national and local levels:

- **International.** The international federation for amateur aquatic sports is the Fédération Internationale de Natation Amateur (FINA). Because only one national federation can represent the United States at FINA, USA Swimming is affiliated with FINA through United States Aquatic Sports (USAS). USAS also represents synchronized swimming, diving, water polo and masters swimming at FINA.
- **National.** USA Swimming is a member of the United States Olympic Committee (USOC) and has voting representation in the USOC House of Delegates.
- **Local.** Within the United States, USA Swimming is comprised of Local Swimming Committees (LSCs), each administering USA Swimming activities of local clubs in a specific geographical area. Each LSC has its own bylaws for local operations.

USA Swimming has the following classifications for competitions:

- **Senior:** for all registered swimmers
- **Junior:** for all registered swimmers 18 years of age and younger
- **Age Group/Junior Olympic:** for all registered swimmers grouped by ages 10 and under, 11–12, 13–14 and either 15–16 and 17–18 or 15–18. An 8-and-under age group competition may also be conducted.
- **Post Age Group:** for all registered swimmers older than 18 years of age whom an LSC elects to include in its age group program
- **Masters:** for all swimmers 19 years of age and older who register with United States Masters Swimming
- **Long Distance:** for all registered swimmers

United States Masters Swimming

United States Masters Swimming (USMS; www.usms.org) is an umbrella organization with responsibility and authority over the Masters Swimming Program in the United States. Through its local Masters Swimming Committees and swim clubs, USMS offers competitive swimming to swimmers 18 years of age and older. It also provides programs involving swimming for fitness as well as fitness events.

Competitions are organized by age groups of 5-year spans (and one 6-year span). Events are wide-ranging and include individual strokes and relays. Open-water swims are held in many locations in the summer, ranging from 1–10 miles.

Masters Swimming's credo is fun, fitness and competition. Masters swimmers enjoy the benefits of swimming with an organized group, participating in structured workouts, developing friendships and socializing with other adult swimmers. Members participate in a wide range of activities from noncompetitive lap swimming to international competition. Paid and volunteer coaching and officiating opportunities are available at all levels of USMS.

National YMCA Competitive Swimming and Diving

YMCA Competitive Swimming and Diving (www.ymcaswimminganddiving.org) trains people of all ages to compete in YMCA programs that may lead to state, regional and national championships.

YMCA Masters Swimming, a part of this organization, is an age-grouped competitive program for adults, starting at age 18. Groups are divided by age spans, beginning with ages 18–24, and then by 5-year spans 25–29, 30–34 and so on with no top age limit. Some YMCAs also sponsor competitive teams in springboard diving and synchronized swimming. YMCAs may register with U.S. Masters Swimming and represent the YMCA in regional and national competition.

National Collegiate Athletic Association

The National Collegiate Athletic Association (NCAA; www.ncaa.org) is the organization for U.S. colleges and universities to speak and act on athletic matters at the national level. The NCAA is also the national athletics accrediting agency for collegiate competition.

Founded in 1905 when 13 schools formed the Intercollegiate Athletic Association of the United States, the NCAA has grown to more than 1000 member institutions. The NCAA enacts legislation on nationwide issues, represents intercollegiate athletics before state and federal governments, compiles and distributes statistics, writes and interprets rules in 12 sports, conducts research on athletics problems, and promotes and participates in international sports planning and competition (in part through membership in the U.S. Olympic Committee).

The NCAA sponsors the following national championships:

- Division I Men's Swimming and Diving Championships
- Division I Women's Swimming and Diving Championships
- Division II Men's Swimming and Diving Championships
- Division II Women's Swimming and Diving Championships
- Division III Men's Swimming and Diving Championships
- Division III Women's Swimming and Diving Championships

The National Junior College Athletic Association

The National Junior College Athletic Association (NJCAA; www.njcaa.org) was founded in 1937 to promote and supervise a national program of junior college sports and activities consistent with the educational objectives of junior colleges. The NJCAA interprets rules, sets standards for eligibility, promotes academics through the Academy All-American and Distinguished Academic All-American programs, publishes a monthly magazine, provides weekly polls and distributes sport guides.

There are member institutions throughout the United States, ranging in enrollment size from 500–25,000 students. At the Men's and Women's National Swimming and Diving Championships each year, the NJCAA presents All-American Awards, Swimmer/Diver of the Year Award and Swimming/Diving Coach of the Year Award.

The National Federation of State High School Associations

The National Federation of State High School Associations (www.nfhs.org) consists of the high school athletic associations of the 50 states and the District of Columbia. Established in 1920, the National Federation is a service and regulatory organization that provides central record keeping, establishes rules and standards, assists with oversight of high school sports and activities, and conducts educational programs and conferences. It oversees numerous interscholastic sports and lists swimming and diving among the 10 most popular sports. Its goal is to promote the educational values of interscholastic sports for student success.

Diving

USA Diving (www.usadiving.org), a not-for-profit organization, is the national governing body of diving. It is organized through Local Diving Associations (LDAs) encompassing clubs nationwide. USA Diving is organized into three programs:

- **Junior:** provides a developmental diving and physical fitness program for youth; teaches fundamentals of diving and benefits of participation in competitions
- **Senior:** provides further development and identifies American divers of national and international caliber to compete in National Championships, Olympic Games, World Championships, Pan American Games, and other national and international competitions

Image © bikeriderlondon, 2014. Used under license from Shutterstock.com

- **Masters:** provides a continuing physical fitness program for diving enthusiasts 21 years of age and older who no longer compete in the Senior program

The mission of USA Diving is to conduct and promote the sport of diving in a manner that allows each participant to achieve the peak of excellence afforded by his or her ability, effort, desire and dedication. All divers have the opportunity to realize the poise, maturity, grace and strength inherent in diving and to reach their personal goals. Coaching and officiating opportunities are available at all levels of USA Diving.

Water Polo

Water polo is a team sport that combines soccer and rugby skills and is played in deep water. It requires tremendous stamina and skill. It was made a sport in 1885 by the Swimming Association of Great Britain and became an official Olympic sport in 1908. Today, it is played as recreation and is a popular high school, college and Olympic sport. Even beginners who make their own rules can enjoy playing water polo.

USA Water Polo, Inc. (USWP; www.usawaterpolo.org), founded in 1978, is the national governing body for water polo in the United States and oversees the water polo program for the Olympics. Local clubs compete in matches and may progress to regional and zone competition. Qualifying teams from geographic zones compete in national championships. Teams compete

Image © muzsy, 2014. Used under license from Shutterstock.com

in indoor and outdoor tournaments at the Junior and Senior levels. Age-group competition is organized as 13 and under, 15 and under, and 17 and under, although many teams mix ages. Co-ed teams and leagues are sanctioned but do not have national competitions.

Synchronized Swimming

Synchronized swimming combines skill, stamina and teamwork with the flair of music and drama. Coaches, psychologists, physiologists, nutritionists, dance specialists and former champions all contribute their expertise. This sport is increasingly popular with both spectators and participants. Noncompetitors can participate as coaches, volunteers and judges.

© iStockphoto.com/amriphoto

United States Synchronized Swimming (USSS; www.usasynchro.org), also known as Synchro Swimming USA, is the national governing body of synchronized swimming. USSS, a not-for-profit organization, was established in 1977 to promote and support all competitive and noncompetitive levels of the sport. It also selects and trains athletes to represent the United States in international competition.

Registered members, ranging in age from 6–80, belong to registered clubs. Masters swimming for USSS includes participants who are 20 years old and older. International Masters competition includes participants who are 25 years old and older and is based on rules set by FINA. Clinics, camps and training programs are available for every level of swimming ability. There is also a training and certification program for coaches.

Three synchronized swimming events are recognized internationally: solo (one swimmer), duet (two swimmers) and team (up to eight swimmers). Synchronized swimming premiered at the 1984 Olympic Games in Los Angeles. The team event debuted in the 1996 Olympic Games in Atlanta. The 2000 Olympic Games in Sydney included the team event, as well as the duet event. There are also compulsory figure competitions.

esynchro.com is an education partner and provider to USA Synchro. The mission of esynchro.com is to research and produce skills, technique and training information for the aquatics and synchronized swimming communities around the world.

Open-Water Swimming

Open-water swimming is defined as any competition that takes place in rivers, lakes or oceans. In 1986, FINA, the world governing body of swimming, officially recognized open-water swimming. The first official competition was staged at the 1991 World Swimming Championships in Perth, Australia. Open-water swimming is now an Olympic event. Open-water swimming is roughly divided into long-distance swimming, with distances of less than 25 kilometers, and marathon swimming, with distances of more than 25 kilometers. Typically, events are held for both men and women at distances of 5, 10 and 25 kilometers.

© iStockphoto.com/iom

Multisport

USA Triathlon (www.usatriathlon.org) is the national governing body for the multisport disciplines of triathlon, durathlon, aquathlon, aquabike, winter triathlon, off-road triathlon and paratriathlon. The organization is a member federation of the U.S. Olympic Committee and the International Triathlon Union. Membership includes athletes of all ages, coaches, officials, parents and fans working together to strengthen multisport.

Participants range from age 15–70 or older and compete at regional, zone and national levels. Some triathlons are team events. For beginners, completing the course is seen as a tremendous personal achievement. Fitness enthusiasts participate in the sport to gain the benefits of cross-training.

© iStockphoto.com/TarpMagnus

Competition and Fitness for Athletes with Disabilities

Special Olympics

Special Olympics (www.specialolympics.org) is an international not-for-profit organization dedicated to empowering people with intellectual disabilities to become physically fit, productive and respected members of society through sports training and competition. Special Olympics, established in 1968, offers children and adults with intellectual disabilities year-round training and competition in more than 30 Olympic-type summer and winter sports, including swimming. More recently, open-water swimming was introduced in 2011.

Courtesy of Special Olympics, Inc.

Because of the wide array of swimming events offered, swimming is appropriate for a range of ages and ability levels. Swimming competition events are based on a variety of strokes. Athletes are grouped in competition according to age, gender and ability:

- **Freestyle events:** 25, 50, 100, 200, 400, 800 and 1500 meter
- **Backstroke, breaststroke and butterfly events:** 25, 50, 100 and 200 meter
- **Individual medley events:** 100, 200 and 400 meter
- **Freestyle and medley relay events:** 4 x 25, 4 x 50, 4 x 100 meter and 4 x 200 meter freestyle relay

Special Olympics also offers athletes with lower ability levels the opportunity to train and compete in fundamental events, including:

- 15-meter walk
- 15-meter kickboard
- 15- and 25-meter flotation race
- 10-meter assisted swim
- 15-meter unassisted swim

U.S. Paralympics

U.S. Paralympics (http://www.teamusa.org/US-Paralympics) is a division of the U.S. Olympic Committee, the organization responsible for underwriting the expenses of U.S. teams in the Olympic, Pan American, Parapan American and Paralympic Games. The Paralympic and Parapan American Games are elite sport events for athletes from different disability groups. Swimming for men and women has been included since 1960. Individuals swim in 50-meter pools and are not allowed to use any prosthesis or assistive device when competing. As in the Olympic and Pan American Games, competitors in the Paralympic and Parapan American Games compete in freestyle, backstroke, butterfly, breaststroke and medley events.

Through education, sports programs and community partnerships, U.S. Paralympics strives to make a difference in the lives of individuals with physical disabilities. U.S. Paralympics operates community, academy, military and elite programs to provide individuals with physical disabilities opportunities to participate in sports.

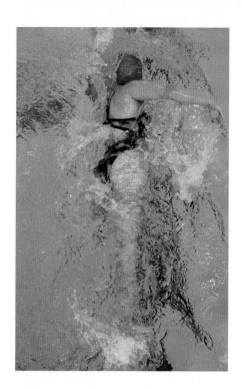

Employment

Lifeguard

Lifeguarding is a challenging and important job. The American Red Cross (www.redcross.org) trains more than 250,000 lifeguards each year to work in pool, waterfront and waterpark settings. Through classroom learning and hands-on practice, participants in American Red Cross lifeguarding courses learn:

- Surveillance skills.
- Rescue skills for in the water and on land.
- First aid, cardiopulmonary resuscitation (CPR) and automated external defibrillation (AED) skills.
- The responsibilities of a professional lifeguard.

Water Safety Instructor

Water Safety instructors teach people of different abilities and needs—infants and preschoolers, children and youth, people with disabilities, adult beginners and older adults—how to swim and how to be safe in, on and around the water. The American Red Cross (www.redcross.org) offers a Water Safety Instructor course to provide instructor candidates with the training needed to teach courses in the Red Cross Swimming and Water Safety program. This course helps develop instructor candidates' understanding of how to use the course materials, how to conduct training sessions and how to evaluate participants' progress.

Aquatic Fitness Instructor

Aquatic Exercise Association

The Aquatic Exercise Association (AEA; www.aeawave.com) is an internationally recognized organization of aquatic fitness education for professionals who conduct aquatic exercise programs. AEA offers certification as an Aquatic Fitness Professional (considered the gold standard in the industry), numerous education programs from beginner to advanced professional levels and continuing education workshops.

© iStockphoto.com/OJO_Images

United States Water Fitness Association

The United States Water Fitness Association (USWFA; www.uswfa.com) is a not-for-profit educational organization committed to excellence in education and promoting aquatics, including water exercise. The USWFA offers the following National Certifications at the primary and masters level:

- Water Fitness Instructor
- Primary Water Walking Instructor
- Aquatic Fitness Personal Trainer

Certification is also available for:

- Aquatic Director
- Senior Aquatic Director

United States Navy

Swimming and aquatic skills are an integral part of the U.S. Navy (www.navy.mil). All naval personnel must meet minimum swim qualifications. Successful completion of a higher-level swim test is required for naval duties, which require increased exposure to water hazards. The most arduous swimming and aquatics programs include special warfare schools, dive schools, rescue swimmer schools and aviation water survival training.

© Associated Press Photos

Recreation

Scuba

Some 3–4 million scuba divers enjoy the beauty and excitement of the underwater world. Scuba divers wear a mask and fins and carry a compressed air supply and regulator for breathing underwater for extended periods. Scuba divers also use buoyancy control devices, weights, wet suits and a variety of instruments to monitor depth, time and direction underwater. Divers enjoy a variety of underwater

© iStockphoto.com/JociJacobson

activities, such as shore diving, boat diving, reef diving, night diving, underwater photography and underwater archeology.

Recreational scuba diving by certified divers has a good safety record because of the comprehensive training required. At least 40 hours of instruction in the pool and the classroom are required before students start supervised training in open water. A medical examination and a swim test are strongly recommended and often required before learning scuba. The Professional Association of Diving Instructors (PADI; www.padi.com) offers certification in scuba diving.

Boating

As an agency of the Federal government and a servant of the public, the U.S. Coast Guard (www.uscgboating.org) is a leader in improving the boating experience of the maritime public. It is the mission of the Coast Guard to use preventive means to maximize safe use and enjoyment of America's waterways by the public and minimize the loss of life, personal injury, property damage and environmental impact associated with the use of recreational boats. The Coast Guard offers boating safety education to teach people how to stay safe on the water and prevent accidents, injuries and fatalities while boating.

© iStockphoto.com/Photomick

Other Activities that Involve Aquatics

Boy Scouts of America

Boy Scouts of America (www.scouting.org) is a year-round program available to boys between the ages of 11 and 18 years. Core objectives of the Boy Scout program include developing character, citizenship and personal fitness. Aquatics-related merit badges for Boy Scouts of America include Swimming, Lifesaving and Sports.

Girl Scouts of the USA

Girl Scouts of the USA (www.girlscouts.org) is a program that helps girls between the ages of 5 and 18 build character and skills for success in the real world. In partnership with committed adult volunteers, girls develop qualities that will serve them all their lives, for example, leadership, strong values, social conscience and conviction about their own potential and self-worth. Projects that can be completed with aquatics as the emphasis include Leadership and Water Sports.

The President's Council on Physical Fitness and Sports—President's Challenge

The President's Challenge (www.fitness.gov) is a program that encourages all Americans to make being active part of their everyday lives. People of all activity and fitness levels are able to participate in the President's Challenge. People can win Presidential awards for daily physical activity and fitness efforts, including swimming.

GLOSSARY

Aerobic exercise: rhythmic, physical exercise that is sustained for a continuous period and requires additional effort by the heart and lungs to meet the body's increased demand for oxygen, also known as "cardio"

Air sparging system: a system that creates a cushion of aerated water on the surface of the pool, allowing divers to practice new dives while reducing the risk of severe injury as a result of a poor landing

Anaerobic exercise: short-lasting, high-intensity activity, where the muscles' demand for oxygen exceeds the available supply

Aquatic exercise: an in-water fitness activity generally performed in a vertical position with the face out of the water

Arm cycle: the time it takes for one hand to enter the water, begin the pull and then return to that position

Bobbing: the skill of repeatedly submerging and pushing off from the bottom to return to the surface; used to practice breath control

Body mass index (BMI): a calculation made based on a person's weight and height that is commonly used to screen for overweight and obesity

Body roll: a rotating movement around the midline of the body, an imaginary line from head to feet that divides the body equally into left and right parts

Breaststroke kick: a kick in which both heels are brought toward the buttocks while separating the knees, the feet are flexed and the feet and knees are forcefully pressed backward until the legs are extended; used primarily in the breaststroke

Buoyancy: the upward force that water places on an object when the object is in water

Cadence: the number of kicks in an arm cycle

Catch: the stage in an arm stroke when the swimmer first engages the water in a way that starts movement; the start of the power phase

Center of buoyancy: a theoretical point in the body where the entire buoyancy of that body can be considered to be concentrated; the location of all upward force

Center of mass: a theoretical point in the body where the entire mass of that body can be considered to be concentrated; the location of all downward force (also called the center of gravity)

Circle swimming: a technique that allows multiple swimmers to swim in the same lane simultaneously, swimming counterclockwise in the lane with approximately 5 seconds between swimmers

Diving board: a recreational mechanism for entering a pool; consists of a flexible board on a rigid stand with a stationary fulcrum

Diving platform: a rigid structure for diving that extends horizontally over the water at a height of 5 meters, 7.5 meters or 10 meters

Dolphin kick: a kick in which the legs move up and down together; used primarily in the butterfly stroke

Drag: the force that opposes movement through the water

Drowning: the process of experiencing respiratory impairment from submersion or immersion in liquid

Emergency action plan (EAP): written procedures for dealing with specific potential accidents or emergency situations

Finning: a technique for moving through the water on the back using a pushing motion with the arms underwater

Fitness swimming: a fitness activity during which swimming strokes are used to reach a specified level of intensity sustained for a set time

Flexibility: the range of motion in a joint or group of joints

Flip turn: a fast and efficient turn done in a tuck position; used in fitness swimming and in the freestyle and backstroke events in competition

Flutter kick: a continuous, alternating upward-and-downward kicking motion of the legs; used primarily in the front crawl and back crawl

Form drag: the resistance created by a swimmer's body shape as the swimmer moves through the water

Freestyle: a competitive event that allows any stroke; often used as a synonym for front crawl because front crawl is the stroke most often used in the freestyle event

Frictional drag: the resistance created by a swimmer's body surface as it moves through the water

Fulcrum: a pivot near the center of a diving board or springboard that lets the board bend and spring

Glide: the stage of a stroke after the power phase when the body keeps moving without any additional swimmer effort

Grab start: a racing start in which both feet and both hands are placed at the front of the starting block

Heat: a race in which times are compared with those from other races to determine overall ranking; often used when there are more entrants in a swimming event than there are lanes in the pool

Hydraulics: vertical whirlpools that occur as water flows over an object, such as a low-head dam or waterfall, causing a strong downward force that can trap an unwary swimmer

Hydrodynamics: the science that studies the physics of fluids

Hyperventilation: rapid, deep breathing; a dangerous technique in which swimmers try to swim long distances underwater by taking a series of rapid breaths in succession and forcefully exhaling in order to increase the amount of oxygen that they breathe

Jump board: a recreational mechanism for entering a pool; consists of a flexible board on a flexible stand that includes a coiled spring

Leading arm: when arms work in opposition, the arm reaching farthest beyond the head (also called the bottom arm in sidestroke)

Lift: the force of the springboard pushing the diver into the air

Longshore currents: currents that run parallel to the shore

Midline: an imaginary line from head to feet that divides the body equally into right and left parts

Muscular endurance: the ability of the muscle to contract repeatedly with the same force over an extended period

Open turn: a simple turn used in noncompetitive swimming

Open-water swimming: any competition that takes place in rivers, lakes or oceans

Overload: a training principle that states that a body system improves only if the system is regularly worked at loads greater than normal

Pike position: a position in which the body is bent at the hips, with the legs straight and the thighs brought close to the chest

Pitch: the angle at which the hand moves through the water when swimming

Power phase: the part of the stroke where the arm or leg is moving the body in the right direction

Press: the diver's final downward push on the springboard assisted by the landing from the approach

Propulsion: the action of pushing or driving forward

Racing start: a long, shallow entry from starting blocks used by competitive swimmers

Rate of perceived exertion (RPE): a subjective method for determining the intensity of a workout based on how hard the person feels he or she is working

Recovery: the part of the stroke where the arms or legs relax and return to their starting position

Recreational water illness (RWI): an illness that is spread by swallowing, breathing or contacting contaminated water

Rip currents: currents that move water away from the shore and out to sea beyond the breaking waves

Rotary kick: a kick in which the swimmer rotates the lower legs at the knees, one leg at a time, making large circular movements with the foot and lower leg; used when treading water and in lifeguarding, water polo and synchronized swimming; also called the eggbeater kick

Scissors kick: a kick in which the legs move apart and then together again in a scissor-like action; used primarily in the sidestroke, the trudgen strokes and for treading water

Scratch: withdrawing from an event for which one was previously entered

Sculling: an out-and-in movement of the arms and hands in the water that provides almost constant propulsion

Shallow-angle dive: a headfirst entry in which the body enters the water at about a 45° angle in a streamlined position

Specific gravity: the ratio of the weight of the object to the weight of the water it displaces

Springboard: a flexible plank used for competitive diving that extends horizontally over the water at a height of 1 meter or 3 meters

Starting block: a raised platform from which competitive swimmers begin a race

Straight position: a position in which the torso is straight or arched slightly backward with the legs together and straight; there is no bend at the hips or knees

Streamlined position: a position in which the arms are extended in front, pressed against the ears with the hands clasped together, and the legs are together and extended, with the toes pointed

Stroke frequency: the number of complete arm cycles in a specified length of time

Stroke length: the distance traveled in one complete cycle of the arms (from the time the hand enters the water, through the pull phase, to exit and reentry)

Stroke mechanics: the basic elements of a swimming stroke (body position and motion, breathing and timing, arm stroke and kick)

Surface diving: a technique used to go under the water when swimming on the surface

Swim meet: a competitive event in swimming; may be a contest between teams or between individuals

Synchronized swimming: a sport in which a team of swimmers perform coordinated or identical movements in time to music

Target heart rate range: the ideal heart rate range that a person must maintain during exercise to achieve the greatest cardiovascular benefit

Track start: a racing start in which the hands grasp the front of the starting block and the feet are staggered on the block

Trailing arm: the arm that rests on the hip in the glide phase of the sidestroke; also called the top arm

Training: a physical improvement program designed to prepare a person for competition in sports

Treading: a basic aquatic skill that combines arm movements (sculling or finning) and leg movements (a scissors, breaststroke or rotary kick) to keep the body upright and the head above the surface

Triathlon: a sporting event consisting of three different activities, usually swimming, biking and running in that order

Tuck position: a position in which the body is bent at the hips and knees, with the thighs drawn to the chest and the heels kept close to the buttocks

Water competency: possessing the basic, minimum skills needed for water safety and survival

Wave drag: the resistance caused by turbulence in the water

SOURCES

American Academy of Dermatology. Understanding Skin Cancer. Available at http://www.aad.org/spot-skin-cancer/understanding-skin-cancer. Accessed December 2013.

American Academy of Pediatrics. Sun and Water Safety Tips. Available at http://www.aap.org/en-us/about-the-aap/aap-press-room/news-features-and-safety-tips/pages/Sun-and-Water-Safety-Tips.aspx. Accessed December 2013.

American College of Sports Medicine. ACSM Issues New Recommendations on Quantity and Quality of Exercise. Available at http://www.acsm.org/about-acsm/media-room/news-releases/2011/08/01/acsm-issues-new-recommendations-on-quantity-and-quality-of-exercise. Accessed January 2014.

American College of Sports Medicine. Resistance Training for Health and Fitness. Available at http://www.acsm.org/docs/brochures/resistance-training.pdf. Accessed January 2014.

American College of Sports Medicine. Selecting and Effectively Using Free Weights. Available at http://www.acsm.org/docs/brochures/selecting-and-effectively-using-free-weights.pdf. Accessed January 2014.

American National Red Cross. Emergency Medical Response. Yardley, Pennsylvania: StayWell, 2011.

American National Red Cross. First Aid/CPR/AED. Yardley, Pennsylvania: StayWell, 2011.

American National Red Cross. Lifeguarding. Yardley, Pennsylvania: StayWell, 2012.

American National Red Cross. Safety Training for Swim Coaches. Yardley, Pennsylvania: StayWell, 2013.

Besford, P. Encyclopedia of Swimming. New York: St. Martins Press, 1977.

Canadian Red Cross. Drown-Proofing Toddlers: Safe Practice or False Security? Available at http://www.redcross.ca/article.asp?id=025216&tid=024. Accessed December 2014.

Centers for Disease Control and Prevention. Defining Overweight and Obesity. Available at http://www.cdc.gov/obesity/adult/defining.html. Accessed January 2014.

Centers for Disease Control and Prevention. Home and Recreational Safety. Unintentional Drowning: Get the Facts. Available at http://www.cdc.gov/homeandrecreationalsafety/water-safety/waterinjuries-factsheet.html. Accessed December 2013.

Centers for Disease Control and Prevention. Measuring Physical Activity Intensity. Available at http://www.cdc.gov/nccdphp/dnpa/physical/measuring/target_heart_rate.htm. Accessed January 2014.

Centers for Disease Control and Prevention. Pools & Hot tubs. Available at http://www.cdc.gov/healthywater/swimming/pools/. Accessed December 2013.

Centers for Disease Control and Prevention. Six Steps for Healthy Swimming. Available at http://www.cdc.gov/healthywater/pdf/swimming/resources/six-steps-healthy-swimming-poster.pdf. Accessed December 2013.

Consumer Product Safety Commission. Pools and Spas. Available at http://www.cpsc.gov/en/Safety-Education/Safety-Guides/Sports-Fitness-and-Recreation/Pools-and-Spas/. Accessed December 2013.

Collis, M. and Kirchoff, B. Swimming. Boston: Allyn and Bacon, Inc., 1974.

Colwin, C.M. Swimming into the 21st Century. Champaign, Illinois: Human Kinetics Publishers, 1993.

Counsilman, J.E. Competitive Swimming Manual. Bloomington, Indiana: Counsilman Co., Inc., 1977.

Counsilman, J.E. The Science of Swimming. Englewood Cliffs, New Jersey: Prentice-Hall, Inc., 1968.

Environmental Protection Agency. Before You Go to the Beach. Available at http://www.cdc.gov/healthywater/pdf/swimming/resources/epa-before-you-go-to-beach-brochure.pdf. Accessed December 2013.

Environmental Protection Agency. Ozone Layer Protection. Benefits of the CFC Phaseout. Available at http://www.epa.gov/ozone/geninfo/benefits.html. Accessed December 2013.

Environmental Protection Agency. SunWise. Action Steps for Sun Safety. EPA sunwise. Available at http://www2.epa.gov/sunwise/action-steps-sun-safety. Accessed December 2013.

Firby, H. Howard Firby on Swimming. London: Pelham, 1975.

Flewwelling, H. "Sparging System," in Gabriel, J.L., editor. U.S. Diving Safety Manual. Indianapolis, Indiana: U.S. Diving Publications, 1990.

Florida Museum of Natural History. Ichthyology. Reducing the Risk of a Shark Encounter: Advice to Aquatic Recreationsts. Available at http://www.flmnh.ufl.edu/fish/sharks/attacks/relariskreduce.htm. Accessed December 2013.

Gabrielsen, M.A. Diving Injuries: A Critical Insight and Recommendation. Clayton, R.D., editor. Indianapolis, Indiana: Council for National Cooperation in Aquatics, 1984.

Gabrielsen, M.A. Diving Injuries: Prevention of the Most Catastrophic Sport Related Injuries. Presented to the Council for National Cooperation in Aquatics, Indianapolis, Indiana, 1981.

Giesbrecht, G.G., McDonal, G.K.: Operation ALIVE (Automobile Submersion: Lessons in Vehicle Escape). Available at http://umanitoba.ca/faculties/kinrec/media/VehicleSubmersionCARSP06.pdf. Accessed March 2014.

Hay, J.G. The Biomechanics of Sports Techniques. Englewood Cliffs, New Jersey: Prentice-Hall, 1985.

International Life Saving Federation: Lifesaving Position Statement LPS 06. Swimming and Water Safety Education. Available at http://www.ilsf.org/sites/ilsf.org/files/filefield/LPS-06WaterSafety_0.pdf. Accessed January 2014.

Katz, J. Swimming for Total Fitness: A Progressive Aerobic Program (2nd edition). New York: Bantam Doubleday Dell Publishing Group, 1993.

Katz, J. The W.E.T. Workout. New York: Facts On File Publications, 1985.

KidsHealth from Nemours. Overweight and Obesity. Available at http://kidshealth.org/parent/general/body/overweight_obesity.html. Accessed January 2014.

Knopf, K., Fleck, L., and Martin, M.M. Water Workouts. Winston-Salem, North Carolina: Hunter Textbooks, Inc., 1988.

Krasevec, J.A. and Grimes, D.C. HydroRobics. New York: Leisure Press, 1984.

Leonard, J., editor. Science of Coaching Swimming. Champaign, Illinois: Leisure Press, 1992.

Lepore M., Gayle, G.W., and Stevens, S. Adapted Aquatics Programming: A Professional Guide (2nd edition). Champaign, Illinois: Human Kinetics Publishers, 2007.

Maglischo, E.W. Swimming Faster. Palo Alto, California: Mayfield Publishing Company, 1982.

Maglischo, E.W. and Brennan, C.F. Swim for the Health of It. Palo Alto, California: Mayfield Publishing Co., 1985.

Malina, R.M. and Gabriel, J.L., editors. USA Diving Coach Development Reference Manual. Indianapolis, Indiana: USA Diving Publications, 2007.

McArdle, W., Katch, F., and Katch, V. Exercise Physiology: Energy, Nutrition and Human Performance (7th edition). Philadelphia: Lippincott Williams & Wilkins, 2009.

McEvoy, J.E. Fitness Swimming: Lifetime Programs. Princeton, New Jersey: Princeton Book Company Publishers, 1985.

Medline Plus. Health Topics—Disabilities. Available at http://www.nlm.nih.gov/medlineplus/disabilities.html. Accessed December 2013.

Medline Plus. Health Topics—Water Safety (Recreational). Available at http://www.nlm.nih.gov/medlineplus/watersafetyrecreational.html#cat22. Accessed December 2013.

Messner, Y.J. and Assmann, N.A. Swimming Everyone. Winston-Salem, North Carolina: Hunter Textbooks, Inc., 1989.

Minnesota Department of Natural Resources. Ice Rescue Claws. Available at http://www.dnr.state.mn.us/safety/ice/claws.html. Accessed December 2013.

Montoye, H.J., Christian, J.L., Nagle, F.J., and Levin, S.M. Living Fit. Menlo Park, California: The Benjamin/Cummings Publishing Company, Inc., 1988.

National Oceanic and Atmospheric Administration. Ocean Facts. Available at http://oceanservice.noaa.gov/facts/population.html. Accessed December 2013.

National Oceanic and Atmospheric Administration. Rip Current Safety. Available at http://www.ripcurrents.noaa.gov/signs-brochures.shtml. Accessed March 2014.

National Pool and Spa Institute. American National Standard for Residential Inground Swimming Pools ANSI/NSPI-5 2003. Alexandria, Virginia: National Pool and Spa Institute, 2003.

Ostby, S. and Skulski, J. Making a Splash: Inclusion of People with Disabilities in Aquatic Venues. Access Today, Spring 2004 - Special Volume, Issue 12.

Paralympic Games. Paralympic Games. Available at http://www.paralympic.org. Accessed January 2014.

President's Council on Fitness, Sports & Nutrition. Physical Activity Guidelines for Americans. Available at http://www.fitness.gov/be-active/physical-activity-guidelines-for-americans/. Accessed January 2014.

Swimming Pools: A Guide to Their Planning, Design, and Operation. Champaign, Illinois: Human Kinetics Publishers, Inc., 1987.

United States Access Board. Accessible Swimming Pools & Spas: A Summary of Accessibility Guidelines for Recreation Facilities. Available at http://www.access-board.gov/attachments/article/594/pools.pdf. Accessed December 2013.

United States Army Corps of Engineers, National Water Safety Program. Safety Tips. Available at http://watersafety.usace.army.mil/safetytips.htm. Accessed December 2013.

United States Coast Guard, Boating Safety Division. The Main Channel. Available at http://www.uscgboating.org/. Accessed December 2013.

United States Coast Guard, Office of Boating Safety. Children and Personal Watercraft. Available at http://www.uscgboating.org/assets/1/Publications/childrenandPWC_brochure.pdf. Accessed December 2013.

United States Consumer Product Safety Commission. Guidelines for Entrapment Hazards: Making Pools and Spas Safer. Available at http://www.cdph.ca.gov/HealthInfo/injviosaf/Documents/DrowningEntrapmentHazards.pdf. Accessed December 2013.

United States Consumer Product Safety Commission. Safety Barrier Guidelines for Home Pools. Available at http://www.cpsc.gov/cpscpub/pubs/pool.pdf. Accessed December 2013.

United States Department of Health and Human Services, Physical Activity Guidelines Advisory Committee. Physical Activity Guidelines Advisory Committee Report. Available at http://www.health.gov/paguidelines/Report/Default.aspx. Accessed January 2014.

United States Department of Homeland Security. United States Coast Guard Office of Auxiliary and Boating Safety. 2012 Recreational Boating Statistics. Available at http://www.uscgboating.org/assets/1/News/2012ReportR2.pdf. Accessed December 2013.

United States Department of Justice, Americans with Disabilities Act ADA Home Page. Americans with Disabilities Act of 1990. Available at http://www.ada.gov/pubs/ada.htm. Accessed December 2013.

United States Lifesaving Association. Beach & Water Safety: Tips for a Safe Day at the Beach. Available at http://c.ymcdn.com/sites/www.usla.org/resource/resmgr/docs/uslabrochurefinal.pdf. Accessed January 2014.

United States Lifesaving Association. United States Lifesaving Association Rip Current Survival Guide. Available at http://www.usla.org/?page=RIPCURRENTS#Survival. Accessed December 2013.

USA Diving. Who is USA Diving? Available at http://www.usadiving.org/about/. Accessed January 2014.

USA Swimming. Saving Lives Through Make a Splash. Available at http://usaswimming.org/DesktopDefault.aspx?TabId=2092. Accessed January 2014.

USA Swimming. Butterfly: Both Kicks Should Be Created Equal. Available at http://www.usaswimming.org/ViewNewsArticle.aspx?TabId=2175&itemid=4178&mid=11657. Accessed March 2014.

USA Swimming: Butterfly: Pull Pattern. Available at http://www.usaswimming.org/ViewNewsArticle.aspx?TabId=2175&itemid=4447&mid=11657. Accessed March 2014.

USA Swimming. What is USA Swimming? Available at http://www.usaswimming.org/DesktopDefault.aspx?TabId=1398&Alias=Rainbow&Lang=en. Accessed January 2014.

USA Synchro. About USA Synchro. Available at http://www.teamusa.org/USA-Synchronized-Swimming/About-USA-Synchro. Accessed January 2014.

USA Triathlon. About USAT. Available at http://www.usatriathlon.org/about-usat/about.aspx. Accessed January 2014.

USA Water Polo. About Us. Available at http://www.usawaterpolo.com/InsideUSAWaterPolo.aspx. Accessed January 2014.

Vandervort, D. Swimming Pool Accessories, Diving Boards & Slides. Available at http://www.hometips.com/buying-guides/swimming-pool-jump-diving-boards.html. Accessed January 2014.

World Health Organization. Drowning. Available at http://www.who.int/mediacentre/factsheets/fs347/en/index.html. Accessed January 2014.

INDEX